HIGH BUILDINGS
LOW MORALS

HIGH BUILDINGS
LOW MORALS

ANOTHER SIDEWAYS LOOK AT
TWENTIETH-CENTURY LONDON

ROB BAKER

AMBERLEY

To Joanna

Cover illustrations: Front: Piccadilly Circus in the fog, 1952, by Carl Mydans. (Courtesy of Getty Images). *Back:* Piccadilly, 1969, by Bernd Loos. (Courtesy of Bernd Loos)

First published 2017

Amberley Publishing
The Hill, Stroud
Gloucestershire, GL5 4EP

www.amberley-books.com

British Library Cataloguing in Publication Data.
A catalogue record for this book is available from the British Library.

ISBN 978 1 4456 6625 9 (paperback)
ISBN 978 1 4456 6626 6 (ebook)

Typesetting and Origination by Amberley Publishing.
Printed in the UK.

Contents

Author's Note

Thank you to the following for your help, inspiration and support: Albie Bairamian, Wilfred Bairamian, Mary Baxandall, Beth Blunt (mum), Joanna Hide, Kate Humphreys, Miles and Luca Leonard (for all the times I've escaped to Parsons, amongst much else), Sarah Mead, John Pearson, Olly Roy, Andrew Michael Sears, Steven Tate and Allan Warren.

1

The Headless Polaroids, Mrs Sweeny, Mussolini and P. G. Wodehouse

'Always a poodle, only a poodle! That, and three strands of pearls! Together they are absolutely the essential things in life.'

Once dubbed by John Paul Getty, a very frequent guest, as 'Number One, London',[1] 48 Upper Grosvenor Street was the salubrious address where one of the most celebrated sex scandals of the sixties took place. A series of Polaroid photographs, taken in the mirrored art deco bathroom, were used as evidence in a very expensive, bitter and acrimonious divorce case between the Duke and Duchess of Argyll. In May 1963, after four years of legal wrangling, the judge, Lord Wheatley, issued a damning verdict. In an extraordinary four-and-a-half-hour judgement that some say was unprecedented in its severity, he described the duchess as 'wholly immoral'.

Immoral or not, the sexual dalliances of Margaret, Duchess of Argyll, together with the Profumo Affair (John Profumo, after admitting that he had slept with Christine Keeler and thus had lied to the House, resigned just a month after Lord Wheatley's judgement) meant that by the end of 1963, the deference paid to what seemed a jaded, outmoded upper class was never quite the same again. Keeler herself would later say, 'The more rich and influential people I met, the more amazed I was at their private lives.'[2]

The Polaroids featured Margaret, the duchess, a former debutante of the year, dressed in nothing but her signature three-strand pearl necklace. More shockingly, one showed her performing fellatio on a naked man, whose identity was concealed because his head was not captured within the frame. Other Polaroid photographs showed a man masturbating for the camera in the same bathroom. The prurient press, already overexcited with the ongoing affairs of Christine Keeler and Mandy Rice-Davies, started to wonder at the identity of the headless man. There were very strong rumours that it might be a cabinet minister, or even a famous film star ...

Margaret, Duchess of Argyll, was born Ethel Margaret Whigham in 1912, the only child of Helen Mann Hannay and George Hay Whigham, a Scottish millionaire and chairman of the Celanese Corporation of Britain and North America. Celanese made cellulose acetate fabrics as a substitute for silk. Margaret later wrote that she remembered her father bringing a sample home for the first time: 'It was ugly, shiny stuff. Hideous. Horribly shiny, and he said, "These are going to be our new curtains," and my mother said, "Over my dead body."'[3] Mr Whigham's hunch about the value of the new material, however shiny and nasty, proved accurate, and in 1926 the Celanese shares jumped from 6 shillings to £6 overnight, making him a very rich man indeed.

Margaret Whigham at eighteen, December 1930.

Due to her father's involvement in the Celanese Corporation, much of Margaret's childhood was spent in America where she was schooled at 'Miss Hewitt's Classes' in New York (Christina Onassis and Barbara Hutton would be future alumnae). Back in London, she went to 'Miss Wolff's' on South Audley Street in Mayfair (Baba and Nancy, Cecil Beaton's sisters, were fellow classmates), followed by a stint as a day-girl at Heathfield School in Ascot. Every day Margaret was picked up by a chauffeur-driven car and, before she was taken back home to nearby Queen's Hill, she would say of her fellow pupils: 'Bye-bye, you poor things, playing in your galoshes and white tunics', and later remembered, 'I had no *esprit de corps*, and certainly didn't want to play hockey or lacrosse or cricket with anybody.'[4] Her education came to an end at 'Mademoiselle Ozanne's Finishing School for English Girls in Paris', where she was carefully groomed for her introduction to London society. Each summer, meanwhile, she holidayed at Baden-Baden, while winter, of course, was invariably spent at St Moritz.

In May 1930, at the age of seventeen and a half, Margaret was launched as a debutante in London. The extravagant coming-out ball for 400 people was at a rented Mayfair house at 6 Audley Square. The music was provided by Bert Ambrose & His Orchestra, and Margaret wore a dress, designed by a young Norman Hartnell, of a delicate forget-me-not blue tulle with a bodice trimmed with crystals and a skirt composed of four deep tiers. She became debutante of the season, and according to *Bystander* magazine 'Margaret Whigham was quite the smartest *jeune fille*' in London. She would write years later: 'I wore make-up, nail polish, and was extremely well-dressed. I was out every night, and nobody dressed like I did.'[5] Theoretically she was chaperoned, but in reality she went where she liked when she liked. The family chauffeur was always on hand to take her from party to party, and then back home again. Margaret remembered that she used to see one man for dinner, plead tiredness and go home, only then to go out with another young man to the Embassy Club or the Café de Paris. At closing hour she and her partner would then 'float on' to late nightclubs such as Meyrick's Silver Slipper.[6] Her father's only rule was that she absolutely *must* be dressed for the family breakfast at nine.

With rumours that her father employed a press agent, Margaret was never out of the newspapers and it has been said that she

Margaret Whigham, at the 'Jewels of Empire' Ball at Brook House, Park Lane, 1930.

singlehandedly invented what came to be known as the 'deb-ballyhoo industry'.[7] She was the first to wear pearl-coloured nail varnish, which was luminous at night, and the press reported with glee when she wore flowers on the right and not on the traditional left.

Her striking looks and svelte figure soon made her the toast of many a hapless young man that year, including a nineteen-year-old Prince Aly Salman Aga Khan, known as Aly Khan, who, after just a few weeks of courting, confidently asked Margaret's father's consent to propose. 'My father almost threw a fit. I was too young and he was Persian.'[8] Khan, who had been born in what would become Pakistan, was devastated and wrote a letter to Margaret dated 27 June 1930: 'When I left you yesterday I would have given anything to have been run over. I thought of killing myself but realised that you loved me and that everything was far from being impossible and that by dying I would forever lose you on this earth.'[9] He must have taken it hard because when the 'Talk of the Town' column in the *Daily Express* wrote about him at a re-launch of the Embassy Club on Bond Street, it was fifteen months later:

Miss Margaret Whigham looking very nearly as lovely as ever, attracted many an admiring glance. Her presence seemed to inspire Jack Harris's band to an even more perfect rhythm, and so alluring a spectacle can hardly have failed to console Prince Aly Khan, who sat entirely alone over a bottle of champagne.[10]

The prince was spending almost every night at the Embassy, and without fail always asked the band to play the Gershwins' 'I've Got a Crush on You'. It took a while, but eventually he got over Margaret, and then made up for lost time and started to cement his lifelong reputation as a playboy and ladies' man.

In May 1936, Khan married the Hon. Joan Barbara Guinness, later saying, 'I had been involved with several women. I was tired of trouble. Joan was a sane and solid girl, and I thought if I married her, I would stay out of trouble.'[11] He didn't, of course, and the couple divorced after his extra-marital affairs came to light, including one with Winston Churchill's daughter-in-law, Pamela Churchill. In May 1949, Khan married the film actress Rita Hayworth at a wedding where '500 guests from the United States and Europe feasted on 50 pounds of caviar, 600 bottles of champagne and other gourmet delights around a swimming pool scented with 200 gallons of *eau de Cologne*'.[12] Just two years later, Hayworth filed for divorce on the grounds of 'extreme cruelty, entirely mental in nature'.[13]

Aly Khan and
Rita Hayworth.
They married on
27 May 1949.

In the meantime, Khan had affairs with numerable women, including the film stars Joan Fontaine and Gene Tierney. Just over two years after his appointment as Pakistan's Ambassador to the UN, Aly Khan died on 12 May 1960, not from sexual exhaustion but in a car crash in Suresnes, a suburb of Paris. Five years previously, during a stint in Las Vegas, Noël Coward, reflecting on Aly Khan's playboy ways, rewrote Cole Porter's lyrics for 'Let's Do It' and included the lines: 'Monkeys whenever you look do it / Aly Khan and King Farouk do it / Let's do it, let's fall in love.'

After the brief relationship with Prince Aly Khan, it wasn't long before Margaret, in March 1932, became engaged to the 7th Earl of Warwick. This was so important to the *Daily Mirror* that the whole of their front page was taken up with the news. The couple had met while Margaret was holidaying with her parents in Egypt – a trip she wrote about for the *Daily Sketch*:

'Margaret has gone mad!' My friends really did not conceal their thoughts when I announced, last Autumn, that I was going to Egypt. I mean they have always seen me round Bond Street, in and out of the Ritz, or at Ascot, and they considered the Embassy Club my spiritual home. It is in a way, for I love the gay life of the West End, Ascot, Cannes and all the other fun that comes the way of the modern young woman. I had heard so much about Cairo's gay life that I bade a fond farewell to Jackson – that's the Embassy Club cat – and sallied forth into the big world. Now Egypt really does come up to expectations – but not from a Ritz-Carlton point of view. I had to abandon all that and appreciate it in the light of stepping back into the Bible. The natives are just heavenly in their colourful robes and especially at Assouan … Cairo, you see is only a pretty imitation of London, Paris and Cannes, and though I love that kind of life I only love it at its best … Actually, the thing in Cairo is the Ghezira Club where they have polo, racing, tennis, golf, and everyone who is anyone goes there for tea.[14]

On Wednesday 9 March 1932, Margaret and the Earl of Warwick arrived home together at Waterloo station and, according to an

Margaret Whigham and the Earl of Warwick shortly before their engagement ended, March 1932.

excited *Daily Express* (almost certainly the journalist Tom Driberg having fun), the engaged couple

> stepped into the arms of a crowd of 'bright young things' and exquisite young men. Miss Whigham was handed a great basket of dahlias still in their pots and six months out of season. Lord Warwick twisted his Grenadier moustache and looked correct and timid. Miss Whigham discarded the dahlias with the absent-minded touch of a film star, and rotated before the cameras. Lord Warwick's eyes were hard and courageous.[15]

The next evening the couple dined at the Embassy Club, Margaret's 'spiritual home', where the engagement was honoured with renamed dishes on the menu such as Salmon Welcome Back, Caviare Supreme de Notre Happiness and Petit Pois Prosperity. Thursday evening was *the* night to go to the Old Bond Street club with royalty, socialites and celebrities seen on the dance floor. Once one had got past the one-legged man at the entrance selling buttonhole carnations – and, of course, Jackson the cat – the club inside was decorated in violet, jade green and white. There were pink sofas along the walls and each table had two green electric candlesticks with pink shades, while amber lights hung from the ceiling. In the centre was the dance floor, and at one end of the room, on a balcony, the orchestra played. The novelist Barbara Cartland's description of Thursdays at the Embassy evokes something of the glamour of the women at the time:

> The faces of the women dancing and sitting round the room have an almost monotonous beauty. They all have large eyes with mascaraed eyelashes, full crimson mouths, narrow aristocratic noses and fine bones. Their hair, cut short and styled close to their well-shaped heads, is like exquisite satin, shiny and neat. Everything about them is neat and the expensive perfection of simplicity. Their skins are white – very white.[16]

Not everyone enjoyed their time at the Embassy Club quite as much as Margaret and her friends. Some felt distinctly uncomfortable. Many of the musicians who played there, for instance, were exposed like nobody else to the disparities of the rich and poor, especially during a time of acute economic recession. Billy Amstell, who played with the Ambrose Orchestra at the Embassy Club, wrote that 'people used to come and they were well fed and they used to guzzle into their food and drink and only round the corner people were sleeping in doorways, wrapped in paper'.[17] In 1932 the economic crisis was hitting even the richest, however. It was at the Embassy that King George V telephoned the Prince of Wales, so frequent a guest he had his own permanently reserved table there, and ordered him to 'donate' £10,000 from his personal Duchy of Cornwall funds to the Treasury.

About a month after the engaged couple had returned from Egypt, with invitations sent and Westminster Abbey booked, Margaret suddenly felt that marriage wasn't quite what she wanted. She broke off the engagement on the grounds that she 'did not love him sufficiently' – although it may have had more to do with Fulke Warwick's mother, Lady Warwick, calling Margaret's mother to say, 'If you love your daughter, don't let her marry my son. He's a liar, he's ill-mannered, and he picks his nose.'[18] Like Aly Khan, Lord Warwick was unable to take rejection easily. Within a week of the engagement being broken, he had incurred extensive bills at the Ritz hotel, had a request from the Metropolitan Police for his driving licence after an accusation of driving dangerously, and had lashed out at his family. His mother accused of him of being both 'silly and impertinent' and said, 'I should be furious were I not sorry for you for being so eaten up with conceit.' She reminded him of his duties as a peer of the realm and advised him to 'try and pay some of your debts, instead of incurring new ones with Rolls-Royce cars you can't afford'.[19]

Later in 1932, the gossip columnists noted that Margaret was often seen dancing at the 400 Club, situated in a basement next to the Alhambra Theatre (where the Leicester Square Odeon is now). Despite having a minuscule dance floor the club had an eighteen-piece orchestra, and although it had no menu, guests were able to order anything they wanted. Somehow the kitchen delivered. Margaret was usually seen in the company of Charles Sweeny, a dashing and very rich amateur golfer who also worked in the City at Charterhouse Investment Trust. Six months after they had met, they were married at the Brompton Oratory in

Margaret with fiancé Mr Sweeny at the Embassy Club in 1932.

Above left and right: Margaret's marriage to Charles Sweeny.

Knightsbridge on 21 February 1933. The *Daily Mirror* described Margaret's dress to its readers:

> Making the wedding dress of a fashionable modern bride is no light task. Norman Hartnell tells me that when the gown he has designed for Miss Margaret Whigham is finished, thirty hands will have been at work on it for six weeks. The motif of the dress is the jasmine flower. The form and texture of this blossom are being carried out in embroidery of pearls both embossed and inlaid. The dress itself is of white satin, tightly fitted with a flaring skirt.[20]

Margaret Whigham was fêted like a film star and the wedding drew an estimated 3,000 onlookers. *The Times*, the next day, reported that many had been desperate for a closer look: 'No sooner had the bride procession moved up the aisle than the swing doors on either side of the main entrance were besieged by women who, using elbows and umbrellas freely, forced their way into the church, and for a moment stood swaying in a solid mass, completely cutting off the means of entry of guests who arrived late.'[21]

By now Mrs Sweeny, as she came to be known, was so famous she was even mentioned in a popular song of the time – a very popular song. In most articles, obituaries and biographies written about the future Duchess of Argyll, including her autobiography where the fact is mentioned on the back cover, it was noted that she was so celebrated that Cole Porter included her as a superlative in one of his famous list songs. 'I had wealth, I had good looks,' Margaret would later write, 'As a young woman I had been constantly photographed, written about, flattered, admired, included in the Ten Best-Dressed Women in the World list, and mentioned (as Mrs Sweeny) by Cole Porter in the words of his hit song "You're the Top".'[22]

Along with the title song and 'I Get A Kick Out of You', 'You're the Top' was one of the hit songs from Cole Porter's musical *Anything Goes*, which opened in London at the Palace Theatre on 15 June 1935. Produced by the impresario C. B. Cochran, it starred the French actress Jeanne Aubert in the role of Reno La Grange,[23] Sydney Howard as Moonface Martin and Jack Whiting as Billy Crocker. Although the music and lyrics were by Porter, the original book of the show was a collaborative effort between Guy Bolton and P. G. Wodehouse (albeit heavily revised by Howard Lindsay and Russel Crouse). Before the revisions the musical was to be more of a satire on Hollywood from where Bolton and Wodehouse had recently returned. Wodehouse once joked that it was 'an era when only a man of exceptional ability and determination could keep from getting signed up by a Hollywood studio in some capacity or other'.[24] Wodehouse wrote to his friend William (Bill) Townend in August 1934:

> I'm having a devil of a time with this musical comedy Guy Bolton and I are writing. I can't get hold of Guy or the composer, so have been plugging along by myself. Still, Guy says he will be here on Saturday. What has become of the composer, heaven knows. Last heard of at Heidelberg and probably one of the unnamed three hundred shot by Hitler.[25]

Wodehouse was possibly referring to Porter's homosexuality in the letter. Many of the 300 SA Brownshirts Hitler had murdered during the Night of the Long Knives the previous month were killed for 'abnormal proclivities'.

Benny Green once wrote that Wodehouse's 'brilliant and immensely influential career as a Broadway lyricist is entirely forgotten today except by people like Ira Gershwin and Richard Rodgers, who readily acknowledge him as the pioneer of the colloquial song lyric'. And it was Wodehouse's revised lyrics written especially for the British audiences and not Cole Porter's that used Mrs Sweeny in the song. 'It was flattering,' she later wrote, 'to be included with the Louvre Museum, a Shakespeare sonnet, Mickey Mouse, the smile on the Mona Lisa, Garbo's salary, a dress by Patou and the other things Cole Porter considered "the top".'[26] She was less keen, however, that Mrs Sweeny was rhymed with Mussolini …

Cole Porter's original lyrics, used in the original Broadway version and usually still used today, were:

> You're an O'Neill drama,
> You're Whistler's mama!

Wodehouse's version, and the one sung by Jeanne Aubert on the London stage in 1935, was:

> You're Mussolini,
> You're Mrs Sweeny.

The use of Mussolini as an example of being 'the top' seems more than a little odd these days. Not helped, of course, with the knowledge that seven years after Ethel Merman first sang the song on Broadway Wodehouse was taken prisoner by the invading Germans at his house in Le Touquet in France and subsequently interned for a year. The English writer then made six broadcasts to the US from a German radio station in Berlin. He wrote to a friend at the time, 'I'm living here in the Adlon Hotel in a suite on the third floor – and a very nice one, too! They took me round and showed me Berlin. We went to the Olympic Stadium and Potsdam and back by the steamer on the Wannsee.'[27] The communication betrayed his casual attitude to his plight and sounded more like a jolly postcard home than a letter of a guest of the Nazis in wartime Berlin. The six talks were comic and apolitical, but the broadcasts over enemy radio prompted anger in Britain, along with a threat

P. G. Wodehouse in Berlin
in 1941.

of prosecution. He was seen by many as a traitor and a Nazi propagandist. A front-page article in the *Daily Mirror* stated:

> P.G. Wodehouse has cracked his worst joke. And the laugh is against his own country. IT'S BITTER LAUGHTER ... He lived luxuriously because Britain laughed with him, but ... Wodehouse was not ready to share her suffering. He hadn't the guts (or was it that he hadn't the wish?) even to stick it out in the internment camp.[28]

In *Performing Flea*, a 1953 collection of letters, Wodehouse wrote: 'Of course I ought to have had the sense to see that it was a loony thing to do to use the German radio for even the most harmless stuff, but I didn't. I suppose prison life saps the intellect.'[29] He was shocked by the controversy he had caused, however, and never returned to England. From 1947 until his death he lived in the US, taking dual British-American citizenship in 1955.

Mussolini in 1922 during his visit to London.

In the early 1930s Mussolini was seen by many in a surprisingly good light. The Italian fascist actually visited London, albeit for a rather brief stay, in December 1922 for a conference on German reparations. The *Manchester Guardian*, in an article published two months before his trip, wrote:

> The subtle Italian mind adores a man of action, a man of elemental force. Mussolini, 'The Thunderer,' whose words become deeds as they drop from his mouth, has swept most of young Italy off their feet, and for the time being holds them in the hollow of his hand.[30]

The man of elemental force arrived at Victoria station on 9 December and was met by about fifty black-shirted supporters. The *Manchester Guardian*, like many newspapers of the time, found the uniformed fascists faintly amusing. The correspondent thought all the energetic marching about was to do with the cold, and was worried that the thin 'black shirt (accompanied by a black tie, some war medals, and a black cloth cap shaped like a fez with a tassel and cord) looked poor comfort for eleven o'clock on a slightly foggy December night'.[31] He then described how the Blackshirts started singing the Italian Fascist marching song 'Giovinezza'. This was all repeated half an hour later outside Claridge's Hotel, where Mussolini and his entourage were staying. In fact, during his entire stay and wherever he went, organised groups of Blackshirts greeted him and sang the same fascist marching song again and again.

During their stay at Claridge's there was an unseemly row, reported in the press, when the Italian delegation accused their French counterparts of being allocated better rooms. No one quite knew what to make of the young Italian leader. In London he wore spats, a butterfly collar with a top hat and badly pressed striped trousers. The aristocratic British Foreign Secretary, Lord Curzon, remarked: 'He is really quite absurd.'[32] Most people were also surprised by Mussolini's height (he was only 5 feet 6 inches). The next day, Mussolini and his party, all wearing Fascist party badges, were received at Buckingham Palace by the king. Later, the Italians all drove to the Cenotaph in Whitehall, where Signor Mussolini laid a wreath of remembrance at the foot of the monument. Finally, they visited the Italian Fascist HQ at 25 Noel Street. At one point during the trip Mussolini missed a press conference because he was sleeping with a prostitute back at the hotel. During his stay he complained incessantly about the fog, which he insisted penetrated his clothes, his bedroom and even his suitcases. When he returned to Italy he swore that he would never return to England, and he never did.[33]

Nine years later, while he was touring Europe, Gandhi accepted an invitation to visit Mussolini in late 1931 in Rome. He even reviewed a black-shirted Fascist youth honour guard during his stay. Regarding his visit with Il Duce, Gandhi wrote in a letter to a friend: 'Many of his reforms attract me. He seems to have done much for the peasant class. I admit an iron hand is there. But as violence is the basis of Western society, Mussolini's reforms deserve an impartial study ... My own fundamental objection is that these reforms are compulsory. But it is the same in all democratic institutions.'[34] Gandhi would also hail Mussolini as 'one of the great statesmen of our time'. George Bernard Shaw once declared of the Italian dictator, 'Socialists should be delighted to find at last a socialist who speaks and thinks as responsible rulers do.'[35] Winston Churchill called Mussolini 'the greatest living legislator' and once wrote to his wife in 1926: 'No doubt he is one of the most wonderful men of our time.' Clementine responded a few days later quoting 'our old friend [Augustine] Birrell' who said: 'It is better to read about a world figure than to live under his rule.'[36]

The London transfer of Porter's musical *Anything Goes* opened on 14 June 1935 to generally very favourable reviews, although one pointed out that due to Jeanne Aubert's French accent it was difficult to hear the words she was singing – Mrs Sweeny/Mussolini or otherwise. However, if the audiences didn't raise a collective eyebrow to the Mussolini reference initially, some must have done four months after the premiere when the fascist dictator, keen to create an Italian version of the British Empire, invaded Ethiopia, then known as Abyssinia. The invasion is often seen as one of the episodes that paved the way for the Second World War, and demonstrated the ineffectiveness and weakness of the League of Nations, of which Italy and Ethiopia were both members. During the Ethiopian conflict, the Italians made substantial illegal use of mustard gas, sprayed directly from above like an 'insecticide', including on civilians and Red Cross camps and ambulances. It was Mussolini himself who authorised the use of the gas.

The Italians also instituted forced labour camps, installed public gallows, killed hostages, and mutilated the corpses of their enemies. Captured guerrillas were even killed by being thrown out of planes mid-flight. Italian troops had themselves photographed next to dead Ethiopian soldiers hanging from the gallows or chests full of detached heads. Even during the Abyssinian conflict, however, the Lord Chamberlain's Office, the censors of the London stage, didn't look kindly on any political satire about European leaders, even fascist dictators. They judged Eric Barker's burlesque of the League of Nations ('Intrigue of Nations') at the Windmill Theatre as 'needlessly barging in on a delicate situation', while the Earl of Cromer, the Lord Chamberlain, worried that the character of 'Signor Whale-Blubber', a clear reference to Mussolini, might offend 'sensitive foreigners'. Even as late as 1939, the theatre censors, anxious not to embarrass a government committed to *détente* with Germany, were deleting negative depictions of Hitler and Mussolini, and even words such as 'Nordic' and 'Concentration Camp'.[37]

The year after the London opening of *Anything Goes* in June 1936, Wodehouse received the Mark Twain Medal in recognition of his 'outstanding and lasting contribution to the business of the world'. In a letter to William Townend, he enclosed a list of former winners of the medal saying '[this] will give you a laugh'.[38] The first on the list and first recipient of the medal was none other than Benito Mussolini. His medal bore the inscription 'Mussolini, Great Educator'.

Wodehouse, incidentally, was often critical of Porter's lyric writing. In 1961, he wrote to Guy Bolton enclosing some updated lyrics for a new production of *Anything Goes*:

The trouble with Cole is that he has no power of self-criticism. He just bungs down anything whether it makes sense or not just because he has thought of what he feels is a good rhyme. I have rewritten the verse because Cole's verse seemed to me absolute drivel … I always feel about Cole's lyrics that he sang them to Elsa Maxwell and Noël Coward in a studio stinking of gin and they said, 'Oh, Cole, darling it's just too marvellous.'[39]

After infidelities on both sides, Mr and Mrs Sweeny divorced in 1947 on the grounds of 'constructive desertion', and two years later, on the luxurious Golden Arrow boat train returning from Paris, Margaret met Ian Douglas Campbell, Chief of the Clan Campbell, Hereditary Master of the Royal Household in Scotland, Keeper of the Great Seal of Scotland and Hereditary Keeper of the Royal Castles of Dunoon, Dunstaffnage, Tarbert and Carrick and Duke of Argyll. During their conversation, Ian told her that he and his second wife, Louise, were leading separate lives and were soon to be divorced. He would later confess that he had first seen Margaret coming down the famous curved staircase at the Café de Paris while he was dining there with his first wife, Janet Aitken, to discuss their pending divorce. He turned to her and said, gallantly, 'There's the girl I'm going to marry one day.'[40]

A few months after they first met, Margaret and the duke bumped into each other at Claridge's and Margaret told Ian she was 'a man short' for a luncheon party she was giving the following day – two years later they married at the Caxton Hall Register Office in Westminster. It was the Duke of Argyll's third marriage and he was making a habit of marrying heiresses. The first, and not short of a penny, had been Janet Aitken, daughter of the press baron Lord Beaverbrook. Not long after they had married in 1927, she discovered that he had

The Duke and Duchess of Argyll.

sold off her jewellery to pay off gambling debts. During their ill-fated honeymoon (she was just seventeen), he violently shook her and told her to 'stop snivelling' and then took her to a Parisian brothel, telling her she 'had a lot to learn'.[41] Unsurprisingly, the marriage didn't last long and they divorced in 1934 (their daughter would later briefly marry Norman Mailer in 1962). The following year, in November 1935, and a few months after *Anything Goes* premiered at the Palace Theatre, the duke married a US banker's daughter, Louise Clews. She also later accused him of 'pillaging' her fortune.

By 1957 the duke and duchess's marriage was also crumbling (the duchess would later admit that she was having affairs by 1954). In September 1959 the duke threw her out of Inveraray Castle, publicly branding her an adulterer, and filed for divorce. To prove Margaret was an adulteress he needed evidence. While his wife was out of the country, he 'broke into' Upper Grosvenor Street where he stole diaries, letters and photographs. When he saw the diary for 1956–59 was missing, he returned to Margaret's house, this time with his daughter Lady Jeanne. Margaret, who was now at home, turned on her bedside light after hearing a noise, and saw two people in her room. Later she recalled: 'I immediately began dialling 999, but Ian pinioned my arms to prevent this, while Jeanne snatched up my diary. After this they

48 Upper Grosvenor Street in 2017. The house is now worth something approaching £20 million.

made a rapid exit. It was a horrible experience, and the next day I suffered from delayed shock.'[42]

Margaret sued Lady Jeanne for trespass, which was settled out of court (Ian, by law, still had the right to enter her house, as they were still married at the time). When the Argyll divorce case finally came to court on Friday 1 March 1963, it was already the longest and costliest divorce in Scottish legal history. The judge, Lord Wheatley, was a teetotal, Jesuit-educated Catholic, and was unable to hide his shock over Margaret's behaviour. The duke provided to the Edinburgh court a list of eighty-eight men found in the diaries whom he believed his wife had slept with. Margaret later maintained the names were from her 'dinner-guest book' and that if they were lovers she deserved to be in the Guinness Book of Records. The names in the list included two government ministers and three members of the royal family.

There were also Polaroids found within the diaries. The first had a man standing upright, in more ways than one, with Margaret performing fellatio, crouched on her bended knees, her hand holding his penis. Wrapped around the photographs were sheets of paper in handwritten captions: 'Before', During', 'Oh!' and 'Finished'. Margaret initially denied that it was she in the photographs but closer examination showed that the woman was wearing a ring that only Margaret had worn. What's more, and although her head faced away from the camera, the Asprey necklace of three strands of pearls secured by a diamond clasp around the neck was also a giveaway. The identity of the headless man in the Polaroid was restricted to five possible suspects: Duncan Sandys, then the Minister of Defence and also Winston Churchill's son-in-law; John Cohane, an American businessman; Peter Combe, a press officer for the Savoy Hotel; Sigmund von Braun, diplomat and brother of the Nazi scientist Werner von Braun; and American actor Douglas Fairbanks Jnr. After four years of legal wrangling, it wasn't until May 1963 that the judge, Lord Wheatley, issued his damning verdict, and in a four-and-a-half-hour judgement, read out:

> She is a highly sexed woman who has ceased to be satisfied with normal sexual activities and has started to indulge in disgusting sexual activities to gratify a debased sexual appetite. A completely promiscuous woman whose sexual appetite could only be satisfied by a number of men, whose promiscuity had extended to perversion and whose attitude to the sanctity of

Margaret Campbell, Duchess of Argyll
outside the law courts in the Strand on
the second day of her case, 3 May 1960.

marriage was what moderns would call enlightened, but which in plain language was wholly immoral.

The press, of course, had a field day and the duchess's reputation was ruined, not only because of the Polaroids, but because she was accused of sleeping with eighty-eight men. It was said that during the war, while visiting her chiropodist on Bond Street, she fell down a 40-foot lift shaft, which left her not only with a lack of taste and smell but also, her friends noted, a voracious sexual appetite bordering on nymphomania. 'Go to bed early and often,' she once said; words she lived by.

Margaret, Duchess of Argyll, complete with her three strands of pearls, at home at 48 Upper Grosvenor Street. (Photo by Allan Warren)

Within two weeks of the Wheatley verdict on 5 June, John Profumo resigned after admitting that he had slept with Christine Keeler. The duke and duchess and the headless man photos were for a short while almost forgotten. At a stormy cabinet meeting on 20 June, however, the Defence Secretary, Duncan Sandys (pronounced Sands), confessed that he was rumoured to be the headless man and offered to resign. He was dissuaded by Prime Minister Macmillan who, not least because of the Profumo affair, was terrified of yet more scandal for his government. Lord Denning, who had already been commissioned to investigate the Profumo scandal, was also asked to investigate the identity of the headless lover as part of the remit.

Denning knew that if he could match the handwriting he would find his man. He cunningly invited the five key suspects – Sandys, Fairbanks Jnr, Cohane, Combe and von Braun, to the Treasury and asked for their help in a 'very delicate matter'. On arriving they all signed the visitor's register and later their handwriting was analysed by a graphologist. The result proved conclusive. Although Denning didn't include it in his report, the headless man was identified by the handwriting expert. 'Lord Wheatley was right in his judgment,' Lord Denning later commented. 'The duke and duchess were very prominent and if they fell short they could expect to be criticised.'[43]

Thirty-seven years later, in the year 2000, a Channel 4 documentary about the case featured a man called Paul Vaughan, a friend of the duchess. He reported that she had once said to him: 'Of course, sweetie, the only Polaroid camera in the country at this time had been lent to the Ministry of Defence.' The programme analysed the film and found that it was taken in 1957 (Sandys was the Defence Minister at this time) and concluded, with this new evidence, that there had been two men in the photos and that Duncan Sandys had been one of them. In 1957, however, Polaroid cameras had been selling commercially for eight years and the company had actually sold their millionth camera the year before. It seems unlikely that the Ministry of Defence would have had the only Polaroid camera in the entire country – luckily for Sandys' posthumous reputation.

The duchess's reputation, however, was severely damaged after the divorce and the ensuing scandal. Nonetheless, her life was still several levels of comfort above most. The *Sydney Morning Herald* in 1963 gave an example of her life at the time:

> She is a regular client at the slimming specialist consulting rooms in Harley Street and eats sparingly. Her daily routine is as cosseted as that of a Hollywood beauty queen. She raises late in the peach bedroom with its adjoining peach-mirrored bathroom in the luxurious Upper Grosvenor Street apartment. Her clothes are laid out ready by a personal maid who also gives the duchess her daily manicure and pedicure. She goes out to have her facials but also has a masseuse call at the flat to give her regular treatments. Her days are spent visiting friends, shopping in London and Paris for clothes or holding lavish dinner parties – usually for about eighteen guests at a time. St Moritz, Nassau and the south of France are her favourite holiday haunts – always with an extensive wardrobe designed by Balenciaga, Balmain, Dior, Hartnell and Stiebel.[44]

The money she had left didn't last forever, and in the 1970s she was forced to open up her Mayfair house to paying visitors. This wasn't enough to support her, and in 1978 she sold it and moved into an apartment in the Grosvenor House hotel. Twelve years later she was evicted for unpaid rent and placed in a nursing home in Pimlico. She did, however, maintain her standards. When luncheon was served in the home at midday she refused to eat it: 'Only servants eat their meal at 12,' she said, and then waited, defiantly, until one o'clock to eat her now cold lunch.[45]

After three years at the Pimlico nursing home, now penniless and alone, she suffered a fall in her bathroom that broke her neck and killed her. She was buried next to her first husband, Charles Sweeny, with whom she had kept friendly relations all his life.

Almost fifty years before, and not long after Mr and Mrs Sweeny were married, the Embassy Club found that its more fashionable members were starting to dance elsewhere. Barbara Cartland, a friend of Margaret's, was employed to get them to return. She lured back Ambrose and his orchestra, softened the lighting and threw away the 'ghastly cubist carpet'. Essentially, and as you would expect, she tried to make the nightclub more romantic, saying:

'What designers forget is that smart restaurants and night clubs are full of unhappily married people – the happily married ones stay at home, the young unmarried ones are not good payers.'[46]

Cartland, famous of course for her 700 novels, most of which feature romanticised virginal heroines, had her first encounter with someone of the opposite sex when a randy major invited her to his bedroom to show her 'how his revolver worked'. Not long after, she was engaged to a handsome young man in the Life Guards but such was her disgust on finding out the 'facts of life' from her mother, she broke off the engagement. The jilted fiancé was devastated, blamed himself and late one night beside the popular coffee stall at Hyde Park Corner he threatened to shoot himself with his service revolver. Some seventy-five years later, at the age of ninety-two, Cartland had a far more modern take on the antics of the Duchess of Argyll than many others, especially Lords Wheatley and Denning. Cartland was interviewed in 1992 and spoke of Margaret:

She was very beautiful and every man wanted to go to bed with her and she wanted to go to bed with every man. And why not? There's nothing wrong with that. She did go from man to man. She didn't have love affairs which lasted a long time. I think men found her rather boring after a time.

This wasn't entirely accurate, as Margaret's last proper relationship, her 'third husband' as she would call him, was with William 'Bill' H. Lyons, an American executive for Pan-Am. They met in about 1957 and saw each other regularly for nine years, after which he returned to his Portuguese wife. Margaret later wrote, 'Our affair ended in 'sixty-eight. No it didn't just peter out. He wouldn't come near me now, because he knows if he did, it would just start all over again.'[47]

In 2013 Lady Colin Campbell, the duchess's stepdaughter-in-law, revealed, after fifty years of intrigue and gossip, that it wasn't a cabinet minister, a member of the royal family or even a film star in the Polaroid photographs. It was her lover, Bill Lyons, who was the 'Headless Man'. He had rigged up the timer on the Polaroid camera and, as Lady Colin Campbell put it, took photographs that were nothing else but 'in all innocence, to record a loving encounter with the man who replaced Big Ian in her affections'.[48]

Margaret with her lover Bill Lyons.

Recipe for Bananas and Cointreau
This is from Margaret, Duchess of Argyll's *My Dinner Party Book* –
another attempt to make some money after falling, relatively, on hard
times. Of the recipe, she wrote: 'It's very rich, but quite delicious.'

4 bananas
1 oz butter
Lemon juice
1 oz sugar
1 teaspoon cinnamon
2 tablespoons Cointreau
2 tablespoons fresh orange juice
1 carton double cream

Peel and split the bananas in half lengthways. Place flat side upwards
in a buttered serving dish and sprinkle immediately with lemon juice
to prevent browning. Mix the sugar and cinnamon and sprinkle over
the bananas. Pour on the Cointreau and orange juice and marinate
for two hours. Dot with butter and bake in the oven at 350F (180C,
gas mark 4) for 15 minutes. Serve hot with double cream.

2

Scott's Restaurant, the Balcombe Street Gang and the Second Blitz of London

Four men, on 10 May 1998, made a dramatic appearance on the platform at a special *Sinn Féin* conference in Dublin. There was 'stamping of feet, wild applause and triumphant cheering' during a ten-minute ovation, while the men stood grinning with clenched fists in the air. To more applause at the same conference, Gerry Adams, without a discernible sense of overstatement, described the four men as 'our Nelson Mandelas'.[1]

A little over fifty-eight years earlier, on the other side of Ireland and with the Second World War only one month old, a German U-boat captain sailed his submarine into an isolated harbour in County Kerry on the Atlantic coast. U-boat 35 launched a collapsible dinghy and, with the help of locals, began bringing ashore twenty-eight sailors rescued from the Greek merchant ship MV *Diamantis*. Two days earlier, after spotting the U-boat 40 miles off Lands' End, the Greek seamen had panicked and, despite the rough weather, abandoned ship. The U-boat had come to pick them up after one of the Greek lifeboats had capsized and thrown the men into the sea. The Greek steamer, carrying manganese ore from Freetown in Sierra Leone and bound for Barrow-in-Furness, was then torpedoed and sunk. The sailors were offered dry clothes, warm beds and given cigarettes, tea and other refreshments. Before they left for the shore, the captain of the U-boat, Werner Lott, later recalled: '[When] the Greek sailors said goodbye to me on the conning tower, they went on their knees and kissed my wedding ring as if I were a bishop.'[2]

A few weeks later, on 29 November, Captain Werner Lott was taken prisoner. He had given orders for U-35 to be scuttled after it was badly damaged by depth charges dropped by the destroyers HMS *Kingston* and HMS *Kashmir* in the North Sea – part of a flotilla under the overall command of Captain Lord Louis Mountbatten. Lott was the last but one of the crew to be brought to safety when, blue with cold from the North Sea and with a damaged life jacket, he had been unable to hold on to the rope thrown down to him and a boat had to be lowered. After a hot bath and a bottle of whisky held to his lips, the U-boat captain made a good recovery. Over the next few days he was surprised how well he was treated (on the ship that brought him to Glasgow he was given the cabin of an officer on leave, and then given beer on his thirty-second birthday on the night train down to London). Lott had the dubious honour of being held prisoner in the Tower of London and was placed in a very cold basement cell with a rusty bedstead as its only furniture. Pinned to the wall was a piece of paper containing the regulations of the Geneva Convention in broken German. Years later Lott still remembered its literal translation: 'Please your holding power and do what they say.'[3]

German submarine U-35 was a Type VIIA U-boat of Nazi Germany's *Kriegsmarine*. She was built three years before the start of the Second World War.

The British, including Louis Mountbatten, knew exactly who Commander Lott was. It was why he was treated so well for a prisoner of war, even for a senior officer. *LIFE* magazine, in the issue dated 16 October 1939 and with a huge international circulation, made Lott the most famous U-boat commander of the entire Nazi fleet. At a time when *LIFE* was occasionally treating the beginning of the Second World War rather flippantly (in the same issue it began a report on baseball: 'While Germany, France and England continued their World Series in Europe, another World Series was taking place in New York's Yankee Stadium...'[4]) – it featured Lott's U-boat 35 on the cover while inside it told the story of the Greek sailors' rescue.[5] This act of humanity was to be one of only two recorded instances during the Second World War of a German submarine risking its own safety to protect the crew of a vessel they had torpedoed and sunk.[6] A few days after Lott had been picked up by HMS *Kashmir*, he got a chance to express his appreciation to Mountbatten. 'I thanked him for the extraordinary efforts his destroyer made to pick us up,' Lott recalled. 'That is how life is,' Mountbatten replied, 'You were extraordinary picking up the Greeks.' 'I could not help thinking,' Lott later remembered, 'why are we fighting each other?'[7]

Captured U-boat 35 crew. The U-boat was scuttled on 29 November 1939 in the North Sea but all forty-three crew were rescued and taken prisoner. They all survived the war.

The story of the rescued Greek seamen and the fact that a German U-boat had entered Irish waters encouraged persistent rumours that U-boats were being refuelled at secret Irish bases on the Atlantic coast. Guy Liddell, part of counter-intelligence at MI5, noted in his operational diary on 20 September: 'Frequent reports coming about submarine bases on the west coast of Éire.' Three weeks later on 12 October he wrote, 'Éire neutrality is rapidly becoming a farce. A German submarine sailed into Dingle Bay with the crew of a cargo steamer which had been torpedoed.'[8] Even before U-35 dropped the Greek sailors to safety, Winston Churchill, the new First Lord of the Admiralty, had already warned the Deputy Chief of Naval Staff of the danger of German submarines off the Irish coast. 'There seems to be a good deal of evidence, or at any rate suspicion, that U-boats were being succoured from West of Ireland ports by the malignant section with whom de Valera dare not interfere.'[9]

Following the establishment of the Irish Free State eighteen years previously, three deep-water Treaty Ports at Berehaven, Queenstown (now called Cobh, and the *Titanic*'s last port before setting off on its final voyage) and Lough Swilly were initially retained by the United Kingdom in accordance with the Anglo-Irish Treaty of 6 December 1921, but returned to Ireland in 1938. At a cabinet meeting on 24 October 1939, just eight days after *LIFE* magazine's U-boat article, Churchill argued that the Dublin government should be told 'the use of the ports in Ireland by the Royal Navy was essential to the security of the Empire, and that the present attitude adopted by Ireland in that matter was intolerable'[10]. De Valera, the Irish Taoiseach, was not to be moved, claiming that Irish public opinion would not stand for any concession to the British, and the ports were to be retained by Ireland. Churchill wanted to insist on their use, by force if necessary, but Neville Chamberlain, who was still Prime Minister at the time, argued that it was not certain the use of the southern Irish ports was 'a matter of life and death' and that it 'would have the most unfortunate repercussions in the United States'.[11]

Not long after Commander Lott was taken prisoner, he went on hunger strike in protest at the cold in his austere Tower of London cell. On 8 December, Captain Lord Louis Mountbatten came to visit Lott at the tower and later recalled: 'I was taken round, in the dark, somewhat dramatically by a Guardsman carrying a candle lantern. I asked for the Captain and was told he was in solitary confinement in the old Dungeons (I believe) and I insisted on being conducted to his cell. There was no furniture except one decrepit old bedstead on which we both sat talking for some time.'[12] Mountbatten arranged for Lott's complaint of the cold to be rather imaginatively resolved. By way of an apology, Lott and his second-in-command were taken, in civilian clothes and at Admiralty expense, for a 'splendid meal' at Scott's Restaurant and Oyster Bar at 18–20 Coventry Street. Some accounts say that this was the idea of future James Bond author Ian Fleming, then working as the aide to the Director of the Naval Intelligence Division that operated out of Rooms 38 and 39 of the Admiralty in Whitehall. He thought that if the German officers got drunk enough, they would reveal Nazi secrets and, specifically, how they had managed to evade British mines in the Skagerrak – the strait running between the south-east coast of Norway, the south-west coast of Sweden, and the Jutland peninsula of Denmark.

After a very fine lunch, albeit with no military secrets spilled, the German naval officers were returned to their now suitably heated cells, but not before Scott's Restaurant had filled with Special Branch police officers after the head waiter had called the police when he overheard the lunch party speaking in German. During and after the war Fleming had a regular spot at the restaurant, a right-hand corner table for two on the first floor. It was also to be the favourite of his creation James Bond and it is said that it was at Scott's that Fleming first heard the request for a Martini that was 'shaken not stirred'. In *Moonraker*, Bond has a date to meet Gala Brand. He heads to Scott's and waits:

> Bond sat at his favourite restaurant table in London, the right-hand corner table for two on the first floor, and watched the people and traffic in Piccadilly and down the Haymarket.

In *You Only Live Twice*, Bond is happy to have finally got an assignment from M, and as he exits M's office he has a request for Miss Moneypenny:

> Be an angel, Penny and ring down to Mary and tell her she's got to get out of whatever she's doing tonight. I'm taking her

Postcard featuring Scott's, *c.* 1930. The restaurant began life in 1872 when Charles Sonnhammer and Emil Loibl, the owners of the London Pavilion music hall, established an 'oyster warehouse' at 18 Coventry Street – although a 'Scott's oyster rooms' existed on the Haymarket from at least 1853. In that year a Paul Shoreditch of Devereaux Court, Temple, was brought before a judge for trying to pass a forged £5 note at the establishment.

Coventry Street featuring Scott's Restaurant on the right, April 1956. (Photo by Allan Hailstone)

out to dinner. Scott's. Tell her we'll have our first roast grouse of the year and pink champagne. Celebration.

In *Diamonds Are Forever*, Bond speaks to Bill Tanner, the Chief of Staff and Bond's best friend in the service, and offers to take him out:

I'll take you to Scott's and we'll have some of their dressed crab and a pint of black velvet ...

Scott's started in 1872 as an 'oyster warehouse' in the London Pavilion Music Hall. Because of its popularity, it expanded from 18 Coventry Street into both nos 19 and 20 before there was a major rebuilding in 1893 in the style of 'Early French Renaissance' by the designers Treadwell and Martin. Over the next fifty years Scott's was always seen as one of the finest fish restaurants in London and was the traditional place for the more affluent Oxbridge undergraduates to eat and drink on Boat Race night. Every Sunday from 1955 the four panellists, the question master, and the producer of *The Brain's Trust* (initially a popular radio programme that began during the war, but which transferred to television in 1955) would meet at mid-day at Scott's where 'they'd eat a good lunch with

Commander Ian Fleming in Room 39 at the Admiralty during the Second World War. He joined Naval Intelligence full-time in August 1939 with the code-name 17F. He was promoted from Lieutenant to Commander a few months into the war.

a fair amount to drink' before they were driven to the television studios at Lime Grove in time for a 4.15 p.m. start. Luminaries such as William Golding, John Betjeman, Rebecca West and Jacob Bronowski (described as 'some of the finest intelligences in the country' by the *Radio Times* in September 1958) were paid £50 a programme, particularly generous in those days, as this included a free lunch, drinks after the programme, and free transport home.[13]

Scott's was seen as a glamorous place to eat in the 1950s and 60s. Winston Churchill, Marilyn Monroe and Charlie Chaplin all visited, and the restaurant was mentioned in the 1963 film *The Great Escape*, when two POWs speak of Scott's Bar in Piccadilly as the first place they wish to go when the war is over. In 1967 the restaurant moved to Mount Street in Mayfair where, according to Kingsley Amis, the restaurant was 'luxurious to the safe side of vulgarity' and although he felt 'conspicuous and flashy in his tweed jacket' it was the sort of establishment where 'nobody is noticeable except the ladies, and they only by their rarity'.[14] Amis had anticipated the move of Scott's restaurant in his James Bond continuation novel, *Colonel Sun*, where Bond is at Scott's lunching on 'Whitstable oysters, cold side of beef and potato salad, and a well-chilled bottle of Anjou rosé' and fearing the worst: 'Bond had recently heard that the whole north side of (Coventry Street) was doomed to demolition,[15] and counted every meal taken in those severe but comfortable panelled rooms a tiny victory over the new hateful London of steel and glass matchbox architecture.'[16]

Surrounded by large classical French paintings and tarnished mirrors with fish and shellfish designs on the bar-panels and blinds, there were about seventy people dining in Scott's Restaurant and Oyster Bar on the evening of 12 November 1975. The general chatter of the comfortably off while consuming oysters, crab and Chablis suddenly turned to screams when at 9.28 p.m. a large object came crashing through one of the two large round plate-glass windows. As soon as they heard the sound of breaking glass many of the customers feared the worst and threw themselves to the stone-clad floor. Seconds later the 5-pound shrapnel-laced gelignite throw bomb exploded. It killed one man, John Batey, aged fifty-nine, and injured at least fifteen others, some very seriously. The explosion at Scott's was caused by only one of the forty bombs that an IRA Active Service Unit (ASU) exploded in the capital in a fourteen-month campaign during 1974 and 1975. It was a campaign that some called 'The Second Blitz of London' and it left thirty-five people dead and many more seriously injured.

On 22 October 1975, three weeks before the bomb exploded at Scott's restaurant, four people had been wrongly convicted of murder for carrying out the Guildford and Woolwich pub bombings where seven people were killed and over ninety people injured. The judge, Justice Sir John Donaldson, declared that he regretted that the four found guilty had not been charged with high treason, which then still carried the death penalty. On the very same day that the 'Guildford Four' were sent down, not coincidentally, a man telephoned the elegant four-storey Holland Park home of the Conservative MP Hugh Fraser and his wife, the writer Antonia Fraser. The maid who answered the phone was asked what time the MP usually left home in the morning and she answered, innocently, that it was usually around eight. Later that night, someone planted a large 14-pound gelignite bomb underneath one of the wheels of Fraser's car that was always parked outside his house on the tree-lined Campden Hill Square.

The next morning, Professor Gordon Hamilton-Fairley, a neighbour of the Frasers and an eminent cancer specialist at St Bartholomew's Hospital, was out walking his two dogs. He noticed something odd underneath Fraser's Jaguar XJ6 and bent down to investigate. Meanwhile, one of his poodles started urinating against a wheel. This caused the sensitive 'anti-handler' switch to override the timer, and suddenly the peace of Campden Hill Square, with its elegant houses around a beautifully kept private garden, was crudely broken. The bomb exploded in a sheet of flame and sent jagged pieces of the Jaguar hundreds of yards in all directions. The main body of the car was thrown high into the air and landed on its roof while Hamilton-Fairley's torso was flung into the Frasers' front garden. He and his two poodles, Emmy-Lou and Bimmy, were killed instantly. For some while afterwards a cloud of dark smoke hung over the appalling scene.

A tyre from the car was blown right over Mr Fraser's home and into the garden of the Countess of Liverpool's house in the adjacent Aubrey Road. James Warren, a freelance hairdresser who was cutting her hair at the time, told a reporter: 'The Countess dropped her cornflakes all over the floor.' The actor Jeremy Brett, who lived near the square, said: 'It takes something like this for people to talk to each other. Most of the people in the square haven't spoken to another person from the square for years. Now they are all out there, countesses and princesses with no makeup.'[17] Hugh Fraser, who had been blown off his chair by the blast, had long been a friend of the Kennedy family and had been due that morning to drive his house guest, seventeen-year-old Caroline Kennedy (her mother Jackie had long been a friend of Fraser's), to Sotheby's where she had enrolled in an art-appreciation course. They had been delayed by a phone call from another Conservative MP, Jonathan Aitken, and the conversation almost certainly saved both Fraser and Kennedy's lives. It will never be known what would have happened to the Provisional IRA's substantial US donations should they have murdered someone from the world's most famous Irish-American family.

The IRA Active Service Unit responsible for the professor's death included Edward Butler, Hugh Doherty, Martin O'Connell and

Gordon Hamilton Fairley DM, FRCP was born and raised in Australia. He moved to the United Kingdom, where he became Professor of Medical Oncology at St Bartholomew's Hospital and contributed a great deal to the chemotherapy and immunology of malignant disease. He was married and had four children, the youngest of whom was just twelve years old when he was killed by the IRA.

Harry Duggan, all of whom were in their early twenties and all from the Irish Republic. A week after the Campden Hill Square 'mistake' the ASU reverted their attention to what they called 'ruling-class' restaurants, and on the 29 October they detonated a bomb at Trattoria Fiore on the corner of Mount Street and South Audley Street near the American Embassy in Grosvenor Square. The bomb was placed behind some railings and it exploded just before 9.30 p.m. when about twenty people were dining in the restaurant, including one ten-year-old girl. Seventeen people were injured, eight very seriously. One American tourist had her scalp

Caroline Kennedy the day after she narrowly avoided being killed by the IRA bomb in Campden Hill Square, October 1975.

ripped off and another woman lost her foot while others were scarred for life, lacerated by razor-sharp shards of flying glass.

Three weeks later, on 18 November, it was the turn of Walton's on the corner of Walton Street and Draycott Avenue in Chelsea. A stolen Cortina screeched to a halt outside the restaurant and a 5-pound bomb containing ball bearings and bolts was flung through the window. With a crash it landed on a table where two couples were dining. Two of them were killed instantly in the blast and the other two sustained terrible injuries along with fifteen other people. Walton Street 'sparkled in a sea of splintered glass and blood as the un-laminated windows of the restaurant shattered'. After a period of silence all that could be heard was moaning from the victims, with one woman staggering around screaming: 'My eye, there's something in my eye.'[18]

In 1975, Londoners over the age of forty remembered the London Blitz all too well, and if most weren't panicking they were starting to think twice about going for something to eat in Chelsea, Mayfair or the West End. Restaurants in central London, much less common than today, were becoming virtually empty. There was a definite sense of public helplessness at the situation. At a press conference called 'Beat the Bombers', Ross McWhirter, who with his brother

Norris was the co-founder of the Guinness Book of Records but who was also known for his right-wing views, offered £50,000 for information leading to the arrest of the IRA terrorists and said:

> When people have a price on their heads they are much more quickly brought to justice. That's what happened in the Wild West, in Australia – and even to our own Special Operations agents in the war, who were sold almost to a man to the Gestapo for money.[19]

In a pamphlet that he presented to the cameras and reporters called 'How to stop the bombers', McWhirter advocated that all Irish Republic citizens who were living in Britain should have to register with their local police station and be issued with a pass if they wanted to leave and enter Britain. He also wrote, echoing the words of Justice Sir John Donaldson, that IRA bombers should be charged not with murder but with treason, so they could be executed. In the introduction McWhirter wrote: 'Unless something is done, some of those reading these words are going to be killed or maimed in the next few weeks.' Ross knew all too well that he was a marked man: 'I live in constant fear of my life,' he said at the press conference. 'I know the IRA have got me on a death-list.'

Just three weeks later, on the evening of 27 November, Ross's twin brother Norris answered the phone at his house and a serious voice said, 'Is that Mr McWhirter? It's Enfield Police here.' After a pause, the voice continued: 'I don't quite know how to put this, sir, but your brother has just been shot.'[20] Duggan and Doherty had staked out Ross McWhirter's house in Enfield and when his wife arrived home they confronted her with two handguns and demanded her keys. She ran past them and rang the house's doorbell. When Ross opened the door, Duggan, in front of Mrs McWhirter, shot her husband in the abdomen and then at point-blank range in the head. Leaving him bleeding profusely on his doorstep, they made their escape in Mrs McWhirter's blue Ford Granada, which was later found abandoned in Devonshire Hill in Tottenham. Ross McWhirter died not long after he was admitted to hospital. *The Observer* reported that a man using a special code word had called them claiming that the Provisional IRA in England was responsible

Ross (right) and Norris McWhirter on the *Record Breakers* BBC show. The photograph was taken four days before the IRA assassinated Ross on 27 November 1975 on the doorstep of his home and in front of his wife.

and had added: 'People like McWhirter can expect no mercy.'[21] Duggan later said: 'He thought it was the Wild West. He put a price on our head. The man thought he was living in Texas.' The Provisional *Sinn Féin* spokesman in London said of the killing: 'By his attitude he was encouraging people to inform on the Irish. He was the target for any Irishman, politically motivated or not.'[22]

By now the ASU was acting as if it *was* the Wild West. It seemed to many Londoners that a brazen IRA were able to drive round bombing or shooting at restaurants and hotels at will. The police by now were recognising that there were patterns to the campaign, and bombs were being activated in roughly the same areas of London. Under the name Operation Combo, uniformed and plainclothes officers, some armed, flooded Chelsea and the West End every evening, looking out for anything unusual. Many officers complained that they were standing out like beacons on otherwise deserted streets. On 6 December 1975 the gang had stolen a blue Ford Cortina but were spotted by Police Constable John Cook when he saw the car being driven unnaturally slowly down a road in Mayfair. The policeman, incredulous, then watched someone in the car open fire with a Sten gun at Scott's – the same Mount Street restaurant that had been attacked less than four weeks earlier. The customers, some of whom must have presumed that lightning wouldn't strike twice, dived to the ground expecting the worst. This time they were in luck. The terrorist's gun jammed and only two bullets were fired, causing no injuries or real damage. The Sten gun, initially produced cheaply during the Second World War, was a notoriously unreliable weapon, prone to jamming and inaccurate beyond 30 metres. The last time the gun was used in combat by the British was with the RUC during the IRA border campaign (codenamed 'Operation Harvest') of 1956–62.

After hearing the constable's radio call, two unarmed detective inspectors, John Purnell and Henry Dowswell, followed the Cortina in a waved-down black cab despite the poor driver having no idea that he was being asked to follow a car full of dangerous, heavily armed terrorists. Armed police were now arriving on the scene and the gang abandoned their stolen car near Marylebone station and started exchanging gunfire. Passers-by were literally diving out of the way of the bullets.

Armed police during the Balcombe Street siege which took place between 6 and 12 December 1975.

In a council flat at 22b Balcombe Street, a road near Marylebone station that runs down to the Marylebone Road, John and Sheila Matthews were watching an episode of *Kojak*. They presumed the loud gunshots they kept on hearing were coming from their television set. Suddenly four ruthless Irish terrorists burst in through the front door and took the middle-aged couple hostage. Mr Matthews had his legs tied together with his wife's tights while Mrs Matthews was dragged by Harry Duggan into the hall with a gun at her throat. He shouted at the police who were following them into the building: 'Fuck off, you bastards!'

The building was soon surrounded by police and, with a telephone dropped into the flat and loud-hailers from outside, the police continually kept in contact with the Irishmen. It was a testament to how successful the ASU had been that the police at this stage had no idea how many were in the Balcombe Street flat or who they were. For several days the terrorists refused food both for themselves and their hostages despite a cauldron of bubbling chicken soup cunningly placed a few feet away from the front door of the flat. One of the gunmen was assured over the field telephone link by the police negotiators: 'We'll give you soup as a gesture of good faith. There will be more substantial food if you release the woman. Cigarettes, too.'[23] At one point one of the gunmen asked for a plane to take them out of Britain, to which Sir Robert Mark, the Metropolitan Police Commissioner at the time, angrily announced: 'There will be no deals. They will not get a plane to Ireland. They are not going anywhere except Brixton Prison.' Presumably used to more polite and sophisticated bombers, he added that they were nothing more than 'vulgar criminals' and 'low-class terrorists'.[24]

On the sixth day, with the gang becoming hungrier and hungrier, some sausages, Brussels sprouts, potatoes and tinned peaches and cream were lowered down to the flat by the police.[25] Within twenty-five minutes the whole gang had surrendered. After the siege had ended the police began to realise that they had arrested the men for whom they had been searching since the autumn of 1974. The four well-trained terrorists had been wary and disciplined and did absolutely nothing to attract the attention of neighbours or the police. During the sixteen months they spent in London they didn't take jobs or make any attempt to mix with the Irish community.

At two addresses in north London (Butler and Doherty lived at 61 Crouch Hill while Duggan and O'Connell stayed forty-five minutes' walk away at 99 Milton Grove in Stoke Newington) the police found target lists containing names and addresses of prominent politicians, judges, and police and army officers. They also discovered bomb-making equipment, an Armalite rifle and, at Milton Grove, the two cartridge cases which had been fired from the gun which had killed Ross McWhirter.

The IRA ASU were soon given a Wild West-style moniker: the Balcombe Street Gang. It sounded almost romantic, but they had been responsible, in a ferocious, bloody burst of IRA terrorism during five months in 1975, for fifteen deaths and dozens of serious injuries. It was noted by many, however, that all charges against them relating to the period from August to December 1974 were dropped by the prosecution. It was the same period of time when the Guildford and Woolwich pub bombings had taken place and the charges were dropped because Paul Michael Hill, Gerard 'Gerry' Conlon, Patrick 'Paddy' Armstrong and Carole Richardson – collectively known as the Guildford Four – had already been convicted for the crimes.

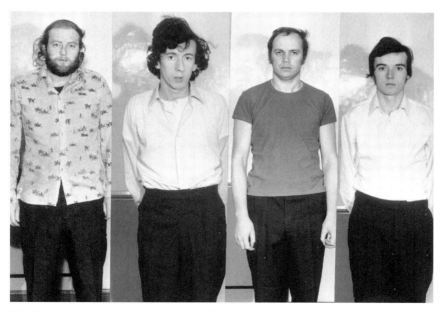

The Balcombe Street Gang, from left: Hugh Doherty, Martin O'Connell, Edward Butler and Harry Duggan, in a lineup in London.

The Balcombe Street Gang didn't call themselves terrorists: 'We are soldiers,' Butler and O'Connell later told the police. 'We are at war. Just as you are.'[26] During the sentencing for their crimes, the bearded twenty-six-year-old Hugh Doherty grinned and gave a clenched-fist salute. Edward Butler bowed his head in silence, but as he was taken to his cell gave the judge a defiant V-sign. Martin O'Connell shouted, 'Up the Provos!' while Harry Duggan, the man who had shot Ross McWhirter in the head in front of his wife, looked pale and tense and said, 'I don't want to listen to any of this English rubbish – I wish to make a statement from the dock, I am not going to listen to what you have to say. I will continually interrupt you.' He didn't, though, and stayed silent.[27]

The four men were convicted of eight killings and up to fifty bombings and shootings in public areas. Among those they murdered were Ross McWhirter and the father-of-four Gordon Hamilton-Fairley, the neighbour of Hugh Fraser. Eschewing the IRA policy of refusing to recognise the British courts, they told the trial that three of them, along with the IRA man Brendan O'Dowd, already jailed, were responsible for bombing the pubs in Guildford and Woolwich. O'Connell stated that the Director of Public Prosecutions had been told about their involvement in December 1975 but had not acted upon it. 'From the moment the police caught the real IRA bombers, the authorities knew the Guildford Four were innocent,' said the former MP Chris Mullin, who had campaigned against this and other miscarriages of justice. 'In order to obtain and sustain these convictions, the judicial process had to be bent from top to bottom.'[28]

In December 1977, two years after the Balcombe Street Gang were arrested, Lord Louis Mountbatten wrote to Werner Lott to wish him happy birthday adding: 'I should like to take the belated opportunity of congratulating you on your magnanimous behaviour when you landed the crew of the Greek ship *Diamantis* at considerable risk. Those were the days when the two navies behaved particularly well to each other and to others at sea during the war.'[29] Mountbatten had obtained the address of Lott via Gerhard Stamer, the chief engineer of U-boat 35, who had kept up correspondence with Mountbatten after the war. He wrote to him initially after the crew members had been brought

The Trattoria Fiore restaurant on the Corner of Mount St and South Audley Street. It was bombed on 29 October 1975. The 14-pound gelignite bomb containing shrapnel was placed outside one of the restaurant windows.

back from a POW camp in Canada to be interrogated, recalling: 'In summer 1946 we came back to England ... I thought of the former visit to The Tower and wrote: "You brought me in, please get me out!" Of course he couldn't but he was friendly enough to answer at once.'[30] Over the years they continued to correspond, and in June 1977 Stamer invited Mountbatten to a reunion the former crew of U-35 were going to have in England. Mountbatten wrote back: 'I am glad to hear you are coming to England in August but I am afraid that I and the whole of my family, fifteen of us in all, always go to my place in Ireland, Classiebawn Castle [Mullaghmore], and spend the entire month of August there, so I am very much afraid I shall miss you but hope you have a wonderful time.'[31]

George, formerly the Trattoria Fiore, Mount Street in 2017.

It was in August two years later in Mullaghmore, a small seaside village in County Sligo and just 12 miles from the border of Northern Ireland, when Thomas McMahon slipped onto a 30-foot wooden boat called *Shadow V*, and attached a 50-pound radio-controlled bomb. The next morning, when Mountbatten was aboard and just a few hundred yards from the shore, the bomb was detonated. Mountbatten, then aged seventy-nine, was pulled alive from the water by nearby fishermen, but died from his injuries before he was brought to shore. The IRA soon claimed responsibility, saying it was designed to 'bring to the attention of the English people the continuing occupation of our country'.[32] Six weeks later, *Sinn Féin* vice-president Gerry Adams said of Mountbatten's death: 'The IRA gave clear reasons for the execution ... As a member of the House of Lords, Mountbatten was an emotional figure in both British and Irish politics. What the IRA did to him is what Mountbatten had been doing all his life to other people; and with his war record I don't think he could have objected to dying in what was clearly a war situation.'[33]

Mountbatten wasn't alone on *Shadow V*, however, and Nicholas Knatchbull, fourteen, one of his twin grandsons, and Paul Maxwell, fifteen, a local boat boy, were also killed that morning. Another passenger on the boat, the Dowager Lady Brabourne, eighty-two, died the day after the attack. At the time of the explosion, McMahon, then thirty-one, was 70 miles away, in police custody – by chance he had been stopped at a checkpoint after he had laid the explosive. It was later found that McMahon had flakes of green paint from Lord Mountbatten's boat and traces of nitroglycerine on his clothes. He was jailed but released nineteen years later in August 1998 as part of the Good Friday Agreement.

On 19 October 1989, fifteen years after the Guildford and Woolwich pub bombings had taken place, Court No.2 at the Old Bailey was packed to capacity. There was utter silence, however, as the Lord Chief Justice, Lord Lane, finished his summing up: 'These appeals are allowed and the convictions are quashed.' After a few moments of stunned silence the courtroom erupted, relatives cheered, reporters smiled and the four defendants kissed, whooped and threw carnations across the courtroom. The long, dark nightmare of the Guildford Four was over. For fifteen years, three young Irishmen and an English woman, a minor at the time of her arrest, had been imprisoned for horrific acts of terrorism they didn't commit. The prison file of one defendant, Paul Hill, had even been stamped 'Never to be released'.[34] All four, the British Government admitted, were innocent. No one else was ever charged with the Guildford and Woolwich bombings, and although three police officers were charged with conspiracy to pervert the course of justice, they were found not guilty.

Scott's Restaurant in Mount Street, 2017.

In 1996, Martin Joseph O'Connell, known as Joe, wrote from jail to *Sinn Féin*'s *An Phoblacht* newspaper, declaring the IRA ceasefire to be 'the most stupid, blinkered and ill-conceived decision ever made by a revolutionary body'.[35] Two years later, with the offer of parole on the table, he must have changed his mind because it was O'Connell, along with Harry Duggan, Edward Butler and Hugh Doherty, who made that dramatic appearance on the platform at the special *Sinn Féin* conference in Dublin, called in May 1998 to vote on the Good Friday Agreement.

Sir Hugh Fraser, the original target of the IRA ASU, died of lung cancer in 1984. His wife Antonia, who had left him not long before the assassination attempt, went on to marry the playwright Harold Pinter. The Frasers' house guest, Caroline Kennedy, who was lucky to escape with her life, became the first female American Ambassador to Japan from 2013 to 2017.

Four days after the Balcombe Street Gang were being fêted at the *Sinn Féin* conference in Dublin, and twenty-three years after they had murdered her father, Diana Hamilton-Fairley (by now a doctor herself but at the time of his death a nineteen-year-old medical student) spoke at a Belfast conference in support of the Good Friday Agreement. She said that she accepted the early release of the gang as part of the agreement and that she was aware that the peace process would be long and painful. She then added:

> All sides will have to give up some of their most precious tenets in order to gain the ultimate goal of peace. It was incredibly hard for me last Sunday to see my father's killers walk into that *Sinn Féin* gathering. They are alive, and my father is dead. Nothing can change that: nothing will bring him back.[36]

Her father has a plaque in the crypt of St Paul's Cathedral, the inscription of which reads:

> Gordon Hamilton-Fairley DM FRCP, first professor of medical oncology, 1930–75. Killed by a terrorist bomb. It matters not how a man dies but how he lives.

Recipe for a Black Velvet

This famous drink that James Bond and his friend Bill Tanner had with their dressed crab at Scott's was invented in 1861 at Brooks's Club in St James's. The story is that the steward at the club, overcome with emotion after the death of Prince Albert, ordered that even the champagne should be put into mourning and mixed it with Guinness.

A Black Velvet is made by mixing equal parts of stout and champagne in a Pilsner glass. It can also be made by filling a champagne flute halfway with champagne and then floating the chilled stout beer on top of the wine. The differing densities of the liquids cause them to remain in separate layers. This is best achieved by pouring over a spoon turned upside down over the top of the glass so that the liquid runs gently down the sides rather than splashing into the lower layer and mixing with it.

In Germany, there is a version of this mixed beer drink called a Bismarck and made with Schwarzbier (a dark lager) and served in a beer stein or beer mug. According to *Brewer's Dictionary of Phrase and Fable*, the 'Iron Chancellor' supposedly drank it by the gallon.

3

The Trial of Schoolkids OZ, the Downfall of the 'Dirty Squad'

Eugene Schuster, a young and brash American who owned the London Arts Gallery in New Bond Street, boasted to the *Observer* in 1969 that he expected to become the ultimate art dealer of them all – 'I'll probably make Lord Duveen, who was the greatest dealer of all time, look like a drawing-room hustler.'[1] It was Joseph Duveen, whose clients included William Randolph Hearst, J. P. Morgan and John D. Rockefeller, who had once said that 'Europe has a great deal of art, and America has a great deal of money'.[2] He was a salesman of genius and managed to persuade his prestigious clients that buying works of art, in particular Italian Renaissance paintings, would do nothing but show their discerning taste and judgment to the world – essentially, buy them class. The works Duveen shipped across the Atlantic in the early decades of the twentieth century remain the core collections of many of the United States' most famous museums. At the end of the sixties, thirty years after the death of Duveen, the cocksure Schuster was not making his fortune by selling paintings by Giotto, Titian or Bellini. Not exactly, anyway. He was making his fortune by selling art prints, which, due to modern advances in colour printing technology, could now be produced relatively quickly and cheaply. One newspaper called it a 'licence to paint money', and Schuster was riding an international art boom that even at the end of the sixties had an estimated annual turnover of £1 billion.[3]

On 15 January 1970, Schuster opened a new exhibition called 'The Bag One', which consisted of fourteen 'intimate and erotic' lithographs by the soon to be ex-Beatle John Lennon. The drawings depicted Lennon and his wife Yoko Ono in various sexual poses. Each lithograph was on sale for £40 each or, if you were inclined, a whole set was available for £550 (approximately £8,000 in 2017) which, to make it more of a bargain, included an extremely handy leather holdall to keep them in. Two days after the opening of the exhibition the gallery was raided by the Obscene Publications Squad, known colloquially as the 'Dirty Squad' and led by Detective-Inspector Patrick Luff. This nickname stuck, not only because of the so-called dirty books it was meant to constrain but because of the moral grubbiness and decaying corruption that was said to permeate the squad. The gallery was immediately closed down, and Schuster was charged under the Obscene Publications Act – legislation introduced by a young Roy Jenkins ten years previously, which for the first time, as far as pornography was concerned, permitted a defence of 'public good'. Penguin Books, prosecuted in 1960 for publishing *Lady Chatterley's Lover*, successfully relied on this defence when academics and literary critics such as Richard Hoggart and Helen Gardner testified at the

Eugene Schuster in 1970.

The leather hold-all which came with fourteen of John Lennon's Lithographs at the cost of £550.

trial that the book was one of literary merit – although, as Clive James has pointed out, 'the Lady Chatterley acquittal gave the notion of obscenity substance and was therefore catastrophic'.[4]

Not long after the forced closure of the London Arts Gallery, the Director of Public Prosecutions received a letter from a member of the public, signed Mr P.F.C. Fuller Esq., who warned that if the court case went ahead there was a chance other art collections throughout the country could potentially be in trouble: 'I understand that HM the Queen has some highly erotic work by Fragonard ...' At the beginning of February, the police burst into the Open Space theatre club on Tottenham Court Road and stopped the showing of Andy Warhol's film *Flesh*. Mr John Trevelyan, secretary to the British Film Censors, arrived in a taxi shortly after the event and told reporters: 'This raid is a strange business. It comes just after the action over the Lennon exhibition. Who started this? Who's behind it all? What's happening? I wish I knew.'[5]

On 1 April, less than three months after the raid and the confiscation of John Lennon's lithographs at Schuster's gallery, Ringo became the last Beatle to play at the group's recording session at EMI's Abbey Road studios. In the presence of producer Phil Spector, he overdubbed the drum parts for 'Across the Universe' and 'The Long and Winding Road'.[6] John and Yoko, meanwhile, issued a false press release which announced that 'they have both entered a London clinic for a dual sex-change operation'. It was an April Fool joke; in reality, partly because Lennon's Ascot mansion was being renovated and overrun by builders, the couple had enrolled themselves in a month-long course of Primal Therapy (a treatment for mental illness that involves repeatedly descending into feeling and experiencing long-repressed childhood pain) with the American psychologist Dr Arthur Janov at his private London hospital at 20 Devonshire Place in Marylebone.[7]

About a mile away from where John Lennon and his wife were primally screaming, the court case over his erotic lithographs was opening at Marlborough Street Magistrates' Court. Mr Schuster was now being charged, not with the Obscene Publications Act, but with a law that was 130 years old and which alleged that the gallery had 'exhibited to public view eight indecent prints to the annoyance of passengers, contrary to Section 54(12) of the Metropolitan Police Act, 1839'. This ancient law, originally brought into force just two years after Queen Victoria had begun her reign, was intended to increase the powers of the police in London and regulated activities such as bear-baiting, cockfighting, 'furious' driving, the blowing of horns, knocking on doors wantonly (or ringing the bell in the same manner), making slides out of snow or ice, flying kites or beating a carpet before eight in the morning.

The original charge using the Obscene Publications Act was dropped to avoid the troublesome defence of 'public good' or 'artistic merit'. Not that Detective Inspector Frederick Luff, who had led the raid, thought there was any when he brought the case to court, saying:

Many toilet walls depict works of similar merit. It is perhaps charitable to suggest that they are the work of a sick mind. The only danger to a successful prosecution, as I see it, is the argument that they are so pathetic as to be incapable of influencing anyone and therefore unable to deprave or corrupt.[8]

The defence team concentrated on the word 'annoyance' in the ancient law, arguing that it was an integral part of the offence, to which Detective Inspector Frederick Luff said: 'I saw a number of people shaking their heads and obviously embarrassed. One middle-aged gentleman said, "Shocking, isn't it?" and left the gallery.' Mr St John Harmsworth, the magistrate, then asked the Detective Inspector, drily: 'Did he stamp his foot?' To which Luff replied, 'Anger was registered on his face!' The police had only been able to obtain two statements from witnesses who found the lithographs obscene. One had insisted that the police did not disclose that she was a justice of the Peace as she feared being labelled a 'neurotic busybody', while the other, a grey-haired accountant called George Brown from Wandsworth Common, was 'a little over-ardent in his criticism':

> I felt a bit sick that a man should draw himself and his wife in such positions. They were exaggerated, distorted caricatures depicting intimate sexual relationships of a repulsive and disgusting nature. To think that a man could use his own wife, not even using a model hitherto unknown to him, was to me making the marriage a farce.[9]

Amid much laughter in court, the case was dismissed. The magistrate decided that there were no 'passengers' in the gallery, annoyed or otherwise – 'they had, for the time being, finished passaging', and thus Lennon's prints were 'unlikely to deprave or corrupt'. It wasn't just Detective Inspector Luff who found it difficult to find any artistic merit in the lithographs. Schuster himself was not over-enamoured: 'They are bad art, but after all it's the name that sells them.'[10] A few days later, the world learnt that the band that had made Lennon's name had broken up when the *Daily Mirror* splashed on its 10 April front page the headline 'Paul Quits the Beatles'.

The following month, in response to accusations that the magazine was losing touch with younger readers, one of John Lennon's favourite magazines, *OZ*, published the 'SCHOOL KIDS ISSUE', *OZ* No. 28. It was so called not because it was aimed at children, but because it was written by around twenty secondary school students who had answered an advert in *OZ* No. 26, which read:

> Some of us are feeling old and boring. We invite our readers who are under 18 to come and edit the April issue. We will choose one person, several or accept collective applications from a group of friends. Oz belongs to you.

The young would-be journalists, who included the music writer Charles Shaar Murray and Deyan Sudjic, later founder of *Blueprint* magazine and Director of the Design Museum, met at the editor Richard Neville's flat in Palace Gardens Terrace, by Notting Hill Gate, and over a few weekends the magazine took shape. The finished issue (selling for 48p) had a provocative blue soft-focus cover, featuring naked women with 'OZ – SCHOOLKIDS' ISSUE' in yellow lettering. Inside the magazine looked much as it always did, containing a surreal mix of graphics and cartoons, but it also included articles written by the students on subjects

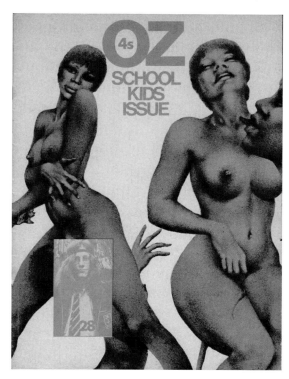

The cover of *OZ* 28, the Schoolkids Issue.

such as pop music, sexual freedom and hypocrisy, drug use, corporal punishment, and the eternal student complaint of exams. ('Examinations are a primitive method of recording a tiny, often irrelevant, section of the behaviour of an individual under bizarre conditions.') One notable item was a racy Rupert Bear parody produced by fifteen-year-old Islington schoolboy Vivian Berger (Byline: '16, Aries. Smoked at 9, first tripped at 11. Interested in mysticism')[11] where he had simply pasted the iconic head and scarf of Rupert the Bear onto an X-rated cartoon by Robert Crumb, while retaining below the rhyming couplets from the Rupert strip. There were also adverts, many of which were adult in nature, such as 'the first portable massager uniquely shaped to body contours', sold by Pellen Personal Products of Muswell Hill Broadway at 80/- (incl. P&P) for the deluxe model.

OZ started in 1963 as an underground alternative magazine published in Sydney, Australia. Four years later, Richard Neville and the designer, Martin Sharp, travelled via Asia to England, and produced a second version in London. Aided by the visual brilliance of Sharp and the fact that the costs of offset printing had fallen so low that they could experiment with colour, OZ managed to both reflect and help define the prevailing British counterculture.

Although the magazine had always been about pushing boundaries, the introduction of children into the mix was the trigger for the police to go on the offensive. Jonathon Green noted in his book *All Dressed Up*: 'The Establishment did not like OZ or the counter-culture that it represented – when Neville naively, injudiciously combined "children" with the usual irritants of drugs and sex and rock, they saw their chance.' Detective Inspector Luff, a deeply committed Christian, had long had the 'alternative' magazine in his sights. OZ was one of several 'underground' publications targeted by the Obscene Publications Squad, and their offices had already been raided on several occasions. Luff had once gone up to Debbie Knight, the receptionist at OZ, and said:

Debbie I have come round here many times and I've always tried to behave like a gentleman and I'd like to speak to you as a father now. I don't understand how such a nice girl could possibly work in a place like this, with all this filth and corruption. You could have a very nice job working in the police force.[12]

Debbie ignored the generous offer, and in July 1970 was still on reception when the magazine was raided by Luff and his men, who seized filing cabinets, disconnected phones, and even took the pictures from the walls. The three *OZ* editors – co-founder Richard Neville, Jim Anderson and 'freak with a briefcase' twenty-five-year-old Felix Dennis, who had previously worked as a gravedigger for Pinner County Council but who was now the magazine's business manager, were charged with 'conspiracy to produce a magazine with intent thereby to debauch and corrupt the morals of children and other young persons within the realm and to arouse and implant in the minds of those young people lustful and perverted desires'. The language seemed old-fashioned and it was – the charge hadn't been used for 130 years. Similarly to the Lennon lithographs case the charge was intended as a way of avoiding the pesky 'public good' defence. Troubling for the defendants, however, was that the charge carried a maximum sentence of life imprisonment.

Around the same time as the *OZ* raid, Detective Inspector Luff, who specialised in 'celebrity raids' that gave him maximum publicity, got hold of two tickets for a preview of Kenneth Tynan's (then the *Observer*'s theatre critic) infamous full-frontal nude revue *Oh! Calcutta!*. Luff, who visited the Round House venue in Camden with Sergeant Ann Cox, reported that he was horrified by the performance, during which he noted that three couples 'stormed out'. He also noted that one sketch was 'pathetic, unjustifiable, appalling pornography'. Just to make absolutely sure how much public nudity was on show, Luff visited the revue twice more to confirm his objections to the controversial production. He then wrote to the Attorney General, Sir Peter Rawlinson, asking him to prosecute the revue under the 1968 Theatres Act: 'Sex is not dealt with with respect,' wrote Luff, while 'man is depicted as a performing dog self-indulgently satisfying every whim and thereby debasing any form of dignity and attacking the very roots of the family unit.' The Bishop of Southwark, meanwhile, declared the show as 'boring as a boarding school on bath night', while the author Tynan defended himself against the allegation that he had himself once described *Oh! Calcutta!* as 'tasteful pornography', by declaring that this was very unlikely, as he had 'a horror of the word "tasteful"'. The Attorney General concluded, eventually, that 'it would be impossible to prove that *Oh! Calcutta!* was obscene', let alone persuade a jury to convict.[13]

The following year, Felix Dennis, Richard Neville and Jim Anderson stood trial at the Old Bailey. Geoffrey Robertson, then a fresh-faced Sydney law graduate and an Australian Rhodes Scholar, offered to help with the defence. After several rebuttals by many QCs worried about the effect the trial might have on their careers, John Mortimer, who had no ambitions to be a judge, agreed to defend the magazine. 'Goody, goody – when do we start,' he told Neville and Robertson over their first meeting, at lunch in a restaurant called Jonah's. Mortimer was already well known for his play, *Voyage Round my Father*, but notable, in the legal world, for defending *Last Exit to Brooklyn* by Hubert Selby Jr. The American novel had been found obscene in November 1966 when an all-male jury had returned a guilty verdict – not least because Judge Graham Rigers directed that women 'might be embarrassed at having to read a book which dealt with homosexuality, prostitution, drug-taking

John Mortimer QC in 1966. He was called to the Bar in 1948 and died in January 2009.

and sexual perversion';[14] but in 1968, after Mortimer had issued an appeal, a judgment by Mr Justice Lane reversed the ruling.

The Australian Richard Neville had already met Mortimer several times, and once remembered a party where Mortimer had mingled at a buffet with his girlfriend, Louise Ferrier, also Australian: 'As he chatted about the unconventional sexual proclivities of Melbourne, it took a while for Louise to realise he was talking about the Victorian English Prime Minister and not the city in Australia.' Neville had also met the writer and QC at a dinner party hosted by his sister Jill, a publisher in London. Early in the morning after everyone had left, Jill had been woken at home by a phone call from Mortimer. 'Hello, lovely,' whispered the notable QC, 'as I'm in the area – I thought I might drop by and pop into bed?' She refused the offer but Mortimer was not easily discouraged and added, 'I quite understand, my dear, perhaps another time?'

The OZ trial was held in Court Two at the Old Bailey in front of Judge Michael Argyle, a stern fifty-six-year-old who had stood in two elections as a right-wing Conservative. He was a firm believer in capital punishment and renowned for his lengthy sentencing. A country, betting and sporting man, the judge was so deaf to political correctness that he never understood why his wife's racing colours – 'nigger brown, black cap' – could possibly cause offence. Argyle was infamous for telling a witness in court that she was 'far too attractive to be a policewoman', and he once explained a suspended sentence to an attempted rapist on the grounds, 'You come from Derby which is my part of the world. Off you go and don't come back.'[15] Jeremy Paxman once wrote that, as a young reporter, he asked a more experienced colleague why a defendant had been sent to prison for 'stealing a pencil or something of similar gravity'. The fellow reporter replied, 'He made the critical mistake of appearing before Judge Michael Argyle after lunch on a Friday.'[16]

The OZ obscenity trial eventually became the longest in history, although the prosecution case was actually rather brief and to the point, with their only exhibit being the Schoolkids edition itself. Many of the problems that arose came from the clashes between two very different cultures. Geoffrey Robertson, in his book *The Justice Game*, recalled that when Detective Inspector Luff was giving evidence, he told the court that his interview with Felix Dennis had ended with the suspect exclaiming: 'Right on!' Judge Argyle, taking down the evidence longhand, looked up, puzzled, and said, 'Write on ... but you had finished the interview?' 'Not write on – W-R-I-T-E, my Lord – but R-I-G-H-T on.' The judge still looked mystified, 'It's a revolutionary expression,' helped an exasperated Luff.

The length of the trial had more to do with the myriad of witnesses brought in by the defence to help explain why the magazine was not obscene. George Melly, the jazz singer and film critic, at one point was questioned by the prosecutor Brian Leary: 'If you really believe more openness is better, what do you think is wrong with an advertisement that describes oral sex attractively?' Melly replied: 'Nothing. I don't think cunnilingus could do actual harm ...' Judge Argyle, by now almost permanently confused, interrupted to ask: 'For those of us who don't have a classical education what do you mean by this word "cunnilinctus"?' (Geoffrey Robertson later wondered whether the judge thought it was some kind of cough medicine.)

Jim Anderson, Richard Neville and Felix Dennis on the way to the Old Bailey, June 1971.

Melly apologised: 'I'm sorry my Lord I've been inhibited by the architecture. I will try and use better known expressions in the future: Sucking. Blowing. Or going down or gobbling. Or, as we said in my naval days, "yodelling in the canyon".'[17] Incidentally, twenty-six years later, Kenny MacDonald, who either knew the odd sailor or was a keen student of the *OZ* obscenity trial, wrote the runner-up song to represent the UK in the Eurovision song contest in 1997, called 'Yodel in the Canyon of Love', sung by Do-Re-Mi, featuring Kerry.

During the trial, Brian Leary seemed utterly obsessed with Rupert Bear's erection. At one point he read out Jim Anderson's editorial, which had described Vivian Berger's work as 'youthful genius'. Leary, after carefully describing the simple process of pasting together two artists' work, then asked the *OZ* editor, 'Wherein lies the genius?' Anderson tried to explain, 'Er, I think it's in the juxtaposition of two ideas, the childhood symbol of innocence … ' Leary, apoplectic, shouted: 'BY MAKING RUPERT BEAR FUCK!?'

Another defence witness was John Peel, who was surprised to find himself discussing with Leary whether it might be possible to induce an orgasm by listening to classical music. John Peel spoke about 'making love', to which Leary said: 'So we take it that you would consider it bad taste to use the word "fuck" rather than "making love"? Which would you prefer?' Peel looked nonplussed and said, 'The expressions are not different,' adding, 'I just felt because I was in court I should say "make love" but everybody else seems to say "fuck" so I will say "fuck" as well … '[18]

Later in the trial Leary was still occupied with Mary Tourtel's cartoon character's penis, and asked the lateral-thinking defence witness, Edward de Bono, 'What do you suppose is the effect intended to be of equipping Rupert Bear with such a large-sized organ?' 'I don't know enough about bears to know their exact proportions,' replied de Bono gravely. 'I imagine their organs are hidden in their fur.'

At one point Leary asked Neville: 'The cover of the magazine portrays, does it not, a series of lesbian poses?' 'Yes, there are depicted three or four ladies enjoying themselves,' Neville replied. Leary then pointed at a phallus strapped to one of the women: 'I think it's called a dildol.' 'Er, I don't think so,' Neville pointed out. At this point Judge Argyle interrupted: 'I think we'd better call it an "imitation male penis" to avoid confusion.' 'Your Honour,' Neville responded, 'I think the word "male" is unnecessary.' Richard Neville once admitted that he was rather pleased with this comment, but it's worth noting that *OZ*, and the underground press generally, often published objectifying and sadistic images of women; and, as Marsha Rowe, founder of *Spare Rib* magazine, who helped work on the defence during the *OZ* obscenity trial, has pointed out, women who worked on the 'alternative' magazines and newspapers at that time 'served the men and did the office and production work, rather than any editorial work'.[19] Only four of the twenty students who worked on the Schoolkids *OZ* were girls, and one of them, fifteen-year-old Berti, featured in a full-page pull-out poster entitled 'Jailbait of the month'.

It was obvious to anyone at the trial that Judge Argyle wanted no other outcome than that the defendants should be convicted. At one point, after the jury had retired to consider their verdict, they asked Judge Argyle if he could help determine the exact meaning of 'indecency'. Argyle answered: 'If a woman takes her clothes off on a crowded beach, we think that is indecent in this country.'[20] After a total of four hours and armed with this helpful explanation, the jury of nine men and three women acquitted the three editors on the conspiracy to debauch and corrupt the morals of young persons, but the judge directed them to bring back a verdict of guilty on an obscenity charge. 'Send them down!' ordered a gleeful Argyle, happy with the fact that he had rescued, almost single-handedly, the very fabric of western civilisation.

The three *OZ* editors were detained in prison and sent for psychiatric examination. They also had their heads shaved. In the early seventies, long hair was still seen as anti-establishment and the shaving only prolonged the already considerable outcry surrounding the trial and verdict. At the sentencing a week later, the judge announced to a shorn Richard Neville, 'I have no alternative but to sentence you to fifteen months' imprisonment.' Dennis, meanwhile, was given a lesser sentence because Justice Argyle considered the future publishing magnate and billionaire 'very much less intelligent' than the other two defendants, and thus less culpable. As they were taken downstairs another prisoner told

Neville, 'Christ. That's how long I got. And I tried to murder my wife.'[21] The sergeant who took them away quipped, 'You can find more porn in Soho than what's in the pages of *OZ*.' The court sergeant wasn't the only person to notice this, and it was once alleged by Geoffrey Robertson that at the appeal the Lord Chief Justice, Lord Widgery, sent his clerk, a former merchant seaman, to Soho one lunchtime to buy £20 worth of the hardest porn he could find. The contents of *OZ* 'paled in comparison'.

At the appeal trial (where the defendants appeared wearing long wigs) it was found that Justice Argyle had grossly misdirected the jury (some have said an extraordinary seventy-eight times). His contemptuous and biased summing-up at the end of the original trial has now gone down in legal history, but the defence also alleged that the fifteen-year-old Berger had been harassed and assaulted by police. This may or may not have had anything to do with his mother being Grace Berger, at the time the Chair of the National Council for Civil Liberties. The convictions were all quashed and the three editors walked free. Years later, Felix Dennis told author Jonathon Green that on the night before the appeal was heard, the *OZ* editors had had a clandestine meeting with the Lord Chief Justice, Lord Widgery,[22] who reportedly said that Argyle had made a 'fat mess' of the trial, and told them that they would be acquitted. But only, he insisted, if they agreed to give up working on *OZ*. Dennis also said that, in his opinion, MPs Tony Benn and Michael Foot had interceded with Widgery on their behalf.[23]

Despite the Lord Justice's wishes, *OZ* continued to be published and, after the highly publicised trials, the circulation rose to an incredible 100,000 copies. Buoyed by this success, the magazine moved to expensive offices off Tottenham Court Road, but within two years the magazine's popularity faded, and the extraordinary, ground-breaking psychedelic designs started to look dated. By the time the last issue (*OZ* No. 48) was published in November 1973, *OZ* Publications was £20,000 in debt and the magazine had 'no readership worth the name'. Felix Dennis went on to become one of Britain's wealthiest and most prominent independent publishers as owner of Dennis Publishing (publisher of *Maxim*, *PC World* and other magazines) and died in 2014, at home in Warwickshire, aged sixty-seven. Neville eventually returned to Australia, where he became a successful author, commentator and public speaker, and died in 2016.

After the *OZ* trial, Reginald Maudling, the Conservative Home Secretary, hauled in Detective Chief Inspector George Fenwick, head of the Obscene Publications Squad, and asked him if he could in any way explain exactly why the porn barons in Soho seemed to be operating with seeming impunity while there were continuous raids on relatively innocuous 'alternative' magazines. Fenwick blamed the press for the huge publicity of the *OZ* trial and others like it, and claimed it was only this that gave the impression that the police were doing nothing about Soho. Fed up with Fenwick's lame excuses, the Home Secretary immediately initiated a major corruption inquiry into the Metropolitan Police.

After the Second World War there had been many rumours, and even acknowledgment by an occasional senior police officer, that there was endemic corruption throughout the Metropolitan Police. In 1955, the *Daily Mail* reported that a Detective Superintendent had sent a report to the Metropolitan Police Commissioner, John Nott-Bower, regarded by many as a pleasant but ineffectual man, revealing a vast amount of bribery and corruption among uniformed officers at the West End Central station. It involved 'club proprietors, prostitutes, gaming house owners, brothel keepers and men living on immoral earnings'.[24] Nott-Bower's reaction was not only to ignore the report's findings, but to go personally to the West End station, jump on a table and give a 'pep talk' to the assorted officers, telling them that any corruption allegations had 'no foundation in fact' and were 'grossly unfair'.[25]

Fourteen years later, in November 1969, *The Times*, at the time considered the absolute mouthpiece of the Establishment, claimed that it had proof that two Detective Constables, and even a Detective Inspector, had taken bribes, given false evidence for money, and had 'allowed a criminal to work unhindered'.[26] The newspaper had even recorded one of the bent detectives saying, 'We've got more villains in our game than you've got in yours, you know.' The same officer went on to talk about corrupt officers in London being 'a firm within a firm'. The allegations were so serious, *The Times* maintained, that the decision was made to publish the story rather than hand over the evidence because they simply had no faith in the Met's integrity. The exposed corruption was shocking in its scale, and one leading criminal lawyer likened it to catching the Archbishop of Canterbury in bed with a prostitute.[27]

The Home Secretary, James Callaghan, appointed Frank Williamson, one of the Inspector of Constabulary officials appointed by the Home Office to oversee the police, to head the enquiry. This was all well and good, but under him, and in operational charge, was a senior officer in the Metropolitan Police, Detective Chief Superintendent Bill Moody, head of the Vice Squad. On his first day in charge of the squad, based in Savile Row, Moody roared up in an Alfa Romeo sports car, which he called 'a real bird puller'. He sneered at an officer with a modest family saloon and said, 'Is that the best you can do?'[28] Williamson went on to divide the entire Metropolitan Police Force into three types: a) corrupt police officers; b) police officers who knew about corruption and did nothing about it; and c) those who were too stupid to realise there was any corruption. Williamson soon came to the conclusion that his investigation was going nowhere. The 'firm within a firm' watching over him meant that important material was leaked to the officers being investigated, essential files mysteriously disappeared, and many senior policemen, including Bill Moody, conducted a campaign of lies against him. Deliberately obstructed by detectives, Williamson became utterly disheartened and resigned in 1971.[29]

The following year, Maudling appointed Robert Mark to be the new Commissioner of the Metropolitan police. To the old guard in the Met he was a provincial outsider and had a reputation as 'Mr Clean'. In the same year as Mark's appointment, the *Sunday People* tabloid, under the headline 'Police Chief and the Porn King', exposed a connection between Jimmy Humphreys (who openly ran strip clubs in Soho and was one of the biggest operators of pornographic bookshops there) and Commander Kenneth Drury, then in charge of the infamous Flying Squad – known as the Sweeney – the Metropolitan Police unit responsible for dealing with armed robberies and organised crime. Drury and Humphreys had together enjoyed a luxurious two-week holiday in Cyprus accompanied by their wives, all paid for, of course, by the Soho pornographer. Drury even had the confidence, or stupidity, to sign the hotel register with his police rank, and even included his address as 'New Scotland Yard'. Drury was hopelessly

Walker's Court in 1966.

compromised, and concocted a yarn that he was in Cyprus looking for the train robber Ronnie Biggs and had paid for the trip himself. Nobody believed his story.

South Londoner Jimmy Humphreys was a handsome and softly spoken man who always dressed smartly. Born in 1930 in Bermondsey, he left school at fourteen and became friends with 'Mad' Frankie Fraser. Fraser was not someone to inhibit anyone's journey into lawbreaking, and Humphreys found the money for his first date with his first wife, June Driscoll, via a stolen television set. At the beginning of the sixties, after a few prison sentences, he decided to try to emulate the Soho success of Paul Raymond, who had opened his Raymond's Revue Bar in 1958. Humphreys had operated a couple of small strip clubs – one on Old Compton Street and another on Macclesfield Street – but then opened one more at 5 Walker's Court, an alleyway connecting Brewer and Berwick Streets, and just a few metres from the Revuebar. In the meantime Humphreys had married a feisty, red-headed stripper who had performed at one of his clubs under the name Rusty Gaynor, in reality born June Packard. The couple became good friends with Paul Raymond and his wife Jean.

Rusty once told a story about Raymond attempting to buy the freehold of his Revuebar in 1960. Raymond had initially been renting the property, once known as the Doric Ballroom, which sounded grand but was in reality a rundown building that was occasionally used for down-at-heel wedding receptions. The landlord was Jack Isow, a rotund, balding Polish Jew born Joseph Isowitski, who ran the large and sumptuous Isow's restaurant on Brewer Street (the Ivy of the day and *the* showbiz restaurant, later to become the infamous Madame JoJo's). At this time, it was assumed by most that this part of Soho, close to Piccadilly Circus, would soon be massively redeveloped. The property developer Jack Cotton had recently bought the Monico site on the north side of Piccadilly Circus, and had plans for a huge tower block in the area. Most contemporary newspapers reported on the proposed redevelopment as almost a *fait accompli*. This meant that property value in this part of London was relatively low, and most properties were rented out on short leases. After Jack Isow had agreed the price of the Walker's Court venue (£14,000, and more than it was worth) Raymond arranged to meet Isow at his restaurant to deliver the money. Rusty recounted:

> When Paul went round to Jack's restaurant to finalise the deal, Jack was expecting him to hand over a cheque. Instead, Paul, who would eventually become one of the richest men in Britain, gave him this briefcase full of cash. Jack said it must've been buried somewhere because it was all green and mouldy. The money smelt really damp and musty. God knows where he'd been hiding it.[30]

Jimmy and Rusty's club at Walker's Court did well and with the profits they bought and renovated a large building on the corner of Berwick and D'Arblay Streets. Soon they opened the Queen's Club,

Queen's Club, owned by Jimmy Humphreys
on Berwick Street in 1972.

which offered a modern brand of striptease in a style that owed more to the new-fangled discotheques than cabaret or theatre. Many at this time thought Soho was rapidly changing, and not for the better. Old retailers and workshops were being forced out by pornographic bookshops and strip joints that would happily take on what were now expensive short-term leases. By the end of the 1960s, there were more than fifty strip-clubs and pornographic bookshops operating around Soho. No one had seen anything like it, and they all seemed to be operating with impunity. It's worth noting, however, that this wasn't the first time residents of Soho were complaining of this (and it won't be the last): 'Our respectable workers are in many cases being driven out of house and home to make room for traders in vice who can afford to pay exorbitant rents,' complained a delegate at a conference held in 1895.[31]

The deregulation of pornography in Sweden and Denmark, together with the reduced cost of colour printing (an unheralded technical revolution that touched upon many aspects of modern life), contributed to extraordinary profit margins. One man who tasted the fruit of this cornucopia said: 'The money comes in so fast it makes you dizzy. The profits are so enormous that you don't even worry about details like overheads, they are minuscule by comparison.'[32] Jimmy Humphreys was in the right place at the right time, but to get a firm foothold in the business of pornography there were considerable hidden costs. In particular, expensive deals with Soho power brokers such as Bernard 'Bernie' Silver – a 'working-class East Ender with a taste for fine restaurants and flashy clothes'[33] and a leading crime boss, active in prostitution, pornography and racketeering. However, the main thing that enabled Humphreys to become one of Soho's prominent porn shop and club owners, and the inspiration for Malcolm McDowell's character Bennie Barratt in the acclaimed television series *Our Friends in the North*, was the massive pay-offs to senior Metropolitan Police detectives.

After the *Sunday People* headlines, most of Drury's colleagues closed ranks and tried to protect him, but Robert Mark soon ordered his suspension and subsequent disciplinary proceedings. Drury resigned, and promptly sold his story to the *News of the World* for £10,000. Humphreys soon realised the danger of appearing to have been a police informant and announced that

Drury had set up the whole thing. After a police raid at his house, a diary belonging to Humphreys was found in a wall-safe and, open-mouthed, the corruption investigators found that it had detailed payments to seventeen different senior policemen; one was Drury, but there was also DCI George Fenwick, head of the Obscene Publications Squad.

As the ensuing corruption investigations widened, the infamous Obscene Publications Squad was replaced in its entirety with a new group of officers drawn from the uniformed branch, and over twenty detectives were dismissed or required to resign. Soon it was realised that corruption went almost to the top, and policemen such as Bill Moody – now head of the Obscene Publications Squad – and, incredibly, his superior Commander Wallace 'Wally' Virgo – a man who had overall control of nine squads including the Flying, Drugs and the Porn Squad – were all being paid

Robert Mark in 1974.

off. It was estimated that Jimmy Humphreys was paying an extraordinary £2,000 per week to the senior detectives (including a further £2,000 Christmas bonus!), enabling him to continue selling porn unimpeded. Humphreys had been so worried that Drury's expensive lifestyle would give everything away that he had supplied him with expensive slimming drugs and a rowing machine to keep his weight down.

In court it came to light that Humphreys had been living in a world of international travel and luxury. In just one year he had bought three Rolls-Royces, a Mercedes for his wife Rusty, a yacht, a villa on Ibiza and a farm in Kent. When at one point it was suggested that his activities were criminal in the extreme, he disagreed: 'My activities were just anti-social,' he declared.[34]

All this revealed that it had become important for the Dirty Squad to raid exhibitions such as John Lennon's *Bag One* and bust 'alternative' magazines such as *OZ* to look as though they were actually doing something. The corrupt policeman had built a delicately balanced house of cards that soon came tumbling down. Initially, there were just the usual discreet early retirements and resignations, but eventually there were two major corruption trials and George Fenwick, Bill Moody, Wally Virgo and Kenneth Drury (who, when he was arrested at his home in Sidcup in Kent, came walking out of his house with a paper bag on his head) were all given between ten and fourteen years in prison in 1977.

'Thank goodness the Obscene Publications Squad have gone,' said an upset Mr Justice Mars-Jones after Fenwick's trial. 'I fear the damage you have done may be with us for a long time.'[35] After the second trial, Mars-Jones said the case had revealed 'corruption on a scale which beggars description'. Sir Robert Mark, who once said that 'a good police force is one that catches more crooks than it employs',[36] recalled in his autobiography *In the Office of Constable* that when he took over as Commissioner he 'had never experienced institutionalised wrong-doing, blindness, arrogance and prejudice on anything like a scale accepted as routine at the Met'.[37]

Jimmy and Rusty Humphreys were finished in Soho, with their reputations, such as they were, ruined. Humphreys had become what he had most feared and become a 'nark' – a

Above: Walker's Court in 1972.

Below: Rupert Street looking at Walker's Court in 2017.

police informant – although it did get him a royal pardon from an eight-year sentence for assaulting a former boyfriend of Rusty's. Soon after his release, the couple began to sell off their Soho holdings. This, together with the downfall of the Obscene Publications Squad, which in their corruption heyday had done so much to reduce the usual legal risks inherent in the porn business, meant that property prices in Soho started to fall in value. With typically good timing, Paul Raymond chose 1977 as the year for a major round of Soho acquisitions and secretly started buying one freehold a week, including many on Old Compton Street, Dean Street and Brewer Street. Eventually he was the owner of 100 properties in Soho alone. The Humphreys, however, were long gone, first fleeing to Mexico and then to Florida, living off horse and greyhound racing. Homesick, they returned to London in the 1990s and soon reverted to their old ways. In 1993 both were jailed for profiting from high-class West End brothels.

The Home Office, in response to the corruption, and in conjunction with Metropolitan Police Commissioner Sir Robert Mark, appointed the Assistant Chief Constable of Dorset Constabulary, Leonard Burt, to investigate all the corruption allegations. In August 1978, a team of 200 officers began investigating the Metropolitan Police from top to bottom. Referring to Burt's Dorset roots, the enquiry had the nickname Operation Countryman. At first the team were housed at Camberwell police station, but following clumsy attempts to interfere with their documents, records and evidence, they moved to Godalming police station in Surrey. In 1984, after six years and millions of pounds, Operation Countryman presented its findings to the Home Office and the Commissioner. It led to a successful conviction of two City of London officers while eight Scotland Yard detectives were acquitted at the Old Bailey, although three of them were dismissed following disciplinary action.[38] And that was that. Not one Metropolitan Police officer was ever found guilty of a criminal offence as a result of Operation Countryman. It was nothing short of a public relations catastrophe, and the Metropolitan Police Service has never really quite recovered.

4

Captain Sears, the Nazi Wreath at the Cenotaph and the Hitler Paint-throwing Incident at Madame Tussaud's

On Valentine's day in February 1933, Madame Tussaud's began to advertise, rather proudly, their latest model. Anyone paying 1s 6d, or just sixpence if you were under twelve, could now turn up at the Exhibition Galleries on Marylebone Road and view not only King Alfred burning the cakes or Sir Walter Raleigh spreading out his cloak for Queen Elizabeth, but also a wax effigy of Herr Adolf Hitler. After all, he had recently been made the Chancellor of Germany.

Two weeks previously on 30 January, President Hindenburg, albeit reluctantly, had had no real choice but to appoint Hitler as Chancellor. He now led the largest party in the Reichstag and had obtained almost a third of more than 35 million votes in the last election. An excited and breathless *Daily Express* reported the next day that '60,000 young Germans, wearing the khaki uniforms of the Hitler storm troops and the field-grey of the "Steel Helmets", marched through the streets of Berlin with flaming torches held aloft to the President's and the Chancellor's palaces in the *Wilhelmstrasse* – all of them chanting "Hail, victorious Hitler! Hail, Hindenburg! Germany, thou hast awakened!"' Another article in the same newspaper led with the headline 'Fascist Hero Forms Cabinet',[1] while *The Times* wrote that they hoped 'a Hitler in power may prove less dangerous than a Hitler unhampered by responsibility', adding, 'Herr Hitler has now reached the summit of his ambition.'[2]

Three months later on Friday 12 May 1933, Claudia Burton, an attendant at Madame Tussaud's,[3] saw three men loitering around the Grand Hall before one of them ducked under a rope and poured red paint over a wax effigy labelled 'Herr Hitler, German Chancellor' which, for the avoidance of doubt for any visitors, was modelled giving a Nazi salute. The man then placed a placard round the neck which read, 'HITLER THE MASS MURDERER.' Seconds later the three men ran down the stairs with Claudia Burton chasing close behind and shouting for help. Hearing the commotion, a detective walking up Northumberland Street (now called Luxborough Street)[4] started to chase the men down Marylebone Road before a woman, seemingly from nowhere, caught his coat and wouldn't let go. When he told her he was a police officer she promptly kicked him in the shin. Soon, despite the initial struggle, the three men and the woman gave themselves up and they were all arrested. The men, Gerald Bradley, Don Irving and Hugh Slater, were all charged with wilfully damaging a wax model by covering it with red paint, while the woman, Mrs Bradley, Gerald's wife, was charged with 'assaulting Detective Payton by kicking him'. Mr Bradley said: 'Yes, we admit it to save any trouble.'[5]

Madame Tussaud's Hitler waxwork being brought to court, 13 May 1933.

The next day the four appeared at Marylebone Police Court before the magistrate Mr Ivan Snell. Appearing as a witness, Mr Sydney Smith, the manager of Madame Tussaud's, said that the red paint poured over the head of the figure also went over the face, collar, tie and uniform. The replacement of the Nazi uniform alone will cost £12, he told the court, while the damage to the waxwork would cost considerably more, 'as the head will need to be completely remodelled'. The magistrate then asked what the defendants had to say. Bradley and Irving said that their plea was 'not guilty' and they were going to attempt to justify it. Mrs Bradley said that she would also plead 'not guilty' although in her case it was because she hadn't known she was kicking a policeman and thought she was just struggling with a bystander who was interfering with her husband. 'I would like, however,' she announced, 'to associate myself most emphatically with the protest which has been made against the Fascist Government of Germany, which is responsible for the mass murder of German workers, suppression of the trade unions and the Communist and Socialist Parties …'

At this point Mr Snell interrupted Mrs Bradley by ordering her to be removed from the court and he addressed an empty witness box: 'You may be a communist: you may be a truthful woman or a liar. In this particular case you may have not known he was a police officer and I give you the benefit of the doubt. In these circumstances I will discharge you.' Warning them that the court was not a place for propaganda, the magistrate then addressed the three men, saying that he would not allow them to make any more speeches. Mr Bradley then said, 'I am a communist worker,' adding, 'my protest was not an attempt to do malicious damage, it was a protest against Rosenberg, the envoy of Hitler, being allowed to represent a murderous government …' The magistrate interrupted him in full flow to say, 'You are doing what I told you not to do.' Slater then started to say, 'It is the duty of every communist …' The magistrate ordered all the men to be removed but they all grasped the rail of the dock and started yelling: 'Down with Hitler! Down with Rosenberg! Down with Fascism!' at which point supporters in the gallery joined in and chanted, 'Down with Hitler! Down with Fascism! Down with Rosenberg!' After a big struggle with a number of police officers they were all removed from the court.[6]

Dr Alfred Rosenberg, mentioned by the protestors in court, had for the past ten years been the editor-in-chief of the Nazi daily newspaper

Volkischer Beobachter – the 'fighting paper of the National Socialist movement of Greater Germany'. He was an influential theorist and ideologue of the Nazi Party – or at least liked to think he was – and it was Rosenberg who had inspired the protest. Two days before the paint incident at Madame Tussaud's he had laid a wreath at the base of the Whitehall Cenotaph, after which he had stepped back, raised his right arm and given the Nazi salute.

The British public was now becoming accustomed to the fascist salute. Eleven years previously in 1922, when Mussolini visited London, the *Manchester Guardian* had to explain in detail to its readers what exactly Mussolini's followers were doing when they 'held high their right arms, with the hands spread slantingly forward'.[7] The public was also becoming accustomed to fascists themselves, and in 1932, a year before Rosenberg's visit, Oswald Mosley had formed the British Union of Fascists (BUF). Formerly a Labour MP, Mosley had hoped for a cabinet position after the 1929 General Election, but Prime Minister Ramsay MacDonald offered him only the post of Chancellor of the Duchy of Lancaster, a position without portfolio and outside the cabinet. Mosley then produced what became to be known as the *Mosley Memorandum*, which, among much else, called for high tariffs to protect British industries from international finance, state nationalisation of main industries, and a £200 million (approximately £12 billion in 2017) programme of public works to help solve unemployment. When the cabinet, and subsequently the Labour Party Conference (albeit narrowly), rejected the *Memorandum*, Mosley resigned. Richard Crossman, the Labour MP and minister, wrote thirty years later in the *New Statesman*:

> Mosley was spurned by Whitehall, Fleet Street and every party leader at Westminster simply and solely because he was right … this brilliant Keynesian manifesto was a whole generation ahead of Labour thinking.[8]

The historian A. J. P. Taylor concurred (although suspicious that the ideas were possibly too good to be Mosley's own) and wrote in 1965 that the *Memorandum* 'offered a blueprint for most of the constructive advances in economic policy to the present day … an astonishing achievement'.[9] Hardly noticed at the time, the man who replaced Mosley at the Duchy of Lancaster was Major Clement Attlee, who once said of the British fascist leader, 'Why does he always speak to us as though he were a feudal landlord abusing tenants who are in arrears with their rent?'[10]

In 1931 Mosley formed the New Party, but after winning no seats in the election of that year and inspired by a study tour of the 'new movements' of Italy's Benito Mussolini and other fascists, he was convinced fascism was the way forward. The following year when Mosley started the BUF he united the disparate British fascist movements into one party. Just a fortnight before the Hitler and Rosenberg protests at Madame Tussaud's, the *Manchester Guardian* reported a speech where Mosley, wearing a 'regulation black shirt with a row of medals tinkling on his chest', outlined what he thought of a free press: 'I do not think it would be necessary to institute a rigid control of the press. Only if newspapers were acting in a manner harmful to the State would we restrict their liberty.' He then continued, 'I was warned that the black shirt, the fascist salute, and that sort of thing would not go down among English people, but they are just the things which are most popular about our movement. The youth of today asks for discipline.' After Mosley finished speaking, the newspaper reported that 'three of the British fascists in the background gave the fascist salute'.[11]

Rosenberg, who was described by Reuters at the time as 'one of the Nazi "Big Five"', had travelled to London at Hitler's behest and as his unofficial Foreign Secretary, ostensibly to discuss the deadlock of the Disarmament Conference. In reality, the visit was more about gauging British opinion of the new German National Socialist regime. The visit hadn't gone as well as he hoped. The British Foreign Secretary was unimpressed with Rosenberg's defence of the persecution of the Jews, suppression of constitutional freedoms and the establishment of concentration camps in Germany, while the Prime Minister, Ramsay MacDonald, and the Conservative Party leader, Stanley Baldwin, both declined to see the Nazi propagandist. It was the laying of the wreath at the Cenotaph, however, that caused most of Rosenberg's bad publicity.

The wreath was made of lilies and laurel leaves, draped with a band in the German imperial colours and included a black swastika in the centre. At about 11 a.m., not long after Rosenberg had left his wreath, a car drove up Whitehall, pulled over to the middle of the road and

9 September 1934: Sir Oswald Mosley's British Union of Fascists at an evening demonstration in Hyde Park.

stopped at the Cenotaph. A man in his late fifties who had been waiting there suddenly grabbed the Nazi wreath, ran over to the car and placed it on the back seat, at which point the car roared off down Whitehall. Police Constable Hudman, who had seen the entire incident, ran over to the man, who immediately gave himself up and said, 'I was just going to look for one of you chaps.' He was taken to Cannon Row police station and gave his name as Captain James Edmonds Sears, telling the policemen that he was the prospective Labour parliamentary candidate for the South West St Pancras constituency. After he was charged, Sears said, 'The wreath is now on its way to Gravesend and has been thrown into the river on instructions.'[12]

Later in the day, at the Bow Street Magistrates' Court, in front of the magistrate Mr Fry, Captain Sears described himself as a managing director of a building company and explained that he had served throughout the war, entering as a private when he was forty,[13] rising to the rank of captain. He also informed the magistrate that he held the Mons Star (a First World War campaign medal for service in France or Belgium between 5 August and 22 November 1914). Mr Fry told Captain Sears that he had

Left: Captain James Edmonds Sears in 1933.

Below: The receipt from the Police Court acknowledging payment of Captain Sears' £2 fine.

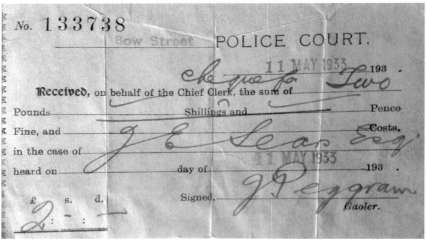

essentially pleaded guilty by admitting that he had taken the wreath and handed it to a waiting car, although as he had informed the authorities exactly where the wreath had been dropped into the Thames, which enabled the Thames River Police to recover it, the magistrate said that Captain Sears would be discharged under the Probation Act. However, as he had also been charged with wilful damage, Mr Fry added: 'It is very ill-mannerly and improper for you to have done what you did, and I must fine you 40 shillings.'[14] Before he left the court Captain Sears read out a statement:

It was a deliberate national protest against the desecration of our national War memorial by the placing on it of a wreath by Hitler's emissary; especially in the view of the fact that Hitler's Government, at the present moment are contriving to do those things and foster the feeling that occurred in Germany before the war in which many of our fellows suffered and lost their lives in fighting.[15]

The Cenotaph on Whitehall had originally been erected in 1919 for the first anniversary of the Armistice. It was intended initially as a temporary monument and had been built of just wood and plaster. It was such a success with the public, who piled wreath after wreath of flowers around the monument, that the architect, Sir Edwin Lutyens, was asked to rebuild it in Portland stone for the following year. Religious imagery was avoided and it was simply inscribed with the words 'The Glorious Dead'. Within five days, a million people visited the monument and left literally tons of flowers piled as 'hedges 5 feet high'. Fabian Ware, the founder of the Imperial War Graves Commission, once estimated that if the British dead from the First World War had marched by the Cenotaph four abreast it would have taken them three and a half days to march by.[16]

The stark facts will never lose their power to shock: there were 9.2 million combat deaths in the First World War and 15 million deaths in total. 750,000 British soldiers were killed, with 1.5 million men seriously injured. Almost a third of all the boys and young men aged between fourteen and twenty-four at the beginning of the war would end up being killed. It is entirely unsurprising that after the war there was an almost tangible sense of a 'lost generation' hanging over the country. Sir Arthur Conan Doyle, whose son Kingsley had been injured at the battle of Somme, but who then, like so many of his contemporaries, had died in 1918 of that peculiar and deadly strain of pneumonia that seemed to affect only the young and fit, wrote in 1926:

The deaths occurring in almost every family in the land brought a sudden and concentrated interest in the life after death. People not only asked the question, 'If a man dies shall he live again?' But they eagerly sought to know if communication was possible with the dear ones they had lost.[17]

Above left: Ada Deane's self-portrait, 1922.

Above right: Sir Arthur Conan Doyle by Ada Deane.

Left: Sir Edwin Lutyens' temporary Cenotaph in 1919.

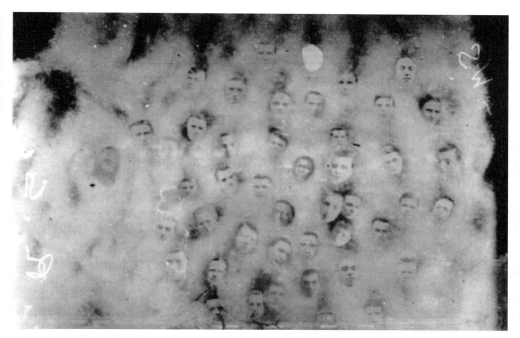

Ada Deane Armistice photograph from 1924 as published in the *Daily Sketch*.

On 11 November 1922, a sixty-year-old woman called Ada Emma Deane, with the help of her nineteen-year-old daughter Violet, set up a camera on top of a wall near the corner of Richmond Terrace and Whitehall. From this position, she took two photographs of the large crowd around Lutyens' Cenotaph. The first picture was taken just before the annual silence commemorating the Armistice, while the second photograph was taken with a long exposure during the entire two minutes. When the photographs were developed one showed a mass of light over some of the audience while the other purported to show a 'river of faces' and an 'aerial procession of men' floating over the bowed heads of the crowd. The images were then commercially printed together and distributed among spiritualists and other believers of spirit photography, of which there were many in the years after the war.

So-called spirit photography had been around for almost as long as photography itself. The long exposures of photography's early days often produced accidental ghostly images as people came in and out of shot. After the First World War, spirit photography was as popular as ever before. Ada Emma Deane lived at 151 Balls Pond Road in

Islington, and was already fifty-eight years old in 1920 when she bought a worn-out old quarter-plate camera for 9p. Her husband had left her a few years previously, and she had brought up three children on her own by working as a servant and a charwoman. When the children had grown, she took up other interests including breeding pedigree dogs, and spiritualism. After visiting a local séance in Islington, a medium predicted that Deane would become a psychic photographer and, lo and behold, in June 1920 she produced her first 'psychic' picture. Her reputation soon spread among the spiritualist community and she became one of Britain's busiest photographic mediums.

According to the Society of Psychical Research, which had been formed by a group of Cambridge Dons in 1882 to investigate, scientifically, the miry world of telepathy, hypnotism and the survival of the soul, Deane would eventually hold over 2,000 sessions. At about the same time as she started her rather odd photography career, a forty-year-old man called Harry Price joined the society. The SPR still exists to this day and has included members such as Carl Jung, W. B. Yeats, Charles Dodgson and Alistair Sim.

Opposite top: Ada Deane's photograph of the Remembrance Ceremony at the Cenotaph in 1922.

Right: Harry Price in 1932.

In 1908 Price had married a relatively wealthy heiress called Constance Mary Knight and decided to use his newfound independent means to become a psychic investigator. He was an amateur but adept conjuror and photographer, and used this expertise to quickly become the society's leading expert at exposing duplicitous and fraudulent mediums – especially 'spirit' photographers.

The most famous of these was a former docker called William Hope, born in 1863 and based in Crewe, who had been producing 'spirit' photographs since 1905 and would have been Ada Deane's major influence. In 1921 Hope agreed to be tested by Price under the auspices of the SPR. Hope wrote to Harry Price requesting him to bring a half-dozen packet of ¼-inch plates for the experiment – 'Imperial and Wellington & Ward are considered preferable,' he said, adding, 'I will use my own camera.'[18] Price visited the Imperial Dry Plate Co. Ltd in Cricklewood and discussed with them a way of devising an incontrovertible test for Hope. Price wrote to the SPR: 'We have decided as the best method that the plates shall be exposed to the X-Rays, with a leaden figure of lion rampant (the trade mark of the Imperial Co) intervening ... Any plate developed will reveal a quarter of design, besides any photograph or "extra" that may be on the plate. This will show us absolutely whether the plates have been substituted.'[19]

On 24 February 1922 Price visited William Hope, bringing with him his special X-rayed Imperial plates. After a verse of 'Nearer my God to Thee' (the nineteenth-century hymn by Sarah Flower Adams and purportedly the last piece of music played by the band on the *Titanic* before it sank), and then a long, improvised prayer by the photographer, Price was taken to the darkroom. He then surreptitiously marked the plate holder he had been given with a pin-pricking instrument on his thumb and also noticed that Hope, while away from the safelight and presumably thinking he couldn't be seen, had slipped the plate holder into his breast pocket and then, it seemed, took it out again.

When they returned to the studio and Hope had developed the print, a strange, ghostly female apparition had appeared on the photograph. Price, however, noticed the Imperial logo had failed to appear and his pinpricks had gone. Later that day Price developed his unused plates and saw the remaining parts of the Imperial logo. He also noticed that the glass of the plate Hope had developed was thinner, despite Imperial confirming that the original plates they had given to him were all made from the same piece. This was, at last, unassailable proof that Hope was a charlatan and a cheat.

Harry Price published the findings in the SPR's journal in May and also printed the exposure in a sixpenny pamphlet called *Cold Light on Spiritualistic Phenomena*. The result became worldwide news and it made Harry Price a national celebrity. William Hope, even after Harry Price had seemingly proved him nothing but a fraudster, retained some loyal followers including Sir Arthur Conan Doyle. Doyle even wrote a book called *The Case for Spirit Photography* in which he went to great lengths to argue the veracity of Ada Deane's and William Hope's work, maintaining in the latter's case that 'with long exposures, such as Hope gave, the X-ray marks vanish, so that this test, as was admitted by the Imperial Company, ceases to be valid'.[20]

Ada Emma Deane was not discouraged by the exposé of William Hope and continued with her supernatural photography. Within two years, however, she had a downfall of her own. In 1924 she again photographed the Cenotaph ceremony during the two minutes of silence. At the request of her spiritual guides she had been 'storing up power' by refusing any other sittings for the preceding three weeks. By now Ada Deane's annual Cenotaph photographs were eagerly awaited and the *Daily Sketch* had to outbid its rival, the *Daily Graphic*, for the right to reproduce her latest picture. At first the newspaper simply asked of the faces: 'Whose are they?' but two days later, the newspaper answered its own question with a front-page headline: 'HOW THE DAILY SKETCH EXPOSED "SPIRIT PHOTOGRAPHY"'.

The newspaper had noticed that the faces in the crowd that Deane had 'photographed' were not brave fallen soldiers but were actually cut-out pictures of footballers and boxers who were all very much alive. The newspaper wrote:

> The exposure of truth in regard to alleged spirit photography, which deeply interests and affects multitudes of people, would not have been possible if the Daily Sketch had not, at the risk of some obloquy to itself, submitted the pictures to the rigorous searchlight of publicity, and thereby set at rest the minds of thousands who at various times have been tempted to believe in 'spirit' photography.[21]

The *Daily Sketch* soon challenged Deane to produce some 'spirit' photographs using the newspaper's own equipment. They even offered £1,000 to charity if she managed to produce them under fair and scientific conditions – not entirely surprisingly, she refused. After the *Daily Sketch*'s exposure of her fraudulent activities, Ada Deane rarely publicly produced her spirit photographs. Arthur Conan Doyle wrote that she was now

> a somewhat pathetic and forlorn figure among all these clever tricksters. She is a little, elderly charwoman, a humble white mouse of a person, with her sad face, her frayed gloves, and her little handbag which excites the worst suspicions in the minds of her critics. When she first pursued the subject her circumstances were such that her only darkroom was under the kitchen table with clothes pinned round it.[22]

Ada Deane died at the age of ninety-three in Barnet in 1956, and as far as anyone knows she has yet to take up the chance of appearing as a ghostly image in someone else's photograph.

The morning after Captain Sears had appeared at Bow Street Magistrates' Court and got off with a paltry £2 fine, the *Daily Telegraph* reported that a female singer at Covent Garden had burst into laughter on hearing of the fate of the Nazi wreath. The singer wasn't named by the newspaper, but it was almost certainly forty-five-year-old Frida Leider, who was married to the Jewish violinist and conductor Professor Rudolf Deman. Sir Thomas Beecham, artistic director at Covent Garden, was due to conduct Wagner's *Tristan and Isolde* at the Royal Opera House and Leider was to play Isolde – one of her most famous roles. The virulently anti-Semitic Wagner was, of course, admired almost fanatically by Hitler who always sought to incorporate the German composer's music into his heroic mythology of the German nation. It has been said that Hitler kept many of Wagner's original scores in his Berlin bunker, all of which perished along with Hitler in the final days of the war. Leider's amusement at the Cenotaph incident, however, infuriated some of her more Nazi-sympathising German colleagues, and this may have had something to do with her refusal to sing on the opening night of the opera the next evening. There was initially no cover, but to save the day the singer Henny

Trundt flew over from Cologne in a specially chartered aeroplane, landing at Croydon Airport three hours before curtain-up. That night a nineteen-year-old Benjamin Britten watched her performance in the third row of the gallery and reported in his diary:

> Henny Trundt V.good; rather ungainly but sings & acts well ... But what music! Dwarfs every other creation save perhaps [Beethoven's] Ninth. The glorious shape of the whole, the perfect orchestration: sublime idea of it and the gigantic realisation of the idea. He is master of us all. Since heard that Beecham was vilely rude to Leider who refused to sing in morning. I am not surprised.[23]

On the same morning, the German newspaper *Berliner Tageblatt* (traditionally a liberal paper that had criticised Hitler and his party, but which two months previously had been taken over by the National Socialists), reported that it was astonished that Captain Sears had only been fined for his behaviour and that a similar act in Germany would surely have been treated far more severely. On the same day as *Berliner Tageblatt*'s criticism of Captain Sears' fine, the British Ambassador, Sir Horace Rumbold, an astute and prescient critic of the Nazi Party, was brought before an incensed Hitler. Why, asked the enraged German Chancellor, had the English court imposed such a pathetic and lenient sentence of just £2 on the wreath's desecrator? Sir Horace responded that there had been an unmistakeable swing in English public opinion, based upon British concepts of freedom of the individual and consideration for other races. A leader in the *Spectator* that week commented on the protests in London and confirmed Sir Horace Rumbold's opinion:

> Herr Hitler's unofficial foreign secretary [Rosenberg] has been in London this week sounding British opinion regarding Germany. He can have had little difficulty in reaching a conclusion. Rarely has this nation been more nearly of one mind on anything than it has been in reprobation of the excesses that have marked the political upheaval which Herr Hitler has inspired ... Everywhere the worship of Germany is proclaimed, a misconceived, disproportioned, deformed Germany shaped after the narrow and myopic idealism of Herr Hitler and his lieutenants.[24]

In Germany Rosenberg's visit was seen as an embarrassment, especially the incident at the Cenotaph and the subsequent protests. Rosenberg had hoped that, following the National Socialists' assumption of power, his explanation of Germany's domestic policies would help shift British public opinion; however, the negative comments in the press (in both countries) led Rosenberg to cut short his trip and return to Germany. The day after Rosenberg had left his Nazi wreath against the Cenotaph on 11 May 1933, the *Daily Sketch* included a joke about Rosenberg's visit.

When Alfred Rosenberg on his return from London ordered a suit from a tailor in Berlin he asked the tailor what it would cost: '950 marks' replied the tailor.
'But,' Rosenberg asked, 'isn't that rather expensive?'
'Not at all,' answered the tailor.
'You are a big man and require a lot of material, that is why the suit costs so much.'
'But in London,' persisted Rosenberg, 'I could have bought the same suit at half the price.'
'Certainly,' explained the tailor.
'In London you were much smaller.'

Rosenberg speaking in 1933.

At the end of the following month, on 30 June 1933, and just before his resignation, Ambassador Horace Rumbold filed his last dispatch. It came to be known as the '*Mein Kampf* despatch' and was an extraordinarily lucid analysis of the Nazi chiefs, Hitler, Goering, and Goebbels, and described them as 'notoriously pathological cases'. He spoke of the Third Reich's militaristic intentions, its avowed extermination of the Jewish race, and its wholly totalitarian social programme and concluded, 'I have the impression that the persons directing the policy of the Hitler government are not normal.'[25]

Alfred Rosenberg was captured by Allied troops after the war. His career hadn't gone as he had hoped. Even Goebbels was purported to have once said, 'Rosenberg almost managed to become a scholar, a journalist, a politician, but only almost.'[26] He was tried at Nuremberg and found guilty of 'conspiracy to commit crimes against peace; planning, initiating and waging wars of aggression; war crimes; and crimes against humanity', and was sentenced to death. Rosenberg was the only condemned man at Nuremberg who, when asked at the gallows if he had any last statement to make, replied with only one word: '*Nein.*' After his execution his body was cremated and the ashes, much like his wreath sixteen years previously, were deposited in a nearby river.

Rosenberg after his execution on 16 October 1946.

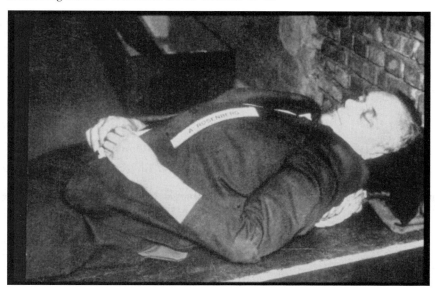

5

The Charming Lord Boothby, His Friend Ronnie Kray and the Humble Woolton Pie

To his face, the writer, campaigner and broadcaster Sir Ludovic Kennedy once called Baron Boothby of Buchan and Rattray Head, his mother's cousin, 'a shit of the highest order'. Boothby's response was to chortle, rub his hands and say: 'Well a bit. Not entirely.'[1] For most of his life, his undeniable charm, along with close friends in very high places, kept any scurrilous rumours, malicious gossip and untoward behaviour of Boothby, much of it true, away from the front pages of Fleet Street. By 1964, however, especially after the Profumo Affair the previous year, Britain's newspaper industry had developed more than a little taste for Establishment blood. In the early 1960s, Boothby, known throughout his life as Bob, was one of the country's more famous politicians, albeit now in the House of Lords; but although he had been in Parliament for over forty years, it was broadcasting rather than high office that had made him truly a household name. During the 1950s his eloquence and avuncular manner meant that Boothby appeared on many current affairs programmes on television and radio: 'I enjoy being recognised in the street,'[2] he once said, and in March 1964 his fame was underlined when he appeared on the BBC's *This Is Your Life* with Eamonn Andrews. Just a few months later, the carefully constructed wall of discretion built around his colourful private life began to break down.

On Saturday 11 July 1964, most of the newspaper offices were finding it rather a dull day for news. Even the weather was

Above: Boothby by Allan Warren in 1972.

Right: Number One Eaton Square in 2017.
It now has a blue plaque for Lord Boothby.

dull – cloudy and mild with the occasional drizzle. The press agency ticker tapes showed no obvious lead stories for tomorrow's Sunday newspapers and, indeed, the variety of headlines the next day reflected this. The *People* went with 'New Birth Pill Row', the *Sunday Citizen* ran with 'True Story of Slum Britain', and the *Observer* reported on 'Rhodesian manoeuvres' at the Commonwealth talks but also had a story about the striking postal workers, as did the *Sunday Times* and the *News of the World*. Only the *Sunday Mirror*'s front page had any prominent sense of fervent excitement, with a headline that proclaimed: 'Peer and a Gangster: Yard Probe – Public Men at Seaside Parties'. The popular Sunday newspaper claimed that the police were investigating 'a homosexual relationship between a prominent peer and a leading thug in the London underworld'. The peer was a 'household name' and the inquiries embraced Mayfair parties attended by the peer and the notorious gangster. A few days later, the *Daily Mirror* announced that it had a photograph – 'the picture that we must not print' – which showed 'a well-known member of the House of Lords seated on a sofa with a gangster who leads the biggest protection racket London has ever known'.

On 28 July, the West German magazine *Stern*, with a circulation of 1.8 million, published an article headlined 'Lord Bobby in a fix'. It reported that the *Sunday Mirror* possessed something which it dare not print – 'a picture of a peer sitting on a sofa with a known degenerately talented criminal'. The magazine not only went on to name the peer as Lord Boothby, but also stated that 'London newspapers give us to understand' that the peer's position in society helps to provide the gangsters with customers who have money to pay for gambling debts and 'more unorthodox pleasures'.

Along with Lord Boothby, the photograph featured Ronnie Kray, one of the infamous East End gangster twins (who at the time, outside of their East End manor anyway, were actually hardly known at all) and Ronnie's friend, a gay, good-looking young cat burglar called Leslie Holt. All three were perched on a sofa in Boothby's flat, which had the prestigious address, even for salubrious Belgravia, of No. 1 Eaton Square. When the story broke, Boothby was holidaying in France, taking the waters at the spa town of Vittel, and would later write that he was initially baffled as to the peer's identity (extremely unlikely, as he was holidaying with Sir Colin Coote, the editor of the *Telegraph* and the man who could be said to have started the Profumo affair when he introduced Stephen Ward to the Soviet attaché Eugene Ivanov). When Boothby arrived back home to a London 'seething with rumours', he called his close friend, the former Labour Party chairman and journalist Tom Driberg, who said, according to Boothby, 'I'm sorry Bob, it's you.'[3]

Robert John Graham Boothby, an only child, had been born to an Edinburgh banker two months into the twentieth century. He was educated at Eton and Oxford University and before the end of the First World War, although too young to see active service, was commissioned into the Brigade of Guards. At the age of twenty-four he became the Unionist MP for the relatively marginal Aberdeen and Kincardine East constituency, and then went on to be returned with large majorities at eight general elections. The young, radical Tory MP was seen as a rising star and had once been tipped as future leader of the Conservative Party, not least because he had, as one biographer described him, 'a lively and independent mind, an easy way with people, and the ability to make compelling speeches enhanced by humour, wit, and a voice well described as "of golden gravel"'.[4]

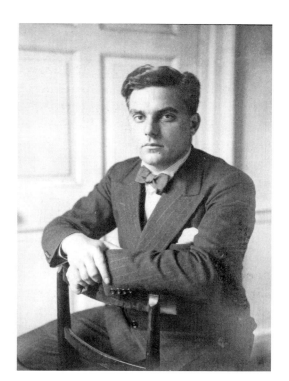

Bob Boothby, aged twenty-four, the new MP for Aberdeen and Kincardine East in 1924.

The Chancellor of the Exchequer Winston Churchill on his way to the House of Commons to present his budget in 1928. He is accompanied by Bob Boothby, his Parliamentary Private Secretary from 1926 to 1929.

He had been a friend and supporter of Sir Winston Churchill at a time when his allies were in relatively short supply, and in the late 1920s Boothby became Churchill's parliamentary private secretary. Boothby was never comfortable in the role of an apostle and was too impulsive and outspoken to be a good party politician, and opinions between the two men often clashed. The Scottish MP, however, was always uncommonly consistent with his anti-appeasement views (in Germany he was once greeted by Hitler's secretary with a 'Heil Hitler', to which Boothby's admirable response was 'Heil Boothby').[5] He was also among only thirty-three Conservatives, including Churchill, who voted against the government over Munich – the settlement in September 1938 that allowed Nazi Germany to annex the German-speaking parts of Czechoslovakia along the country's borders, for which a new territorial designation, 'Sudetenland', was coined.

After Churchill had replaced Neville Chamberlain as Prime Minister in May 1940, he made Boothby Parliamentary Secretary at the Ministry of Food, where he worked under the minister, Lord Woolton. The minister, before the war, had run Lewis's, the large chain of department stores. The Woolton Pie, initially the Lord Woolton Pie, was named after him. This pastry dish of vegetables had been created at the Savoy Hotel by the Maitre Chef de Cuisine, Francis Latry, at a dinner in honour of the new American Ambassador, John Winant, who had been shown to the table by Churchill himself. 'What is this?' the Prime Minister asked the waiter as the vegetarian dish was put in front of him. 'Woolton pie, sir,' he replied. 'It is what?' exclaimed the great man. 'Woolton pie, sir,' he repeated, to which Churchill responded, 'Bring me some beef!' The food minister would hardly have been surprised, and once wrote that Churchill was 'benevolently hostile to anything that involved people not being fed like fighting cocks'.[6] A pragmatic man, Woolton saw rationing and restrictions as an opportunity to improve the country's nutrition (an ambition in which he was successful). Churchill, however, felt that Woolton enjoyed restricting food to the British population just a little too much.

Woolton and Boothby initially got on well and felt that they made a good team. In July 1940, the newspapers reported how Boothby, after an initial idea by Woolton, had come up with a popular national scheme for cheap or free milk for nursing mothers and

Lord Woolton who was Minister of Food from April 1940 until 1943 when he entered the War Cabinet as Minister of Reconstruction, taking charge of planning for post-war Britain.

young children. It was widely praised and, while the evacuation of Dunkirk was taking place, was accepted by the House of Commons without opposition or even debate. Some thirty or so years later, Margaret Thatcher first came to real national prominence (and many thought the possible end of her political career) when, as Education minister, she introduced the beginning of the end of the scheme. Young children, most of whom were perhaps more enamoured with the rhyme rather than any future lack of morning milk that seemed to be either served warm or frozen solid, chanted in the playground, 'Mrs Thatcher, Mrs Thatcher, Milk Snatcher.'

When the Blitz hit the East End of London, Boothby was encouraged by Woolton to visit the air-raid shelters as they were emptying at six in the morning when the all-clear siren sounded. Boothby quickly organised canteens all over the East End, run by volunteers, to provide free cups of tea. One day Boothby came across a small boy crying. When he asked him the matter the boy said: 'They burnt my mother yesterday.' Thinking the boy was referring to an air raid, Boothby said: 'Was she badly burned?' The boy looked up and said through his tears: 'Oh yes. They don't fuck about in crematoriums.'[7]

Later on that summer the *Daily Mirror* reported that a new 'fortified' bread was to revolutionise and increase nutrition with added 'energy-producing' Vitamin B1 and calcium. 'This is an unprecedented and a revolutionary step,' announced Boothby, 'and along with the milk scheme will be hailed by scientists all over the world as a great advance on anything hitherto achieved in this field.'[8] Bread made with fortified white flour, despite wholemeal bread still being far more healthy, was seen by most as a good thing, and it is still fortified today. Boothby rejected pressure to make wholemeal bread compulsory on the grounds that 'a great many people do not like it, and why should they be compelled to take what they do not like even in wartime?'[9] Boothby's passionate evangelising about healthy bread, however, was not totally to do with the population's good health.

It soon came to light that the Welwyn Garden City company Roche was supplying the synthetic vitamin B1 in vast, and highly profitable, quantities. Boothby had once been the chairman of directors of Roche but had stood down when he was given his recent governmental role. As a parting gift from the company, however, he had been given 5,000 shares. When Woolton found out about this Boothby was forced to sell them, making a lot of money in the process. Woolton was shocked that Boothby was allowed to keep the share-selling profits, but when he raised the subject with the Prime Minister found that it only seemed to irritate him. Woolton said to Churchill, 'I will be glad if you would consider whether I should remain as minister,' and added, 'I have no intention of having a Marconi scandal associated with the department of which I am head.'

This was an inflammatory remark: the scandal to which he referred took place in 1912, when senior members of Asquith's Liberal administration, including the Chancellor of the Exchequer David Lloyd George, had bought shares in the US wireless firm in the knowledge that the British government was about to issue the company with a lucrative contract. Woolton continued, 'Unless it is made abundantly clear that Boothby has no sort of financial interest in anything that is being done by the Ministry of Food, then I shall not remain minister.' The Minister of Food left the meeting angry and annoyed: 'I came out of the whole thing with a sort of conviction that it was I who had the shares and done something wrong,' he later wrote. He then heard that the Chancellor of the Exchequer, Kingsley Wood, who had also been at the meeting with Churchill, was going around saying that 'Woolton had been very Wooltonish'.[10] It wasn't just politicians who found Woolton's sometimes patronising admonishments unbearable. A diarist, G. W. King, wrote on 3 December 1940: 'Tonight there has been a talk by the Lord Woolton, the Minister of Food. He has plainly told us that ... there are a good many things we have to do without, and live more plainly, like we used to when he was a boy.' A twenty-year-old woman, a canteen worker, wrote just over a year later:

> I find it hard to tolerate this incessant nagging, these endless exhortations and scoldings, those pompous official lectures from Lord Woolton – whose utterances, far from encouraging us to endure our monotonous and restricted diets with good grace, infuriate us and are anything but conducive to the maintenance of good morale. If carrots and potatoes are the only things we can get to eat, all right we'll eat them; but it really is too much to be lectured all the time about the excellence of carrots and potatoes, and scolded for not having eaten many of them before, and nagged at for having eaten too much of other things ...[11]

Boothby was starting to get a bad reputation at Westminster, and his addiction to gambling and its associated debts meant that he was always looking for more money. His business activities in the arms trade brought him into contact with Richard Weininger (a suspected German agent who was arrested at Boothby's flat before being interned by the British government). Boothby was indebted to the Austrian-Czech émigré and stood to receive a commission if, by using his influence in government, Weininger benefitted from the release of his Czech assets impounded by wartime regulations. After asking questions in the House about the matter in October 1940, Boothby was suddenly suspended from duties when it was found that he had failed to declare his interest. In January 1941 a parliamentary select committee reported that his conduct had been 'contrary to the usage and derogatory to the dignity of the House and inconsistent with the standards which Parliament is entitled to expect from its members'. Boothby had no alternative but to resign.

In his autobiography he wrote of the matter: 'The single sentence "I have an interest to declare" would, it seems, have cleared me. I can only say that it never occurred to me to say it.'[12]

Three months later, Woolton came across Boothby dining with Noël Coward one lunchtime at L'Escargot on Greek Street. Boothby approached Woolton saying that he hoped to join the Air Force and added, discreetly, 'I'm anxious, of course, that I am able to defend myself against any unpleasant charges. Anything that might suggest I was ever dishonest.' Woolton looked at Boothby and said, 'No one thinks you are dishonest. But many people think you are very foolish.'[13] Woolton was kind. Churchill's advice to his former Parliamentary Secretary when he came to him asking what he should now do after his resignation, was, 'Get yourself a job with a bomb disposal unit.'[14]

Despite the scandal, Boothby was successful in his determination to retain his seat and in 1958, after thirty-five years as an MP, nearly all of them as a backbencher, he was made a peer by the Conservative Prime Minister, Harold Macmillan. It was a benevolent act – the first (and last) Baron Boothby of Buchan and Rattray Head had been having an affair with Macmillan's wife Dorothy since around the beginning of 1930. For the first five years they virtually lived together, almost openly. It was even strongly rumoured that Sarah, Dorothy's third child, was Boothby's.[15] At one point Dorothy, besotted with Boothby, wanted a divorce, although her husband, who in his opinion had done nothing wrong, refused to cite her for adultery. Boothby once told a biographer of Harold Macmillan: 'What Dorothy wanted and needed was emotion, on the scale of Isolde. This Harold could not give her, and I did. She was, on the whole, the most selfish and most possessive woman I have ever known ... But we loved each other. And there is really nothing you can do about this, except die. Wagner was right.'[16]

Ludovic Kennedy once asked Boothby what he saw in her, to which he replied, 'Dorothy has thighs like hams and hands like a stevedore, but I adore her.'[17] In 1935, Boothby attempted to extricate himself from this impossible relationship by proposing to one of Dorothy's cousins, Diana Cavendish. The proposal, according to Boothby, came after rather too good a dinner. The next morning he realised he had made a huge drunken mistake, but before he had a chance to make

Dorothy Macmillan, daughter of the 9th Duke and Duchess of Devonshire. She had a long affair with Boothby but was married to Harold Macmillan from 1920 until she died in 1966.

amends Diana's mother, to his horror, had already announced the news to the world, including a delighted Winston Churchill.

It was a doomed and brief marriage, and, as Boothby's biographer subtly put it: 'It was not long before Diana realised that her husband's many qualities did not include those normally associated with a successful husband.'[18] Boothby felt guilty for the rest of his life and once said: 'It is impossible to be happily married when you love someone else.'[19] In May 1937, after just two years of marriage, there was no choice but divorce – a decision not taken lightly in those days, especially for a Scottish MP. Boothby wrote to his friend Lord Beaverbrook, pleading: 'Don't let your boys hunt me down.' The press baron had words with the relevant people and the divorce registered just a few lines in most newspapers, if anything. The affair, however, put an end to any hopes Boothby might have had of achieving high office.

Despite the long relationship with Lady Macmillan and his marriage to Diana, Boothby was bisexual. In his autobiography, published in 1978 (in which, incidentally, he mentions Dorothy not once), he hinted of past gay dalliances. Of his time at Oxford University he wrote: 'As for the homosexual phase, most of the undergraduates got through it; but about 10 per cent didn't. Homosexuality is not indigenous in Britain, as it is in Germany ... but it is more prevalent than most people wish to believe.'[20] In the 1920s and 30s Boothby often visited Germany and wrote: 'Among the youth, homosexuality was rampant; and, as I was very good-looking in my twenties, I was chased all over the place, and rather enjoyed it.'[21]

On the same subject, Boothby also mentions a speech he made to the Hardwicke Society (a senior debating club for barristers) at Cambridge University in February 1954, in which he proposed that the clause that made 'indecency between consenting male adults in private a crime should be removed from the Statute Book'. Boothby sent a copy of his speech to the Home Secretary and called for a royal commission, to which David Maxwell Fyfe replied: 'I am not going down in history as the man who made sodomy legal.'

To many people's surprise, however, Maxwell-Fyfe 'after anxious reflection'[22] established a committee to look into the issue. He had been worried not only about the apparent recent increase in homosexual activity, but had also long been concerned with

Bob Boothby, Ronnie Kray and 'Mad' Teddy Smith at Boothby's apartment at 1 Eaton Square. (Photo courtesy of John Pearson)

impudent female prostitutes soliciting on the streets of London and other large cities. He had no doubt that they were both manifestations of the same moral malaise, and that both needed to be firmly dealt with in the same way – with punitive new laws. The committee was chaired by John Wolfenden – then vice-chancellor of Reading University. Almost no one knew (and it was certainly not reported in the press), however, that John Wolfenden's son Jeremy had admitted to his father five years before that he was, at least as far as you could be in those days, openly gay. He would later claim that his father had written him a note at the time:

> Dear Jeremy, you have probably seen from the newspapers that I am to chair a committee on homosexual offences and prostitution. I have only two requests to make of you at the moment. 1) That we stay out of each other's way for the time being; 2) That you wear rather less make-up.[23]

The committee first met on 15 September 1954, and early on Wolfenden suggested that for the sake of the ladies (there were three on the committee and some additional secretaries present) they use the terms Huntley and Palmer after the biscuit manufacturers – Huntleys for homosexuals, and Palmers for prostitutes. After almost exactly three years, the Wolfenden Committee published its report on 4 September 1957, recommending that homosexual behaviour in private between consenting adults (over twenty-one) should be decriminalised. It was the first progressive piece of proposed legislation, as far as homosexuality was concerned, for over five centuries and essentially said that it was not the law's business 'to settle questions of morality, to interfere in the private lives of the citizens'. The report sold 5,000 copies within hours of publication and had to be reprinted the next day.

The government was horrified. Some recommendations – tougher penalties on women soliciting, for instance – were quickly enacted, but the main part of the report dealing with homosexuality was considered far in advance of what the public would tolerate, and the government decided to put the report to one side. Jeremy Wolfenden, meanwhile, who had been a brilliant scholar at Eton and Oxford, became a journalist for *The Times* and then a *Daily*

Telegraph correspondent in Moscow at the height of the Cold War. His relatively open homosexuality threatened, if publicly revealed, to undermine the path-breaking reforms proposed by his father, and he soon became the victim of KGB blackmail after they had photographs taken of him in a hotel room *in flagrante delicto*. Jeremy initially tried to brazen it out by asking for enlargements of the photographs, but the pressure on him ultimately told. At the end of 1965, while working in Washington, Jeremy Wolfenden died of alcohol-induced liver failure after years of excessive drinking. A few months before he died, a bill for what would become the Sexual Offences Act was introduced by Lord Arran into the House of Lords. Maxwell Fyfe, the former Home Secretary, who was made a peer not long after he had set up the Wolfenden Committee, was now the 1st Earl of Kilmuir and still vehemently opposed to any homosexual liberalisation. He spoke during the debate:

> There is no judge who has to go on circuit, as I did for many years, who does not from time to time find that … there are … 'buggers' clubs' or associations or coteries of people who are given to this particular vice. At these coteries of buggers, the most horrible things go on. As a judge, one has to sit and listen to these stories which make one feel physically sick.[24]

Less than eighteen months later, on 27 July 1967, the Sexual Offences Act received royal assent after an intense late-night debate in the House of Commons. Ten years after the Wolfenden Report was initially published, it decriminalised homosexual acts in private between two men. Lord Arran, in an attempt to minimise criticisms that the legislation would lead to further homosexual civil rights, made the following qualification to this 'historic' milestone: 'I ask those [homosexuals] to show their thanks by comporting themselves quietly and with dignity … any form of ostentatious behaviour now or in the future or any form of public flaunting would be utterly distasteful.'[25]

There had long been rumours that Boothby was comporting himself neither quietly nor with any dignity, but, as usual, the newspapers refused to report anything untoward in his private life. A few hints broke through, however. In 1959, the *Daily Express* reported, with the headline 'THIEF "LETS DOWN" BOOTHBY', that seventeen-year-old Robert Bevan, in the dock at Marlborough Street Magistrates' Court, had been accused of stealing a gold watch and chain and a large gold coin, together worth £50. The court had been told that he phoned Lord Boothby to ask for help in finding a job, and as the lord's manservant Goodfellow was away the young man was invited to help out in his flat in Eaton Square. Boothby was reported to have said: 'He is very young – I think the temptation was too great.'[26]

A few years later, in May 1963, a month or so before John Profumo admitted to having had an affair with Christine Keeler, the *Daily Express* reported about another seventeen-year-old boy who had been sent to borstal, this time for trying to cash a £1,899 cheque of Boothby's at the peer's bank. The boy said that he had found the chequebook on the King's Road, and when told the chequebook was still at Lord Boothby's flat he said, 'I lied about that, but all the rest is true.' The *Express* wrote: 'The riddle: How the cheque came into the possession of Buckley, a cloakroom attendant at Esmeralda's Barn, Belgravia.'[27]

Esmeralda's Barn in Knightsbridge.

Esmeralda's Barn, in the 1950s, was a relatively conventional nightclub run by a man called Stefan de Faye and situated in Wilton Place in Knightsbridge, where the Berkeley Hotel now stands. After the Betting and Gaming Act of 1960 gambling became legal in the United Kingdom, and from 1961 de Faye turned Esmeralda's Barn into a gambling club. The Act, which was intended to drive criminals out of gambling, instead proved a boon to them, as it enabled many of them to expand their empires legally. The Kray twins, who acquired Esmeralda's, found it a lucrative venture. Regular visitors to the club included the artists Lucian Freud and Francis Bacon. David Somerset, Duke of Beaufort, said in the BBC documentary *Lucian Freud: A Painted Life* how Freud had once arrived at his home to ask for a £1,500 loan. When asked why he needed so much money at such short notice he replied, 'Because if I haven't produced it by twelve o'clock they're going to cut my tongue out.'[28]

If customers sometimes got carried away and accumulated large debts, that was not necessarily a bad thing for the Krays, as it put them in their power. At one point one of the twins' associates, David Litvinoff, accumulated debts of £3,000. Ronnie Kray agreed to waive this debt in return for the lease on Litvinoff's flat at Ashburn Gardens in Kensington but also 'access' to Litvinoff's lover, Bobby Buckley (brother of James 'Jimmy' Buckley, who was found with Boothby's cheque), a croupier at Esmeralda's Barn. Litvinoff, meanwhile, continued to live at Ashburn Gardens as part of the deal. Ronnie enjoyed being able to choose waiters and croupiers at Esmeralda's Barn that suited his own preferences for attractive young men. According to the journalist and writer John Pearson, 'the Barn' became the centre of Ronnie's own 'private vice ring' which included private sex shows at Ashburn Gardens but also, with Boothby and Tom Driberg in attendance, at the Krays' flat at Cedra Court in Bethnal Green, 'where rough but compliant East End lads were served like so many canapés'.[29]

After the *Daily Mirror* headline and the subsequent story in *Stern* that actually named him, Lord Boothby was in a tricky situation. If he decided to do nothing it would seem as if he was admitting the accusations; however, if he sued Mirror Newspapers he could be involved in a lengthy and expensive court case, with a real risk that all kinds of revelations would be raked over to support the story. At this stage senior members of the Tory party were terrified that the scandal was likely to rival the Profumo affair (which had also gently simmered under the surface for a while), and as there was a general election looming it was a situation the party could ill afford. Two Tory backbenchers had even reported to their chief whip, Martin Redmayne, that they had seen Lord Boothby and Tom Driberg importuning males at the White City dog track and that they were involved with gangs of thugs who laundered money at the tracks.[30] At Chequers the story and its implications were debated by the Lord Chancellor, Lord Dilhorne, the Home Secretary, Henry Brooke, and the Prime Minister, none of them feeling that Boothby's pleas of innocence were the least bit plausible.

Boothby's connection with Tom Driberg, which was now coming to light, meant that the Labour Party were in no mood to take advantage of the situation. If Boothby went to court then it seemed more than likely that Driberg's private life would also be exposed. It was known to most of Westminster and Fleet Street that over

Lord Boothby and Ronnie Kray at the old 'Society' restaurant in Jermyn Street. Ronnie Kray kept this photo as evidence of his friendship with Boothby. From left to right: Charlie Clark, cat burglar, Boothby's butler, Goodfellow, Boothby, unidentified teenage boy, Ronnie Kray, and gangster Billy Exley with his wife. (Photo courtesy of John Pearson)

the years few attractive men were safe from Driberg's attentions. Driberg made no secret of his homosexuality, although his ability to avoid any consequences for his risky and often brazen behaviour confounded his friends and colleagues. In the autumn of 1935, while he was the writer of the extremely popular William Hickey column in the *Daily Express*, he had actually been charged with indecent assault after an incident in which he had shared his bed with two Scotsmen picked up late one night. With the help of Lord Beaverbrook, who paid for a leading counsel, Driberg was acquitted, and the press baron's influence meant that the case went unreported by the press. This was the first known instance of what writer Kingsley Amis called the 'baffling immunity [Driberg] enjoyed from the law and the Press to the end of his days'.[31]

Driberg's connection to the Boothby scandal meant that Harold Wilson's personal solicitor, the louche, overweight Arnold Goodman, became involved. To Wilson, as well as many others, Goodman was known by the name 'Mr Fixit'. *Private Eye*, however, preferred 'Two Dinners' Goodman', or when mocking his sanctity, 'Blessed' Goodman. The satirical magazine would also regularly mention a firm of solicitors called 'Goodman, Badman, Beggarman and Thief, solicitors and commissioners of Oaths'. Arnold Goodman offered to represent Lord Boothby and advised the troubled peer to write a letter to *The Times* admitting that it was him in the picture but denying all of the *Mirror*'s allegations:

I have never been to all-male parties in Mayfair. I have met the man alleged to be King of the Underworld (Ron Kray) only three times, on business matters, and then by appointment at my flat, at his request, and in the presence of other people. The police deny having made any report to Scotland Yard or the Home Secretary in connection with any matters that affect me. Lastly, I am not, and never have been, homosexual. In short, the *Sunday Mirror* allegations are a tissue of atrocious lies.

The letter ended: 'If Mirror Newspapers possess any documentary or photographic evidence to the contrary, let them print it and take the consequences.'

Boothby also wrote to the Home Secretary explaining that he had not known Kray was a criminal and had in any case turned down the business plan he had been discussing with him. Kray had wanted to be pictured with Boothby because he was a personality, and it would have been churlish to refuse. The Kray twins at this stage were becoming known to the public, not least because they enjoyed having their photographs taken with well-known celebrities, of which Lord Boothby was one.

After *The Times* published the letter, Goodman won a quick agreement from the International Printing Corporation, owners of the *Sunday Mirror*, saving Boothby from the court case he and the government were dreading. This wasn't all: Goodman won his client a record out-of-court settlement of £40,000 (not an inconsiderable sum back then, and approximately £750,000 in 2017) and a grovelling and demeaning public apology signed by Cecil King, the chairman of IPC. Boothby would later say that he had given away the £40,000: 'The whole of it. I regret it bitterly

Bob Boothby, Ronnie Kray and Holt at Boothby's apartment.

now. But I felt I couldn't live with it. I hadn't earned it.' His friend Driberg would later write: 'He was wise to say that the money was entirely gone. Otherwise I might have tapped him.'[32] Boothby had nothing to fear from Driberg, but because he had essentially perjured himself in public, the peer was extremely vulnerable to anyone who could prove he had lied. Thus much, if not all, the money went to Ronald Kray.

Derek Jameson, the *Daily Mirror* picture editor, and future editor of the *Daily Express* and *News of the World*, once recalled that for a long time Fleet Street refused to go anywhere near the Krays: 'Dodgy trouble, £40,000, not very nice,' he said. Subsequently, for years the Twins were known by the *Mirror* and other publications as 'those well-known sporting brothers'. The Commissioner of the Metropolitan Police, Sir Joseph Simpson, also had to deny publicly that there had ever been a police investigation of the Boothby–Kray affair. Since the beginning of 1964, however, the Kray twins and their gang had been under the scrutiny of Detective Chief Inspector Leonard Read, also known by his nickname 'Nipper'.

On 10 January 1965, the Kray twins were arrested and charged with demanding money with menaces from Hew McCowan, owner of a club in the West End called the Hideaway. They were refused bail and sent to court. It was hard enough for Read to find anyone sufficiently suicidal to testify against the Krays, but the case against them wasn't helped when, a month after their arrest, Boothby stood up in the Lords and inquired, shamelessly, whether the government intended to keep the Kray twins in custody for an indefinite period. He added: 'I might say that I hold no brief for the Kray Brothers.'[33] No one believed him, and unsurprisingly there was complete uproar in the house after the question, to which Boothby shouted, 'We might as well pack up.'

At the end of the trial the jury failed to reach an agreement and a re-trial was ordered; the judge eventually stopped the second trial, finding for the defendants. Fleet Street and the Metropolitan police felt that the Krays now had a complete hold over the Establishment, and their control over London's underworld would remain unchecked for four more years.

The Krays were arrested again in 1969 for the murders of George Cornell and Jack 'The Hat' McVitie. At the same time sixteen of their firm were also arrested, which helped witnesses to come forward without fear of intimidation. Ronnie and Reggie were eventually sentenced to life imprisonment with a non-parole period of thirty years for the murders of Cornell and McVitie, at that time the longest sentences for murder ever passed at the Central Criminal Court.

There was, of course, a third man in the famous photograph taken at Lord Boothby's flat – Leslie Holt, Ronnie's sometime driver and lover, who was also used as bait to entrap the likes of Robert Boothby and Tom Driberg. Holt eventually became the partner of a Dr Kells, based in Harley Street, and it was said that the society doctor would supply customers for Holt's cat burglaries. It was a lucrative project that worked well until police became suspicious of the criminal double act. Holt mysteriously died at the hands of Kells when he was under anaesthetic for a foot injury. The doctor was arrested but eventually acquitted.

Lord Boothby and Wanda Sanna outside Caxton Hall Register Office after marrying in 1967.

Lord Boothby was married for the second time in 1967, to a Sardinian woman called Wanda Sanna, thirty-three years his junior. 'Don't you think I'm a lucky boy!' he shouted out to well-wishers outside the ceremony at Caxton Hall around the corner from his flat.

William Deedes, former Conservative MP and editor of the *Daily Telegraph*, once wrote of his friend as someone who 'simply could not resist drinking from brim to dregs every cup offered him'.[34] Sadly at the end of Boothby's life the cups consisted of nothing but whisky and Complan and he told Ludovic Kennedy that euthanasia should be compulsory at the age of eighty-five.[35] Boothby was never very good at taking advice, even his own, and he died in Westminster in 1986, aged eighty-six.

Recipe for the (Lord) Woolton Pie
(This is the official recipe, released to the Press in April 1941.)

TAKE 1lb each of diced potatoes, cauliflower, swedes and carrots; three or four spring onions; one teaspoonful of vegetable extract; and one teaspoonful of oatmeal.

Cook all together for 10 minutes with just enough water to cover. Stir occasionally to prevent the mixture from sticking.

Allow to cool; put into a pie dish, sprinkle with chopped parsley and cover with a crust of potatoes or wholemeal pastry.

Bake in a moderate oven until the pastry is nicely brown and serve hot with brown gravy.

6

The Prince of Wales Theatre and the De-Mob Suit – Starring Sid Field and Featuring Dickie Henderson, Kay Kendall, Terry-Thomas and the Ross Sisters

When the last chord of 'Twist and Shout' came to an end, the Beatles grouped together at the front of the Prince of Wales Theatre stage. The blue curtain swished closed behind them and, from the waist and in unison, they bowed first to the 'cheap seats', then turned and bowed again to the 'jewellery wearers' in the Royal Box. With the orchestra playing and the audience still applauding they skipped and ran off the stage with boyish energy. It was the comedian Dickie Henderson, unenviably, who was next to perform, and after the applause had died down he said: 'The Beatles ... young ... talented ... frightening!' The audience laughed, but it had been said with feeling. He, like most of the other acts on the bill of the Royal Variety Performance in November 1963, including Marlene Dietrich, who couldn't understand why all the camera lenses had been pointing at the four young men from Liverpool, suddenly felt very old-fashioned.

Henderson's fame was at its peak that November, and it was on purpose and as a reassuringly safe pair of hands that Bernard Delfont had asked him to follow the Beatles that night. The theatre impresario had had too many bad experiences with pop groups dying in front of indifferent mink-wearing Royal Variety audiences,

Beatles fans outside the Prince of Wales Theatre Royal Variety rehearsals in 1963.

and when he had booked the Beatles earlier that year, on the advice of his daughter Susan, he had never heard of them. The primetime *Dickie Henderson Show* had recently finished on ITV (it was a staple on the channel between 1960 and 1968) and that summer Henderson had been top of the bill of a popular show called *Light Up the Town* at the Brighton Hippodrome. Today you would almost have to be a pensioner to remember Henderson in his prime, but he was once described by Roy Hudd as 'perhaps the most versatile and certainly the smoothest, most laid-back comedian it had been my pleasure to see', adding that 'he danced, sang and delivered one-liners wonderfully, and even his prat-falls were, somehow, classy … He was, without doubt, the best I ever saw.'[1]

Dickie had come from a 'showbiz' family. Before the Second World War his sisters, Triss and Winnie, were a pair of popular dancers and singers called the Henderson Twins, while his father, Dick Henderson, was a rotund, bowler-hatted comedian and singer known in the music halls, where he had made his name, as 'The Yorkshire Nightingale'. His trademark was his breakneck banter, salty and censorious, and delivered in a strong Hull accent. Part of his act was to tell the audience that he didn't want any applause because he was there 'strictly for the money'. He is perhaps most famous for the first British recording of 'Tiptoe Through the Tulips', with which, accompanying himself on the ukulele, he usually entered and exited the stage.

Dick Senior, like his son, also performed at Royal Variety shows, the first of which was in 1926 when King George V laughed at: 'I went to get married and asked the vicar how much it was. He said, "What do you think it's worth?" I gave him a shilling. He took one look at the bride and gave me twopence back!' Henderson was a fat man and he usually started his performance by standing sideways, showing off his large belly, saying: 'I was standing outside a maternity hospital, minding my own business ... ' He died in 1958, just a few days before what would have been his third Royal Variety show.

Dickie Henderson's first job in show business was, as a ten-year-old, playing Master Marriott in the 1933 film of Noël

Dickie with his father and Max Miller in *Things Are Looking Up* from 1934.

Noel at the time of *Cavalcade.*

Coward's play *Cavalcade*, a movie made while his father was in California performing in vaudeville. Henderson Senior, despite losing most of his life savings in the Wall Street Crash, was earning reasonably good money in the States where he was commanding top billing in the smaller houses, and was a much appreciated feature act in the bigger circuit halls. Even though the popularity of vaudeville was on the wane, Henderson Senior often earned an impressive $1,000 per week. Dickie tells a story in his half-finished autobiography that Hal Roach had once offered his father, a stout gentleman who never performed without his bowler hat, to 'test' with Stan Laurel, another Englishman from the north of England. His father turned him down, however, as the money was only half of what he was earning on stage. Henderson Senior always regretted this decision but later admitted that, compared with Oliver Hardy, 'I would never have been as good.'[2] He did make a few films, however, including *The Man from Blankley's* in 1930, which starred Loretta Young and John Barrymore, now unfortunately lost. It wasn't necessarily an easy life in Hollywood at that time, despite the warm Californian sunshine. Noël Coward, unhappy that everyone seemed to 'work too deuced hard', once described a typical day while working on *Cavalcade*: 'They get up at 6.30 ... stand around all day under the red-hot lights ... eat hurriedly at mid-day, and because they are too tired to sit up, late at night have their supper served on trays. That's no way to live, and certainly no way to work.'[3]

After the young Dickie had completed his part on *Cavalcade*, for which he earned $400 for the month's work, the whole family returned to England on the liner RMS *Lancastria*. Ten years later, on 17 June 1940, the *Lancastria*, sank in twenty minutes after it was bombed by the *Luftwaffe* near the French port of Saint-Nazaire. The sinking of the *Lancastria* has almost been forgotten but it was the largest loss of life from a single engagement for British forces in the Second World War – about 4,000 men, women and children died. It was also the largest loss of life in British maritime history – greater than the *Titanic* and *Lusitania* combined.[4]

Dickie left school at fifteen, and became 'prop boy' with Jack Hylton's Band, with whom his twin sisters, two years his senior, were singing. Two years later, the twins had become 'headliners' throughout the country and Henderson was learning everything about stagecraft, which he would put to good use for the rest of the career. Looking back at this time he once wrote:

> The time on the road, when not performing, we spent learning. Every morning jugglers, acrobats, dog acts and dancers rehearsed. Always rehearsing. In exchange for dance steps from dancers, the jugglers taught dancers how to twirl a cane. Acrobats put you in a harness and taught you back-somersaults. That is why performers, then, could do a bit of everything. I was fortunate to have been part of it, before 'that school closed', to quote the great Jacques Tati.[5]

In September 1939, at the start of the Second World War, all the theatres were instructed to close. Dickie became a messenger boy with Air Raid Precautions (ARP), given a bicycle and told to await instructions. There never were any instructions, and when the theatres reopened, after just two weeks, he was back to his pre-war life and travelling around the country as a junior touring performer.

The Henderson Twins and Dickie *c.* 1938.

Just as he was about to appear, along with Naunton Wayne and the Hermiones Gingold and Baddeley, in *A La Carte*, his first West End show, Henderson was called up. It was 1942 and he was nineteen. In the next three years he had, in his own words, 'an extremely cushy war'.[6] He didn't have to leave Britain and he saw no action.

As just one of over four million servicemen who were demobilised between June 1945 and January 1947 (about 8,000 personnel per day), Second Lieutenant Henderson was not able to rejoin civilian life until 1946. Like thousands and thousands of others, he made his way to Olympia to swap his service uniform for the ubiquitous 'demob' outfit. Most of the servicemen in the queues were grumbling about the length of time it had taken for them to get there. The first illustration in the book *Call Me Mister! – A Guide to Civilian Life for the Newly Demobilised* was a cartoon of an old and decrepit man holding his release book and saying, 'To think I should really live to see myself demobbed.'

By the end of 1945, 75,000 de-mob suits were being made every week and supplied by tailors such as Burton, a company founded by Montague Burton and where, perhaps, the phrase the 'full Monty'[7] came from – meaning the full set of demob clothes supplied by the firm. Anthony Powell, who served in the Welch

Prince of Wales Theatre in 1931.

Regiment and later the Intelligence Corps during the war, used a scene set in the demob centre at Olympia in the closing passages of his 1968 novel *The Military Philosophers*: 'Rank on rank, as far as the eye could scan, hung flannel trousers and tweed coats, drab mackintoshes and grey suits with a white line running through the material'. He pondered whether the massed ranks of empty coats on their hangers somehow symbolised the dead.[8]

The 'full monty', as it were, included socks, a shirt, a tie, a hat, cuff links and collar studs and came in a 'handsome box bound with green string'.[9] The accompanying label featured the magic word – to men who had been in the services for six or more years anyway – 'Mr', followed by their name. The de-mob suit, often ill-fitting due to the lack of the right sizes available, was a subject to which literally millions of people could relate and became an important ingredient of much post-war comedy. The comedian Norman Wisdom, whose suits were always far too tight with 'half-mast' trousers, had been demobilised in 1946 and was once described by John Hall in the *Guardian* as 'Pagliacci in a demob suit'.[10] Frankie Howerd, yet another of the generation of British comedians who came to prominence in the years after demobilisation, performed in a badly fitting demob suit, probably because, like countless others, he had nothing else to wear.[11]

Dickie himself described his new demob clothes as a 'grey double-breasted three-piece pinstripe suit, snap trilby hat and a flannelette shirt affair, rather like pyjamas'. He also mentioned his 'cumbersome

Nineteen-year-old Lieutenant Henderson in 1942.

shoes', and it was often joked by the new civilians that the footwear provided by the government needed to be particularly stout and rugged to stand up to the constant wear and tear as they tramped around endless pavements in search of suitable employment. After his visit to the Olympia De-Mob Centre, Dickie later wrote about how embarrassed he was of his new civilian clothes when, walking down Piccadilly on his way to see his sister Triss, he bumped into a snappily dressed Jack Hylton, who was wearing a suit from Hawes and Curtis in Jermyn Street, a Sulka shirt from the shop on Old Bond Street, and shoes by Walkers of Albemarle Street. Triss Henderson, who had sung with Hylton but was now dancing solo after her sister had met and married a GI during the war, was appearing in a revue called *Piccadilly Hayride* at the Prince of Wales Theatre. The same theatre, located on Coventry Street between Piccadilly Circus and Leicester Square, where Dickie would be compering the 1963 Royal Variety show seventeen years later.

The Prince of Wales Theatre, originally built in 1884, was named after the future Edward VII, and its first production was a revival of W. S. Gilbert's *The Palace of Truth* starring Herbert Beerbohm Tree. Another notable production was the 1928 play *Alibi* based on the Agatha Christie novel *The Murder of Roger Ackroyd*, which was directed by Gerald du Maurier and starred Charles Laughton as Hercule Poirot. Four years later, the theatre started a series of risqué 'Folies'-style revues for which it became known during the 1930s and into the war. They ran continuously from 2 p.m. to midnight, four performances a day, and were the Windmill Theatre's competitor for West End stage nudity, and where, according to Graham Greene, 'peroxided showgirls, as tall as grenadiers, their eyes as empty as statues, walked lazily with a sneer in at one wing and out at the other'.[12]

Greene may have disliked the cynicism of the shows, but they were an enormous success and paid for the theatre to be completely rebuilt in 1937. After the original building had been demolished, Gracie Fields sang to the workmen as she laid the foundation stone of the new art deco theatre, priced at £350,000. The new theatre's seating capacity was increased to about 1,100, and there were improved facilities for both the artists and the public, including a revolving stage and a 14-metre-long stalls' bar. The new theatre, however,

Programme covers for *Les Folies de Paris et Londres* and *Revue Folies de Can-Can*.

continued with its slightly sleazy but money-spinning shows, such as *Les Folies de Paris et Londres*, starring George Robey, and *Revue Folies De Can-Can*. In 1943 the theatre changed tack and put on a revue entitled *Strike a New Note*, notable not only for Zoe Gail's anthem for a blacked-out capital – 'I'm Going To Get Lit Up (When The Lights Go Up In London)' – but for the performances of a newly discovered comedian, to London audiences anyway, called Sid Field.

In the beginning it was meant to be an anonymous revue with no stars, and the programme listed the performers in alphabetical order (including a young Eric Morecambe and Ernie Wise, performing separately) with a footnote that said: 'Here is Youth.' At thirty-nine he was far from youthful, but Sid grabbed his chance and within three weeks the posters were being amended with 'Sid Field – The New Funny-man'. After years and years of playing provincial fleapits and end-of-pier shows, the Birmingham-born comedian made his West End debut to massive acclaim. The journalist Brian Glanville once described Field as 'the funniest man who ever lived', adding that he had 'timing, personality, movement, everything'. He wrote in 1974 about his visit to the Prince of Wales Theatre, as a twelve-year-old, to see Sid Field in *Strike a New Note*:

This big fellow came lolling up on to the stage, wearing an enormous long dark overcoat with padded shoulders, a beaten-up black hat with the brim pulled down, and everyone around me was laughing and clapping, the applause broke out like an explosion, everyone was pleased, everyone was expectant, you could feel it in the air; he'd got the audience before he'd even opened his mouth. And it wasn't just his reputation, though obviously that helped; after all he was the new star, setting the West End alight. More than that, though, it was his presence. Even where we were, that far away, it came across.[13]

Not a venue to fix something that wasn't broken, the Prince of Wales Theatre soon followed *Strike a New Note* with another Sid Field revue called *Strike It Again*, which, like its predecessor, was well received by audiences and critics alike. J. B. Priestley once wrote of Field: 'No comic can ever have had greater immediate success, going up like a rocket that exploded its gold and silver in the darkness of wartime London.'[14] Field had a particular talent: with the slightest glimmer of a smile or glint in the eye he could 'melt the most frigid of audiences'.[15]

Taking advantage of his new-found fame as the great new comedy star, Field was soon signed up as lead in a comedy/musical film to be called *London Town*, shot in Technicolor at Shepperton Studios in the autumn of 1945. J. Arthur Rank was convinced that what the glamour-starved country needed and wanted most was a big, bright million-dollar musical. At great expense, the songwriters Jimmy Van Heusen and Johnny Burke were hired, and Rank imported the American director Wesley Ruggles to take the musical's helm. It was an odd choice, as Ruggles had no experience with the genre, and his best-known films, the Oscar-winning Western epic *Cimarron* (1931) and the Mae West comedy *I'm No Angel* (1933), were both more than a decade old. The screenplay revolved around a comedian, Jerry Sanford (played by Sid Field), who arrives in London believing he has been hired as the star of a major stage production, when in fact he's merely an understudy. Thanks to his daughter Peggy (Petula Clark, at the time just thirteen), who sabotages the revue's star Charlie de Haven (Sonnie Hale), he finally gets his big break. The premise allows for a variety of musical numbers and comedy sketches performed by, among others, Kay Kendall in her film debut and the musical hall star 'Two Ton' Tessie O'Shea.

Shepperton Studios had almost closed down during the war, with many of the skilled technicians being used to make dummy aircraft from wood and canvas. These 'aeroplanes' were then parked on decoy airfields in the hope of luring enemy bombers away from their intended targets. Eventually, the technicians developed lighting effects which mimicked runway landing lights and even aircraft taxiing, so that the pretend aerodromes could be used both day and night. Two of the massive sound stages at Shepperton were used for storing sugar for much of the war, and after the bombing of the Vickers factory at Brooklands in 1940, the other two stages were used by Vickers workers to make bomber parts and spares. Shepperton was also regularly bombed due to its close proximity to the Queen Mary reservoir. Over the course of the war eleven people were killed, including a nurse, May Durrell, who in February 1944 refused to go to the air-raid shelter in case someone needed help. For the courage she showed, Durrell Way in Shepperton is named after her.

Field was never comfortable as a film actor, much preferring the stage. He said of *London Town*: 'When I saw that camera coming at me for the first time like a bloodthirsty dragon waiting to pick up my mistakes, my stomach screwed up. I couldn't get a word out. My inside felt like a cavern of bats.'[16] Field, now forty-two, was sometimes compared to Bob Hope, often not unfavourably, and he was a talented singer and comic, but hardly a potential matinee idol. Watching the film today, Field's stage routines don't age particularly well and certainly aren't helped by Ruggles, who, for some reason, refused to dub audience laughter over the sketches, making them appear particularly flat during the show-within-a-show. The film, however, is the only permanent record of Field's most famous routines, which involved a naive approach to the billiards table and the golf course, both of which included his long-suffering straight man Jerry Desmonde.

For example: Desmonde, (sternly), as golf pro: 'Address the ball!'
Field (trying hard): ' … Dear Ball … '

London Town, artistically and financially, has gone down in history as a disastrous failure but the contemporary reviews were not all bad; the *Daily Mirror*, for instance, called it a 'smash hit' while *The Times* called it 'a triumph in its own class' before contributing the opinion that Sid Field had 'ten times the talent' of Bob Hope.[17] On the whole, however, critics sided with the *Observer*, which thought the film had 'all the sparkle of cold gravy and the taste of a cold in the head';[18] the *Daily Express* thought that the ballet scenes smothered Field's appearances: 'What a relief when the camera at last finished with those seemingly eternal girls galumphing about among the daffodils.'[19]

J. Arthur Rank was wrong. The public may have been glamour-starved but they failed to turn up, both in Britain and the US (where the film was eventually released as *My Heart Goes Crazy*). The hoped-for rebirth of the British musical came to a screeching halt. Any concerns that Bob Hope may have had of Field taking his place certainly disappeared, as did the careers of nearly everyone involved in the film. Wesley Ruggles sloped back to America and never directed again, while Field's film career was essentially over.[20] The choreographer responsible for the 'galumphing', Agnes de Mille, reputedly paid the producers of the film $5,000 to have her name removed from the credits. Petula Clark was young enough to escape any blame, while Kay Kendall, at nineteen, just five years older, was hardly singled out for the film's failure. The brash, hopeful publicity about 'Britain's Lana Turner' certainly didn't help her early career, however, and she was soon dropped by Rank. 'Nobody had ever heard of me but they called me a star,' she later recalled. 'I opened bazaars, signed autographs, went to premieres, did everything a star was supposed to do. My photograph was on magazine covers and front pages of newspapers. And all before we'd even finished the picture.'[21]

A Rank executive, Kendall later claimed, although she didn't name him, called her into his office to release her. 'You are a very ugly girl,' she recalled him saying. 'You have no talent. You are too tall and you photograph horribly. Find some nice man and get married.'[22] In 1946 telling a young woman to go and get married meant, euphemistically, it was time to give up your career. It is worth noting that it wasn't until October 1946, the month after *London Town* was released, that the Civil Service marriage bar was abolished – a ruling that prohibited married women from joining the Civil Service and required women civil servants to resign when they became married. Incidentally, the marriage bar for the Foreign Office wasn't lifted until 1973. In 1947 there was a government enquiry into the end of the marriage bar, with one senior official writing: 'To us, married

women have been, to quote the Treasury – "a perfect nuisance".'
Another recorded: 'Naturally, their home comes first with them, and
if their husbands or children are ill, they regard it as their duty to
remain at home and look after them, especially in these days when
nurses and domestic help are almost unobtainable.'[23]

The Rank executive who released her was an idiot. Kendall was
tall and beautiful, with a delicate turned-up nose and a purr for a
voice. She was also funny – very funny. She was born in Withernsea
in 1926, 15 or so miles east of Hull and not far from where Dick
Henderson Snr was born thirty-five years previously. Henderson
would have certainly known Kay's grandmother, the music hall
star Marie Kendall who, along with Max Miller and Gracie Fields,
performed at the Palladium in the Royal Variety show in 1931. Nine
years later, when she was just thirteen, her granddaughter Kay was
tall enough for the Palladium chorus line and eventually became one
of the students in the Rank charm school. She grew up to be, as the
film critic David Thomson described her, 'not just a beauty, but one
of the most sophisticated-looking women you had ever seen'.[24]

After the disaster of *London Town*, Kendall almost disappeared
but for small parts in Jules Dassin's *Night and the City* and *Lady
Godiva Rides Again* with Diana Dors. In 1953 her luck changed
when she appeared in the charming comedy *Genevieve* about the
annual London-to-Brighton vintage car race. The film, a huge hit
in the UK, showcased her perfect comic timing not least in the very
funny dancehall scene where she joins the band and, much to the
surprise of her friends (and the band), plays a brilliant jazz trumpet.
At last her talent, in some ways so similar to Dickie Henderson's
in that she somehow remained elegant and classy even while
performing pratfalls or comic drunk scenes, was appreciated.

In 1956 Kendall began an affair with Rex Harrison after they had
both appeared in the film *The Constant Husband*. They married in
1957, but not before Harrison was called in by Kendall's doctor,
who told him that she had fatal leukaemia. With the collusion of
the doctor, Harrison took it upon himself to keep it a secret from
her and she died in 1959 aged just thirty-two, not long after she had
completed the comedy *Once More, with Feeling!*, stealing the film
from her co-star Yul Brynner, who played her conductor husband.

Kay Kendall playing the trumpet in *Genevieve*, released in 1953.

The *Piccadilly Hayride* revue at the Prince of Wales Theatre, where Dickie's sister Triss Henderson was performing, was actually Sid Field's triumphant return to the stage after the disappointment of *London Town*. Much to Field's relief, the disastrous reception of the movie didn't at all damage the mutual love affair he now had with the West End audiences and theatre critics. Preceding Field's first sketch of the show, entitled *The Return of Slasher Green*, Triss Henderson performed the opening song called 'Let's Have a Piccadilly Hayride' with fellow performer Pauline Black, the daughter of the theatrical producer, George Black.

At Al Burnett's nightclub *The Stork*, just off Regent Street, Pauline introduced Dickie to a young woman called Dixie Ross, part of an extraordinary American singing, dancing and contortionist act called the Ross Sisters ('Pretzels with Skin' said some of their posters). Dixie Jewell Ross was just sixteen and along with her two elder sisters, Veda Victoria Ross and Betsy Ann Ross, eighteen and twenty years old respectively, had travelled to Britain on the RMS *Queen Mary*, docking at Southampton on the 10 September 1946. Each sister, presumably so they could perform 'legally' in clubs in the US and subsequently the UK, had assumed the identity and birthday of the next older sister, and carried passports to this effect. The eldest of the trio, Eva, managed this by taking the name and birth date of Dorothy Jean Ross, the first-born sibling, who had died just a few months old of whooping cough in 1925. Informally the sisters continued to use their original given names, but formally their 'legal' names became Dorothy Jean, Eva V and Veda V. Confused? You will be, because the Ross Sisters often used the stage names of Aggie, Maggie and Elmira.

Whatever they were called, just four years previously the girls and their parents were all living in a trailer near New York. The Ross Sisters' parents were originally very poor dirt farmers from west Texas. When the dust storms drove them off the land, Mr Ross started working on the Texan and Mexican oil fields, while the girls' amateur acrobatics and singing were good enough to perform at county fairs and such like. Soon word got around about the three talented sisters and they started to perform professionally in theatres around the country. Pooling their money, they bought a trailer to live in. In 1942 they got their big break, being asked to join the cast of *Count Me In*, a musical starring Charles Butterworth at the Ethel Barrymore Theatre on Broadway. Each night after appearing in a glamorous New York show they made their way back to Ray Guy's Trailer Park on Bergen Boulevard, about a mile across the George Washington Bridge in New Jersey. American syndicated newspapers reported that they were 'thrilled about their first trip to New York. "But," says Betsy, who is twenty and the eldest, "we certainly aren't going to give up our trailer until we are sure of the future."'[25]

The Texan-born sisters had been invited to the West End by Val Parnell, the managing director of the Moss Empires theatres network, who thought they'd work really well in *Piccadilly Hayride*. Parnell had seen the Ross Sisters' performance in a film called *Broadway Rhythm*, an MGM hodgepodge of a musical released in 1944. It starred Ginny Simms and George Murphy, who played a Broadway producer looking for big-name stars, while ignoring the talent available around him from his family and friends. The film was essentially a pageant of various MGM speciality acts, including impressionists, nightclub singers and tap dancers. The short *New York Times* review of the film included the line: 'Three little girls,

SID FIELD brings
" Slasher Green "
up-to-date

Sid Field as Slasher Green *c.* 1943 (left) and later in 1946 (right) with Jerry Desmonde.

the Ross Sisters, do a grand acrobatic dance.'[26] The 'grand acrobatic dance' is pretty well all that's remembered of the film these days, and seventy years or so after the film was released, their remarkable performance has been seen by millions on Youtube and certainly by many more people than on its original cinema release in 1944.

If *Broadway Rhythm* wasn't particularly successful, *Piccadilly Hayride*, riding on Sid Field's incredible popularity, certainly was, and it ran for an incredible 778 performances and took over £350,000 at the box office. The original songs for the revue were written by Sammy Cahn and Jule Styne, one of which, 'Five Minutes More', was sung by the Ross Sisters, and a version by Frank Sinatra became one of the most popular songs of the year. Dickie fell in love with young Dixie, and although he was performing in a touring revue entitled *Something to Shout About* (a title it didn't live up to, according to Dickie), when he was in London he took her to nightspots such as the Coconut Grove at 177 Regent Street – a club where the Latin American bandleader Edmundo Ros had performed during the war. Dickie would later appear in cabaret there, and describes it in his autobiography: 'It was like all night-clubs at the time: a cellar where one could drink

Top left: A candid shot of the Ross Sisters, Vicki on the left, Dixie in the middle and Betsy on the right.

Left: The Ross Sisters in a promotional photograph *c.* 1945.

Above: Three headshots of Dixie Ross. (All pictures on this page courtesy of Steven Tate)

scotch or brandy after hours out of a cracked coffee cup in case of a police raid. It was never raided during the three months that I was there, and with Savile Row police station only one hundred yards away, I drew my own conclusions regarding the dogged efficiency of the police surveillance.'[27]

When *Piccadilly Hayride* closed, Dixie and her sisters went to France to perform at the glamorous *Bar Tabarin* on rue Victor Massé with the likes of Edith Piaf and Maurice Chevalier. Meanwhile, Dickie went into pantomime in Brighton with Jewel and Warriss. After the six-week run, a broke Dickie used up his last £10 for a flight to Paris and immediately proposed to Dixie. He assumed that, if she accepted, he had time to save some money as she and her sisters had planned to tour Australia for six months. The next morning they strolled down the Champs-Elysées and Dixie turned to Dickie and said, 'Darling, I have some wonderful news... ' The middle sister, Vicki, had fallen in love with the French ventriloquist Robert Lamouret (who performed with a Donald Duck-a-Like called Dudulle and who had also been part of *Piccadilly Hayride*). Lamouret had proposed to Vicki but she hadn't wanted to be the one to break up the Ross Sisters' act. 'But she can now, as we are getting married too!' said Dixie. Henderson and Dixie Jewell Ross married in the summer of 1948 at Westminster Cathedral, with the comedian Jimmy Jewel as the best man.

Piccadilly Hayride, and it must have been some show, was also notable for Terry-Thomas's big break. The gap-toothed comedian who in the decades to come would encapsulate the idea of the caddish English rotter, acted as compère during the revue. He also featured in a spot called 'Technical Hitch' where he played a smooth BBC DJ who, after an accident, finds that all his records are broken. In the spirit of 'the show must go on', and with the help of a piano accompanist, Terry-Thomas's character looks up at a notice that says 'DO NOT PANIC!' and pretends nothing has happened by impersonating, however unlikely, the vocalists on the broken records. Terry-Thomas would perform this routine, or something like it, throughout his career but always the DJ would finally meet his Waterloo with something utterly impossible to copy like Paul Robeson, Yma Sumac or even the Luton Girls' Choir ...

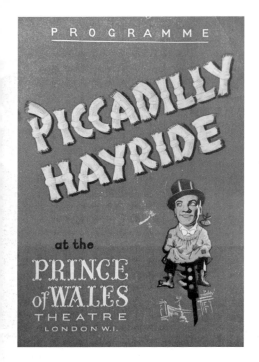

Above left: Cover of the *Piccadilly Hayride* programme from 1946.

Above right: Cover of the sheet music for 'Five Minutes More', sung by the Ross Sisters in *Piccadilly Hayride*.

Below: Dixie Ross showcasing her flexibility.

Opposite: Some of the cast of *Piccadilly Hayride* from the programme.

ACKSTAGE with some of the
tars of "PICCADILLY HAYRIDE"

TRISS HENDERSON
who sings "Let's Have a
Piccadilly Hayride," "The
Coffee Song" and "Make
with the Music"

Photo—Keyst

**ROBERT
LAMOURET**
gives "Dudule"
a final grooming

SID FIELD
appears amazed
by congratulatory
telegrams

Photo—Victor Thompson

TERRY THOMAS
prepares for
"KING JOHN"
Photo—Dudley Harris

Terry-Thomas from the *Piccadilly Hayride* programme.

Terry-Thomas was born Thomas Terry Hoar Stevens in North Finchley in July 1911. His father was a bowler-hatted butcher based at Smithfield Market and it was through him that the young Thomas Stevens got his first job at the centuries-old meat market as a 15-bob-a-week junior transport clerk with the Union Cold Storage Company.[28] On his first day, surrounded by bloodstained butchers' aprons and ash-flecked grey suits, Thomas turned up sporting an olive-green pork-pie hat, a taupe double-breasted suit decorated with a clove carnation, a multi-coloured tie and yellow wash leather gloves, twiddling a long cigarette holder with one hand and twirling a silver-topped malacca cane with the other.[29] He soon joined the firm's amateur dramatic society, and made his debut in AA Milne's *The Dover Road* at the Fortune Theatre in Russell Street. He was surprised by the pleasure he got from the applause: 'The buffoon in me was released ... I was able to get laughs at a twitch of a nostril,' he later wrote.[30]

His first professional engagement as an entertainer was on 11 April 1930 when, at the age of eighteen, he appeared (billed as 'Thos Stevens') at a social evening organised by the Union of Electric Railwaymen's Dining Club in South Kensington. He was paid 30 shillings, not an inconsiderable amount at the time, but despite his best efforts he was a flop and unable to make his boozy audience laugh. He started giving 'exhibitions' of dancing with the sister of the musical star Jessie Matthews, while sometimes helping out at the popular Ada Foster School of Dance in nearby Golders Green. For a short while he became a professional ballroom dancer at the Cricklewood Palais de Dance but, despite the attractive women, he was unable to muster the dedication needed.

His next job was as a guinea-a-day film extra, and his first speaking part came in 1935 in a movie released the following year called *Once in a Million*, when he was heard to shout, 'A thousand!' during an auction scene. He subsequently made publicity cards describing himself as the man who had said 'A thousand!' During the year 1936 alone, he was seen being stabbed to death by fellow extra and future star Michael Wilding (later to marry Elizabeth Taylor, who was just four in 1936); glimpsed in the Jack Buchanan and Fay Wray historical comedy *When Knights were Bold*; spotted falling into a water tank during the musical *This'll Make You Whistle* (which caused him to permanently damage his hearing); dancing in both the Jessie Matthews film *It's Love Again* and *Cheer Up*, written by and starring Stanley Lupino; getting drunk in Vic Oliver's variety revue *Rhythm in the Air*; and briefly appearing in Alexander Korda's version of H. G. Wells' science-fiction novel *The Shape of Things to Come*.[31] At this time he was still uncredited, but was calling himself Thomas Stevens, which he disliked as too 'stiff and stuffily suburban'. After rejecting, thankfully, 'Mot Snevets' (Tom Stevens backwards) and also Thomas Terry, he eventually decided on Terry Thomas. The all-important hyphen, symbolising the gap in his teeth, arrived nine years later.

In 1938 he met and married a 'very neat, vibrant, well-read and enthusiastic' South African ballet dancer and choreographer named Ida Patlanski. Pat, as she called herself, was already twice divorced and nine years TT's senior (at their Marylebone Register Office marriage they both lied about their age, he slightly older, she slightly younger). Together they formed a Spanish dancing cabaret act called 'Terri and Patlanski', but for about '30 bob a week' they were lucky if they were booked at all and had to rely on 'ghastly clubs' such as the Paradise Club. Situated at 189 Regent Street, the

Paradise had opened in 1935. Members paid seven and sixpence for entrance and, to avoid licensing restrictions, had to order bottles in advance from an agent in Bruton Mews. In its advertising the club described itself as 'London's latest and most exclusive niterie', but an anonymous letter written in 1937 to the Metropolitan Police Commissioner described it, possibly more accurately, as 'nothing but a hotbed of "gentleman" crooks, and prostitutes, the whole place savours of evil and immorality'.[32] Thomas himself said it was the type of place known in the business as an 'upholstered sewer'.[33]

The marriage was short-lived, although at the outbreak of the war they performed together for ENSA (the entertainment wing of the forces, set up by the film and theatre producer Basil Dean) in northern France. They returned to England when the Nazis invaded but after affairs by both parties they separated (they eventually divorced twenty years later in 1962). Thomas continued to work at ENSA as a solo act but also became the head of its cabaret section based at the Theatre Royal in Drury Lane. In March 1942, however, he received a brown envelope containing 'a cunningly worded invitation to join the Army'. He accepted the call-up, 'with dignity, if not enthusiasm', and joined the Signals Corps in Ossett in West Yorkshire. After about twenty-four hours, a sergeant asked for TT's number. 'Mayfair 0736' was the Londoner's facetious reply. 'You ain't Terry Thomas any more,' he said, 'You are now just a fucking number!' TT replied, 'Yes mate, Number One!' The insolence meant that for the next five weeks, at an hour when he used to go to bed, TT found himself having to march over a mile to breakfast each morning.

Despite the bad start, TT's natural competitiveness and dislike of being underestimated meant that he was actually a good recruit and contemporaries said he sounded more like an officer than the real ones.[34] Although he was promoted to sergeant, because of a duodenal ulcer and deafness he was offered a place in one of the newly formed services-sponsored touring revues called, collectively, *Stars in Battledress*. Signed up by Captain George Black, father of Pauline, TT's first official contribution was at an Army show based at Olympia. This was where he began performing the precursor of the 'Technical Hitch' sketch, the inspiration for which came from the plight of a well-known newsreader of the time called Bruce Belfrage.

Terry-Thomas in 1947.

At 8 p.m. on 15 October 1940, about five weeks after the start of the London Blitz, a 500 lb delayed-action bomb crashed through the BBC switchboard before coming to rest in the record library on the fifth floor. Staff tried to move it by hand, but during the attempt the timer set off the bomb. Seven BBC staff were killed, while much of the fifth- and sixth-floor frontage of Broadcasting House was blown into Portland Place, with glass and debris scattered as far as the junction with Duchess Street. Covered by dust in his basement studio, Belfrage paused only slightly before finishing the nine o'clock news bulletin.

Despite giving up smoking soon after the war for health reasons, Terry-Thomas always carried a long, expensive cigarette holder. When he started smoking as a teenager he hated the thought of having nicotine-stained fingers, and his very expensive suits, made by the tailor Cyril Castle on Savile Row, all had one very special requirement – the breast pocket had to be 7 inches deep to accommodate the cigarette holder. In January 1960 Terry-Thomas's fame was at its height, and he was appearing at a midnight charity event at the Odeon Theatre in Liverpool. After coming off stage and getting back to his dressing room, he soon realised that his expensive custom-made cigarette holder was missing. It wasn't just any old cigarette holder; this one was particularly ostentatious, decorated with forty-two diamonds and a gold spiral band. It was insured for £2,000. The Liverpool police didn't take long to track down two of the diamonds, which they found at the home of a local unemployed salesman and well-known 'fence' called Alan David Williams.

The other forty diamonds were found inside a roll of carpet at the Queen's Drive home of a twenty-year-old small-time variety comedian called James Joseph Tarbuck. Alan Williams was charged with being an accessory after the fact and Tarbuck with theft, and they were both committed for trial at Liverpool Magistrates' Court in April 1960. At the trial it came to light that Tarbuck had repeatedly asked Terry-Thomas if he too could perform at the charity gig. The star had pointed out to him that they had too many artistes already and it 'would be madness to put anybody else on'. Mr. F. V. Renshaw, the prosecutor, revealed that Tarbuck had said: 'I rang Terry-Thomas and he promised me a three-minute spot on the show, but by the finale I still hadn't been on.' The Liverpudlian, once a classmate of John Lennon, said of his humiliating rebuff, 'I was disgusted. I was walking out of the theatre when I saw the cigarette holder on the dressing table, and took it. I had it broken up and I was going to throw it away.' The defence maintained that it was 'a moment of pique rather than dishonest intent', although they admitted that Tarbuck was deeply in debt. Both men pleaded guilty and James Tarbuck was put on probation for two years, while Williams was given a twelve-month conditional discharge.

At the end of the court case, TT left the building, gave one of his famous broad, gap-toothed grins and conspicuously waved around another very expensive cigarette holder to the waiting reporters. Just over three years after the court case, Tarbuck, the unemployed Liverpudlian pub comedian, now twenty-three, appeared on the ATV show *Sunday Night at the London Palladium*. After his eight-minute joke session, Tarbuck was given one of the biggest receptions the show had ever known. Despite Associated Television staff trying to calm the audience down so that the rest of the production could continue, the cheering just went on and on. It only stopped when the new discovery was brought back to take an extra bow.

Terry-Thomas appeared in dozens of films, especially during the fifties and sixties. Unlike Sid Field and even Dickie Henderson he is still remembered and popular today with people who were not born at the height of his fame. TT's technique of underplaying many of his reactions suited the big screen. He once explained that when filming a close-up in the 1956 film *Private's Progress*, he was required to show his character registering shock, fury and indignation: 'I just looked into the camera and kept my mind blank. It's a trick I've used often since. In this way, the audience does the work.'[35] In 1984, Terry-Thomas, who had been living in Ibiza since 1968 in a villa he designed himself ('I'm allergic to architects'), admitted in an interview that he had been told he had Parkinson's disease and only had a few years left to live. He had remarried in 1963 to a twenty-one-year-old called Belinda Cunningham, whom he had met on holiday in Majorca.

In 1987 the couple could no longer afford to live in Spain and moved back to London. They lived in a series of rented properties before ending up in a three-room, unfurnished charity flat, where they lived with financial assistance from the Actors' Benevolent Fund. Richard Briers was one of his first visitors, and was shocked by the change he saw: 'He was just a mere shadow. A crippled, crushed, shadow. It was really bloody awful.'[36] On 9 April 1989, the actor Jack Douglas and Richard Hope-Hawkins organised a benefit concert for Terry-Thomas, after discovering he was living in virtual obscurity, poverty and ill health. The gala, held at the Theatre Royal, Drury Lane where TT had once worked for ENSA, ran for five hours and featured 120 artists, with Phil Collins topping the bill and Michael Caine as the gala chairman. The money raised allowed Terry-Thomas to move out of his charity flat and into Busbridge Hall nursing home in Godalming, Surrey. The man who personified the Englishman as an amiable bounder died there on 8 January 1990, at the age of seventy-eight.

Fifteen years before Tarbuck's success at the Palladium, in January 1948, Sid Field was topping the bill at the same famous theatre where he had replaced Mickey Rooney. The recently demobbed Kenneth Williams saw him there and wrote in his diary: 'Sid Field was marvellous, and received terrific and well-merited applause – what camping! I simply roared!'[37] The previous year Field had made one more film called *The Cardboard Cavalier* (as Sidcup Buttermeadow), co-starring with Margaret Lockwood, but, like *London Town*, it wasn't a success.

Above left: Sid Field playing snooker in a Littlewoods advert from 1946.

Above right: Sid Field in a promotional photograph for *Harvey.*

Back on stage it was a different matter. In 1949, to more acclaim, Sid Field returned to the Prince of Wales Theatre to perform in Mary Chase's play *Harvey,* in which he played the loveable drunk Elwood P. Dowd, whose best friend was a rabbit – a part which would later be played by James Stewart in the film of the same name. The play ran for 610 performances, but sadly this was to be Field's last part. During the play's run, on 3 February 1950, he died from a heart attack at his home in Richmond at the age of only forty-five. It was an early death, almost certainly brought on by his chronic dependence on alcohol. Field had made his stage debut, singing 'What A Life' at the age of nine, and in an attempt to alleviate the young Sid's stage fright his mother gave him a glass of port to drink. If it worked it came at a cost, for by the age of thirteen he was dependent on alcohol. Field was the special hero of Tony Hancock, also from Birmingham, and on hearing the news of Field's death he wept – the only time his agent saw him cry.[38]

Sid Field is now largely forgotten, perhaps because of the lack of recorded material on film or television. Only three films and

TO THE MEMORY OF THE GREAT COMEDIAN
Sid Field
WHO MADE HIS FIRST APPEARANCE IN THE WEST END OF LONDON AT THIS THEATRE ON MARCH 18TH 1943, AND WHO PLAYED HIS LAST PERFORMANCE HERE ON FEBRUARY 2ND 1950

Memorial plaque to Sid Field in the Prince of Wales Theatre. (Courtesy of the Prince of Wales Theatre)

some recorded variety material survive. He inspired a generation of comedians and pioneered the use of character acting in comedy. He was cited as a comic favourite not only by Tony Hancock (an influence, too) but also Eric Morecambe, Eric Sykes, Frankie Howerd and Tommy Cooper. He was also once described by Bob Hope as 'probably the best comedian of them all'. Laurence Olivier, during an interview with Kenneth Tynan in 1966, cited Field as a strong influence on his acting, saying, 'Of all people I have ever watched with the greatest delight, I think, was in another field entirely, was Sid Field … I still borrow from him, freely and unashamedly.'[39]

One place that hasn't forgotten Sid Field is the Prince of Wales Theatre. Inside, and near one of its loges, there is a highly polished memorial plaque dedicated to the performer whose first, last and greatest London performances were at the famous West End theatre on Coventry Street.

On 10 July 1963, just a few weeks before he followed the 'frightening' Beatles on to the Royal Variety stage at the Prince of Wales Theatre, Dickie Henderson arrived at his home in Kensington, only to be told his wife had died on the way to hospital. The thirty-three-year-old Dixie, after leaving a note for the 'daily' saying that she was not to be disturbed, had taken fifteen or sixteen barbiturate sleeping pills. Whether it was suicide or a tragic cry for help, the coroner gave an open verdict but it was noted that she died on Dickie and Dixie's fifteenth wedding anniversary. In fact Dickie hadn't seen his wife for two weeks, and would write in his unfinished autobiography that they were on a trial separation at the time, and that he was actually returning home to discuss a reconciliation. Dixie was buried in Gunnersbury Cemetery in Acton. On the gravestone it says 'Dixie', but the marriage and death certificate both have her name as Veda Victoria – the name she borrowed from her older sister twenty years before and never officially relinquished.

Invariably a safe pair of hands, the 'classy' Dickie Henderson went on to perform in eight Royal Variety shows. After making his television debut on Arthur Askey's *Before Your Very Eyes* in 1953, he became a much-loved national star during the late 1950s and throughout the 1960s. Some forty-seven years after making his inauspicious stage debut as an 'eccentric dancer', the always neat and dapper Dickie succumbed to pancreatic cancer in 1985.

Dickie Henderson leaping over Dixie at home in Kensington on his thirty-seventh birthday in 1959.

7

A Hungry Graham Greene on the Night of 'The Wednesday', and the Death of Al Bowlly

On 2 April 1941 at the HMV studios on Abbey Road, and with the arranger and accompanist Pat Dodd attending the recording session in his RAF uniform, Al Bowlly and Jimmy Mesene recorded the Irving Berlin anti-Hitler song 'When that Man is Dead and Gone'. Twelve days later, on Easter Monday, Bowlly and fellow singer and guitarist Mesene ('The Anglo-Greek Ambassadors of Song – Two voices and Guitars in Harmony') started a week-long engagement at the Rex Theatre on Oxford Street in High Wycombe. The concerts got off to a bad start when the organist, used to playing solo in a cinema, found it difficult to keep time with the rest of the band. During the first performance, Bowlly, generally a happy-go-lucky man but with an occasional quick temper, had been stamping out the beat as hard as he could to 'Brother, Can You Spare a Dime?'. Suddenly he stopped and, according to the owner of the Rex Theatre at the time, 'advanced to the organist, raised his guitar menacingly, and told him he was killing the act and that if he played another note he would kill him'.[1]

Bowlly, although at first glance not particularly intimidating, was tough, very fit (albeit with a thirty-a-day cigarette habit) and had taken boxing lessons from Johnny Brown, the former featherweight champion of Britain. He had been on the road too long not to carry a brass knuckleduster in his travel suitcase, and his best friend was Harry 'Boy' Sabini, who, with his brother Charles 'Darby' Sabini, ran the infamous and feared racecourse gang, originally based in Clerkenwell.[2] It was Darby Sabini, incidentally, who lived during much of the 1930s in an apartment at Brighton's Grand Hotel and on whom, in his novel *Brighton Rock*, Graham Greene based his character Colleoni, the gangster. After Bowlly's threatening behaviour, the frightened organist left the stage and also left High Wycombe, never to be seen again. The band continued without him and a local church organist was found who, bravely, agreed to play for the rest of the engagement.

After the third night's performance at the Rex Theatre and a quick drink of tomato juice in the local Red Lion hotel, Bowlly, virtually a teetotaller, left the others to continue their drinking and caught the 10.34 Marylebone train back to London. Not long after midnight he was in his bed in his second-floor apartment at Duke's Court, which overlooked Jermyn Street in St James's. Bowlly was often blasé about his safety and frequently ignored the protection of the air-raid shelters, and during what had already been a pretty ferocious Luftwaffe bombing raid he started to read a book of cowboy stories. It was said that Bowlly's relaxed attitude to the Blitz came from one of the first daylight raids of the war, when he

Al Bowlly.

had been walking along Brewer Street in Soho. A bomb exploded in the middle of the road in front of him but all the force of the blast went in the opposite direction – leaving him unscathed. From that point he often ignored the sirens, feeling almost invincible.[3]

Albert Allick Bowlly was an incredibly influential singer during the early to mid-1930s, and he's widely credited as one of the originators of 'crooning' or, as he once called it, 'The Modern Singing Style'. It was a gentle, intimate and romantic form of singing that took advantage of new advances in microphone technology that enabled even a soft vocal performance to be heard live. In the early days of amplified singing, microphones were not always available and Bowlly was featured in an advert in *Melody Maker* in which 'Britain's most outstanding dance vocalist' expounded the 'Al Bowlly ultra compact Megaphone – a new loud speaker for vocalists!' In reality, although he occasionally used them, he disliked megaphones as they would hide his face from the audience. Women, in particular, were susceptible to Bowlly's not inconsiderable charms, vocal or otherwise, and he was known by many as 'the Big Swoon'. Ray Noble, the bandleader, later said, 'He was the very devil with women.' Noble recalled, 'When we went on the road in the States he left a course of destruction among the opposite sex everywhere he went.'[4]

Bowlly was born in January 1898 in Maputo, Mozambique, then a Portuguese colony, to Greek and Lebanese parents who had met en route to Australia but subsequently moved to South Africa. After travelling and busking his way to Europe, he made his first recording in 1927 in Berlin with Irving Berlin's 'Blue Skies'. He then came over to London to sing with Fred Elizalde's orchestra. Their version of 'If I Had You' became a hit in America – maybe the first British 'jazz' record to do so. Initially it wasn't a smooth ride to fame for Bowlly, but by 1931 he had signed two contracts: one with Roy Fox, singing in his live band for the Monseigneur Restaurant in Piccadilly, the other a record contract with Ray Noble and his orchestra. It was Noble who is regularly quoted as saying, 'Al often stepped away from the microphone with tears in his eyes; never mind him making you cry, he could make himself cry!'[5]

During the next four years, he recorded over 500 songs and now, with radio exposure and a successful British tour, Bowlly was inundated with demands for personal appearances and

✌ New Loud Speaker for Vocalists!

The
"AL BOWLLY"
ULTRA COMPACT
MEGAPHONE
(Reg. and Pat. pending).

The only megaphone of its type. It rolls up and occupies very little space. It can be packed in the bell of a saxophone or rolled round the finger board of a guitar.

Recommended by AL BOWLLY, Britain's most outstanding dance vocalist.

HERE for the first time is something new in portable megaphones designed expressly for the dance vocalist and crooner. Not an ordinary megaphone dressed up in some new material, but entirely new, novel and really useful. It has won the instant praise of one of Britain's masters of dance song. It is the invention of an artist possessing a profound knowledge of acoustics. It is made of a new composition and is obtainable in many pleasing and tuneful colours. It is light and weighs only 7 ounces. The illustrations will convey an impression of its portability. The material is finished glossy smooth internally and is strengthened at the bell end with a steel cable. It is fitted with a neat handle and five press studs mounted on steel plates, thus making it definitely air tight.

It packs flat for the drummer, etc. It is the very essence of neatness.

It is the only megaphone that amplifies the natural tonal qualities of the singer's voice without distortion. It is correct acoustically.

Buy an "Al Bowlly" Megaphone and Magnify your voice

NET PRO. PRICE
14/3
Postage 9d. extra.

Al Bowlly megaphone advert from *Melody Maker* in February 1933.

gigs – including undertaking a subsequent solo British tour. In 1934, accompanying Ray Noble, with whom he was still making the bulk of his recordings, Bowlly travelled to New York City. This resulted in more success and their recordings started to achieve popularity in the United States, where he often appeared at the head of an orchestra hand-picked for him and Noble by Glenn Miller. During the mid-1930s the songs 'Blue Moon', 'Easy to Love', 'I've Got You Under My Skin' and 'My Melancholy Baby' all became American hits for Bowlly. For a short while he even had his own radio series on NBC and in 1936 he travelled to Hollywood to co-star with Bing Crosby in *The Big Broadcast*.

The time spent in the States, however, damaged Bowlly's popularity with British audiences, and it also coincided with problems with his voice, affecting the frequency of his recordings. Bowlly moved permanently back to London with his wife Marjie in January 1937, but he had to work hard to regain anything like his former popularity. He moved from orchestra to orchestra, tirelessly touring regional theatres and recording as often as possible. When the Second World War started Bowlly's career was still relatively in the doldrums, and this was when he teamed up with

Al Bowlly.

Jimmy Mesene, whose career had also suffered a downturn (due to a particular fondness for alcohol). Late in 1939, to entertain an already war-weary public, they formed a double act called The Radio Stars with Two Guitars. They had a shaky start – their voices were of a very different style – but by Easter 1941 when they came to play at the Rex Theatre in High Wycombe, the act was getting good reviews, although they weren't always at the top of the bill.

In the early hours of 17 April 1941, a large parachute bomb floated down above St James's. At around 3.10 a.m. it exploded just above the corner of Jermyn Street with Duke Street St James. Parachute bombs, or landmines as they were often called (they were originally designed as mines to be used in water with a magnetic detonator), were built to explode in the air just above their target so that without protective cover the resultant shockwaves would flatten whole streets, with windows breaking up to a mile away. In this particular case the destruction was savage. The famous

Hammam at 76 Jermyn Street, once said to be the finest Turkish bath in Europe, was razed to the ground while other premises badly damaged were Fortnum & Mason, the Cavendish Hotel, Dunhill's and the southern end of the Piccadilly Arcade. Many of the serviced flats in Duke's Court also took the full force of the 1,000 kg bomb.

It wasn't just St James's that suffered during the Luftwaffe bombing raids on the night of 16/17 April. As far as London was concerned, it was one of the worst of the war and became known, simply, as 'The Wednesday'. Over a seven-hour period about 1,000 tons of incendiaries and high explosives rained down on the capital. This time it wasn't the East End that took the brunt, but much of central and west London, with the West End in particular taking a battering. It was estimated that 1,180 London civilians died that night or soon after, with 2,230 seriously injured. The diarist Anthony Heap wrote: 'About the worst "blitz" we've yet experienced broke over London after 9 p.m. last night and lasted a good seven hours. It took us right back to last September, though neither then nor since has there been anything to match the raid for non-stop intensity.'[6]

Based in Finsbury and one of the first women to become a full-time air-raid warden, Barbara Nixon wrote an account of the same 'ferocious night'. She too had heard the sirens sounding at 9 p.m., and recorded that even before they had a chance to put on their coats and tin hats they heard the 'steady drone of aircraft overhead'.[7] At first Nixon and her colleagues only heard bombs whistling down and exploding in neighbouring districts, but after half an hour or so the streets and the buildings nearby 'lit up' and she described the terrible beauty around her:

We looked up, and saw three chandelier flares descending slowly, directly above us. Two gave off the usual reddish amber light, the third was greenish. Three at once would be too many for the gunners to hit before the next plane came in ... The light grew so bright that it paled the full moon; it shone eerily through the empty windows of the buildings opposite, and gleamed green on the charred walls and twisted girders ... Streams of tracer bullets were rising slowly and gracefully towards the flares.[8]

On the same evening the writer Graham Greene also heard the nine o'clock siren. He was surprised – the Luftwaffe raids tended to begin an hour later. The thirty-six-year-old, who by 1941 had already published ten novels, including *The Power and the Glory* the previous year, was drinking in the Horseshoe pub – a vast and cavernous bar at the southern end of Tottenham Court Road. He was with Dorothy Glover, whom he had met almost exactly two years before after he had rented a writing studio from her mother in Mecklenburg Square in King's Cross. Thirty-nine-year-old Dorothy, who had once danced in theatrical revues, was now a theatre designer, and while Greene's wife Vivien and their children lived relatively out of harm's way in Oxford, she and Greene began an affair. David Low, a dealer in rare books and a friend of Greene's, remembered Dorothy as 'happy, small, rather stoutish, not smart but very friendly – she radiated friendliness. She gave you a sense of feeling at home in her company – she had a nice laugh.'[9] By the time the Blitz started, Greene was spending every night at Dorothy's flat in Gower Mews, although Vivien thought he was still living in his house next to Clapham Common. Graham and Dorothy were both serving as neighbourhood fire wardens, and Dorothy as a bomb shelter warden. 'From the very first raid,' Greene later remembered, 'she was courageous, oh yes, and showed no fear of any kind.'[10]

When Graham and Dorothy first heard the air-raid siren they decided to finish their drinks and find somewhere to eat while they had a chance. They both knew from experience that it was likely to be a long night ahead. Most restaurants were serving food in the evening, and the *Manchester Guardian* had reported only the month before that although restaurants, especially foreign ones, had once displayed signs saying 'Open for lunch only', recently they had all been tentatively opening again for dinner after the worst of the bombing had seemed to be over the previous November.[11]

The Horseshoe pub was situated next to the Dominion Theatre in a building that had been in existence from around 1875, although there had been a pub on the location since the seventeenth century. The Dominion had been built in 1928 on the location of the Meux Horse Shoe Brewery, which had closed in 1921 and demolished the year after. This was the brewery of the great beer flood when in October 1814 corroded hoops on a large vat had suddenly given way, releasing about 3,550 barrels of beer (over a million pints) of porter. The brewery was located in a densely populated and tightly packed area of squalid housing (known as the rookery, much of which was cleared away when New Oxford Street was built in the 1840s). In one nearby house a group of Irish immigrants had gathered at the wake of John Saville, the two-year-old son of Ann Saville. As the flood of beer crashed in, five of the mourners were killed, including the grieving mother.[12] Eight people in total died in the disaster while swimming survivors drank the beer flowing down the streets.

At the same time as the Dominion was being constructed an extension was built onto the Horseshoe pub which added a grill room and restaurant to the premises and also a second-floor Masonic temple with a domed room decorated with gold stars. In the 1960s this temple became a music venue and it was where the folk-rock band Pentangle first played. Bassist Danny Thompson once said: 'People have said to me, "Cor you were lucky getting that Pentangle gig!" but Bert [Jansch] and John [Renbourn] had simply asked, "Do you fancy coming down the pub for a play – there's no money." And I went. It was successful because we loved what we were doing. The band was an honest 'ere-we-go – five geezers having a play.'[13] During the 1980s the Horseshoe operated as a music pub playing mostly jazz-funk. After becoming the electrical shop Gultronics, the whole site was demolished in September 2007. The building that replaced it is dull and unmemorable.

At about the same time that the geezers of Pentangle started playing together at the Horseshoe pub, across the road the Lyons Corner House, on the corner of Oxford Street and Tottenham Court Road, was closing down after being sold to Mecca on a ninety-nine-year lease. Eleven Lyons teashops had also closed the previous year, 'mitigated', the company said, by the opening of thirty brand-new Wimpy bars – a brand name they had purchased back in 1954. It was the end of an era – the Lyons Corner Houses had been feeding grateful Londoners for over sixty years. The huge restaurants, over four or five floors, each employed up to 400 staff. Each floor had an individual style, and in their heyday all had orchestras playing to diners through the day and night. The Corner Houses included hair-dressing salons and theatre-booking agencies, and would deliver food to any address in London twice a

Graham Greene *c*. 1939.

day. Although the restaurants looked expensive, the meals, on the whole, were within the price range of most working people. During the war Lyons did particularly well in the mornings, when, after the all-clear was sounded, very hungry people came rushing out of the shelters and, with no wish or time to cook their own breakfasts, made for the Lyons tea shops and corner houses.[14]

It was at the Tottenham Court Road Lyons Corner House opposite the Horseshoe where Graham and Dorothy first tried looking for something to eat. However, at just past nine, with the air-raid sirens sounding, it was full and the doors were closed. The Corner Houses were usually open all night and had air-raid shelters in the basement and their own air-raid spotters on the roof. After the Corner House, Graham and Dorothy tried Restaurant Frascati, situated almost next door on the north side of Oxford Street at number 32.

Frascati's had opened almost fifty years previously in 1893, initially as Krasnapolski's Dutch Restaurant, but was soon renamed after the famous Italian summer resort. It wasn't long before the sumptuous and elegant venue became famous for its international cuisine. There wasn't a restaurant like it in London. The facade, with a large frontage, was made up of a handsome gold portico with large windows sporting gold frames. The entrance into the restaurant was through a yellow-and-gold revolving door into a spacious lounge area with thick red pile carpets with futuristic patterns. On the right was the Grill Room, with large open charcoal grills, while the main restaurant was a spectacular and immense room called the Winter Garden that rose to a huge glass dome and had a wide balcony that overlooked the space below. On the ground floor there were two other large offshoot rooms, both restaurants in themselves. It must have all looked spectacular. In the years up to the war the restaurant's advertising would always say: 'London's floral restaurant – Renowned all over the world for its Charm, Recherché Cuisine and excellent Wines and Cigars.'

Frascati's was always a popular place for banquets and dinners, especially as there were numerous rooms for private functions. In November 1927 the Magic Circle had their annual dinner at the restaurant and the *Observer* reported that 'Mr Gordon Powell, one of the finest amateur conjurers in England, grew a tangerine tree at a moment's notice; real fruits "developed" instantaneously, and a bird's nest with real live birds in it was discovered among the branches'.[15] Another notable dinner five years later in 1932 was a reunion for graduates of the University of New Zealand. The father of nuclear physics, Lord Rutherford, was the main speaker – it was the year that he had discovered the neutron, and he gave an illustration that evening of the process of atomic bombardment: 'The passage of the invisible neutron into the nucleus of the atom,' he said, 'is like an invisible man passing through Piccadilly Circus. His path can be traced only by the people he has pushed aside.'[16] Rutherford at the time thought that anyone who thought it feasible to produce energy from the transformation of atoms was 'talking moonshine', but after reading an article in *The Times* that summarised Rutherford's speech, the Jewish Hungarian physicist Leo Szilard conceived exactly that with the idea of a nuclear chain reaction. The historian Richard Rhodes described Szilard's moment of inspiration:

In London, where Southampton Row passes Russell Square, across from the British Museum in Bloomsbury, Leo Szilard waited irritably one grey Depression morning for the stoplight to change. A trace of rain had fallen during the night; Tuesday,

September 12, 1933, dawned cool, humid and dull. Drizzling rain would begin again in early afternoon. When Szilard told the story later he never mentioned his destination that morning. He may have had none; he often walked to think. In any case another destination intervened. The stoplight changed to green. Szilard stepped off the curb. As he crossed the street time cracked open before him and he saw a way to the future, death into the world and all our woes, the shape of things to come.[17]

The manager of Frascati's at the start of the Second World War was Mr W. G. Cox, a former president of the Gastronomic Society (a society for heads of the chief hotels, restaurants and clubs). The Gastronomes traditionally held their monthly dinner at the restaurant, the last of which had been in December 1939 when 'supper took the place of the annual dinner'. The menu consisted of dishes containing only ingredients which were obtainable in Britain at the time and were felt not to be at risk of any future rationing restrictions. Butter was not served and saccharine came with the coffees. The menu included Whitstable oysters, borscht soup, fillets of sole, wings of chicken with purée of mushrooms, Comice pear cooked in vanilla syrup with vanilla ice, and a savoury composed of Cheddar and Roquefort cheese with chopped almonds on toast dressed with pickled walnuts.[18]

After the war Frascati's never really regained its pre-war reputation, and it was announced in 1953 that the restaurant was to close for good the following year. If there are skilful conjurors and eminent physicists in the building today it would be only to check their bank accounts – the once grand building with the gold windows at 32 Oxford Street is now a Lloyds TSB branch.

Sumptuous and luxurious it may have been, but it was of no matter to Graham and Dorothy, as the restaurant's doors were closed during the air raid. The couple continued their search for food and walked across Oxford Street and then down Wardour Street until they crossed Shaftesbury Avenue and got to Chez Victor's at number 45. Chez Victor's was a mirror-walled restaurant that had originally opened forty years before in 1901. In the years before the Second World War, musicians and singers such as Leslie 'Hutch' Hutchinson serenaded diners with Cole Porter and Rodgers and Hart songs. During and after the war a portrait of

General de Gaulle and Free French souvenirs became part of the decor, and in the sixties the restaurant again became the haunt of fashionable celebrities. In the guestbook David Hockney once drew the plate, the coffee cup and glass at his dinner table while Peter Cook and Dudley Moore joked across the pages: 'Whose that bloke on the other page? I can't read his signature – Dudley Moore', prompting a scrawled reply: 'I'm not famous enough – Peter Cook. And anyway no one can read my signature.'[19]

In 1987 Jonathan Meades, in an article in *The Times* entitled 'The authentic taste of Old Soho', described the restaurant's sad decline:

> Chez Victor has sat in Wardour Street since the beginning of the century. It looks it. This is not your mellow oldster but an embittered misanthrope, a sort of Steptoe père of a restaurant. In its defence you might plead authenticity. But authenticity is, with sincerity, a most overvalued property. At Chez Victor the service is authentically surly, the grime is authentically grimy; the cooking is authentically vieux jeu, which might be a desirable attribute were it not for its ineptitude. The menu – which was gracelessly shoved at me – offers tripes, brains, tete de veau – all the proper bourgeois standbys that are increasingly rare in France and threatened species here.[20]

Tripe and brains became even rarer after 2011 when after 110 years Chez Victor's closed down for good. It's now an Italian restaurant called the Astoria. There was also no tripe or brains for Graham and Dorothy because Chez Victor's was closed that evening as well. Not having much luck, the couple then walked back across Shaftesbury Avenue, but this time up Dean Street to the York Minster at number 45. Again it was to no avail as the chef was about to travel home.

The York Minster had originally opened as the Wine House in 1910 under a German called Schmidt, but he was deported at the start of the First World War. He was replaced by a Frenchman called Victor Berlemont, who changed the name to the York Minster and who was infamous for throwing out troublesome drinkers by shouting, 'I'm afraid one of us will have to leave, and it's not going to be me!'[21] In time the pub came to be known as the French House, and during the war was popular with soldiers and sailors, described by *Picture Post* magazine as the 'lower French ranks'.[22] Although it has been said that Charles de Gaulle drew up his Free French call to arms after lunch in the restaurant upstairs, it was L'Escargot, the Coquille and Chez Victor that were frequented more typically by French officers and people connected with the De Gaulle headquarters. As for many Londoners, Soho at the time was their escape from English cooking, and the French-run restaurants, whatever the proprietor's private opinion of the Vichy government, invariably displayed De Gaulle posters with the words: '*A tous les Français: La France a perdu une Bataille, elle n'a pas perdu la guerre.*' Despite the strict food restrictions, the *Manchester Guardian* reported that in Soho the standard of cooking was still good in the better-class restaurants:

> A good filet de sole is not a rarity yet, nor a navarin d'agneau; and French chefs have always been noted for their ingenuity in making potatoes interesting. And even if the rarer French vegetables are lacking, potatoes and carrots and sprouts are always plentiful, and cooked in the French way ... the raw materials available do not always lend themselves to a characteristically Continental treatment. Even served by a Frenchman, a leg of mutton is a leg of mutton for all that; and there is often little other choice.[23]

Wine, however, especially since the fall of France, was getting expensive and beer was becoming far more popular as an accompaniment to food than was formerly the case.

In the end Dorothy and Graham ended up in the bare-bricked surroundings of Czarda's in Dean Street for their supper. They sat rather apprehensively next to the plate-glass windows, which were bravely still in place despite the Blitz. Czarda's had been opened by Paul Weisz in 1937 and despite the acute shortage of paprika was still serving what must have been a relatively bland and colourless goulash.

Perhaps a little too far in the wrong direction for Graham and Dorothy was another Hungarian restaurant on Lower Regent Street called the Hungaria, which had the added attraction of a very deep basement and also gas and blast-proof doors. The waiters, some of whom slept on the premises, were trained to make a bed and operate as air raid precaution (ARP) wardens and first-aid workers.

HUNGARIA
The SAFE Restaurant
Bomb-proof . Splinter-proof . Blast-proof
Gas-proof and BOREDOM PROOF
We care for your Safety as well as your Pleasure
LOWER REGENT STREET, PICCADILLY CIRCUS, W.I
Tel.: WHItehall 4222

Second World War advert for the Hungaria restaurant on Lower Regent Street.

If staying the night wasn't an option, there was also a fleet of private cars driven by tin-hatted chauffeurs ready to take you through bomb blasts and shell fragments back home.[24] Their advertising during the war read, 'Bomb-Proof. Splinter-proof. Blast-proof. Gas-proof and BOREDOM PROOF – we care for your Safety as well as your Pleasure.' A little over a year after 'The Wednesday', the crews that had returned from the Dambusters raid (fifty-three of the original 133 young men died during the mission) were fêted at the Hungaria. The survivors were wined and dined and entertained by Arthur Askey, Jack Hylton and Elsie Carlisle.

Although Czarda's shook from some nearby bombs, the plate-glass windows stayed intact and Graham Greene later wrote that 'by ten it was obvious that this was a real blitz. Bomb bursts – perhaps the ones in Piccadilly – shook the restaurant. Left at ten thirty and walked back to Gower Mews. Wished I had my steel helmet. Changed, and went out with D, who was fire-watching. Standing on the roof of a garage we saw the flares come slowly flowing down, drilling their flames; they drift like great yellow peonies.'[25] Years later David Low recalled that when one of the largest bombs fell and hit the corner he 'saw Graham and Dorothy walking up Bloomsbury Street. As a result of a bomb, there were papers flying everywhere. Graham and Dorothy were picking up the papers whatever they were and reading them to each other in the street and roaring with laughter.'[26]

Greene, who wrote years later that the night was 'the worst raid Central London had ever experienced', reported to his post at midnight (which must have been around the time Al Bowlly got home after walking from Marylebone station down to his apartment in St James's). By a quarter to two not much had happened in his district and Greene was planning to sign off at half past two. Then the flares came down again, almost directly on top of his group of wardens, and landed west to east across Charlotte Street. A few minutes later there was a massive explosion and glass from a shop window showered down on their helmets. A parachute bomb had fallen, landing on the Victoria Club in Malet Street, where 350 Canadian soldiers were sleeping. All down Gower Street bleeding people, cut by flying broken glass, were emerging from doorways in 'squalid pyjamas grey with debris dust'.[27]

The guns and bombing continued, and Greene came across a body with 'only the head and shoulders visible and a clot of blood by the head. Quiet and slumped and just a peaceful part of the rubble.'[28] 'He's a goner,' someone said. Another 'stick of three bombs came whistling down' and everyone lay down on the pavement. A sailor landed on top of Greene, who now had a bleeding cut on his hand from the broken glass. All this 'belonged to human nature', Greene would write. As he was having his hand dressed, another three bombs came down, blowing in all the windows. He was no longer frightened – 'one had ceased to believe in the possibility of surviving the night'.

At quarter past three it was bright as daytime from the flares and Greene and his colleagues had to rest, despite the cries of the injured. Eventually Greene called in at the shelter in Gower Mews where Dorothy was acting as shelter warden. Greene said that she was 'cheerful but glad to see me. A warden had told her that he had seen me in the Victoria Club. "I think he was all right. He was covered in blood, but I don't think it was his blood."' In the meantime another parachute bomb had landed at the end of Bloomsbury Street and a high-explosive bomb had landed on the Jewish Girls' Club in Alfred Place (more than thirty people were killed and bodies were still being removed days later). And then, after hours of chaos, confusion and noise, at around five the continuous all-clear 'raiders past' siren sounded.[29]

On the same night, the architectural historian and writer James Lees-Milne, thirty-two at the time, had been sheltering in the

Piccadilly Hotel, which had been hit by a bomb. He described the scene when he walked out when dawn broke:

> On pavements and streets a film of broken glass crunched under the feet like the jagged crystals of lush icicles. One had to take care they did not clamber over the edge of one's shoes. The contents of shop windows were strewn over the pavements among the broken glass. Silk shirts and brocaded dressing gowns fluttered upon area railings. The show cases of jewellers's window had sprinkled tray loads of gold watches and bracelets as far as the kerb of the street. I stooped to pick up a handful of diamonds and emeralds – and chuck them back into the shop before they got trodden on, or looted.[30]

After walking along Jermyn Street, Lees-Milne noticed that it was blocked by the rubble from collapsed houses: 'Here I noticed the stripped, torn trunk of a man on the pavement. Further on I picked up what looked like the mottled, spread leaf of a plane tree. It was a detached hand with a signet ring on the little finger.'[31]

A diarist called E. J. Rudsdale wrote that same morning:

> Tremendous raid on London last night. This is obviously the most violent raid ever launched. It has been increasingly the policy of the Government lately to minimise or falsify raid casualties, which are almost always described as 'some', 'slight', 'including a few persons killed' or some such vague term. Thanks to the general narrow-mindedness of the English, these unsatisfactory statements cause little interest or comment.[32]

Although there were no real numbers of casualties, the newspapers on the 18th, despite Mr Rudsdale's cynicism, did acknowledge the devastation across London. The *Daily Express* reported: 'The vicious air raid on London on Wednesday night – it was the worst the capital has experienced – caused heavy casualties, it is officially reported. High explosives and fire bombs were rained down hour after hour until dawn brought relief. One of the districts most affected was the West End, where shop and office workers yesterday morning had to wade through piles of shattered glass and wreckage.' The newspaper added that Lord and Lady Stamp

Piccadilly, not far from Duke's Court the morning after 'The Wednesday', April 1941.

and Mr Wilfrid Carlyle Stamp, their eldest son and heir to the title, were killed in the raid, as was Lord Auckland (an expert in animal taming). Almost as an afterthought it mentioned the death of 'well-known crooner' Al Bowlly.

When the all-clear sounded around dawn on 17 April, the caretaker of Duke's Court went round to check on the safety of his tenants. He found Al Bowlly on the floor by the side of his bed, killed outright by the door of his room smashing on his head from the blast of the parachute bomb. Two friends of Bowlly's also lived at Duke's Court. The pianist Monia Liter, who had fortunately been away in Bangor on the night of the raid, had known Bowlly since 1929. As the leader of his own orchestra, he had employed the young vocalist at Raffles, the famous hotel in Singapore and was subsequently an accompanist on some of Bowlly's recordings.

When Liter arrived back at Duke's Court, he saw the comedienne and actress Beatrice Lillie, another inhabitant of the serviced flats. He later recalled: 'When I got back to Jermyn Street on the morning after the raid, Bea Lillie met me in the hall. She said "We've had a terrible night – look here", and showed me a number of large sacks in the hall with labels on them. "These are the people who were killed last night. I saw that one of the sacks had Al Bowlly's name on the label. It was a terrible shock.'[33] Lillie had experienced the bombing by the Zeppelins during the previous war, and her own son would die a year later, killed in action aboard HMS *Tenedos* in Colombo Harbour, Ceylon (present-day Sri Lanka). An inveterate entertainer of the troops, she heard about her son's death just before she was about to go on stage. She refused to postpone the performance, saying, 'I'll cry tomorrow.' At the theatre she pinned a notice on the board by the stage door, reading: 'I know how you all feel. Don't let's talk about it. Bless you. Now, let's get on with our work.'[34]

Bowlly's remains were taken to the local council's mortuary at Glasgow Terrace and a death certificate was eventually produced which misspelt Bowlly's name and gave the cause of death as 'due to war operations'. He was buried in a mass communal grave on Saturday 26 April at 10.30 a.m. at the Westminster City Council Cemetery on the Uxbridge Road in Hanwell. Jimmy Mesene and several others tried to make arrangements for a proper tombstone for Al Bowlly to be erected. The required licence, however, was refused by Westminster City Council, who claimed that it would set a precedent – that section of the cemetery was designated as a war grave and there could be no private memorials.

Graham Greene, in his autobiographical book *Ways of Escape*, wrote about the night of 'The Wednesday' and remembered the 'squalor' of the night and 'the purgatorial throng of men and women in dirty torn pyjamas with little blood splashes standing in doorways'. After little or no sleep, Greene had to travel to Oxford the next morning as he had promised to give a talk at the Catholic Newman Society. Having had no chance to shave, in Oxford he went into a chemist and asked for a packet of razor blades. The man glared at Greene in fury and said, 'Don't you know there's a war on?'[35]

32 Duke's Court, April 2011 (now demolished).

8

When Tallulah Bankhead Met Gerald du Maurier, and the Eton Schoolboys Scandal

The weather hadn't been great in London during April 1925, and the Easter holiday that month was no exception. The American journalist Christopher Morley wrote in the *Manchester Guardian* that 'the most pathetic thing he had noticed in England was a sign in a shop window that said – WATERPROOFS FOR THE HOLIDAYS'. Despite this, Morley noted that the English thought it 'churlish and poor spirited and against the whole spirit of a holiday' to go out for the day with waterproofs and umbrellas and, thus, on that Easter bank holiday 'the millions that had ventured out to Hampstead Heath and Epping and Hadley Woods or the West End parks for their vernal enjoyments' had all got very badly soaked.[1]

During this 'endless deluge',[2] as she described it, the American actress Tallulah Bankhead went to bed the weekend after Easter intending, perhaps, not to wake up. She had swallowed twenty aspirin and written a suicide note that was made up solely of the flippant line, 'It ain't goin' to rain no moh.' Bankhead always preferred a clever line to any acknowledgment of emotion on her part and she wasn't referring just to the inclement weather in her note. Earlier that day, after watching her audition from a corner of the dark auditorium of the Garrick Theatre, Somerset Maugham had turned her down as Sadie Thompson in *Rain* – a play that had been adapted from his acclaimed short story 'Miss Thompson'.[3] Bankhead had provisionally been given the part by the producer Basil Dean, subject only to the playwright's approval, but an unimpressed Maugham decided to give the part of the 'South Sea slut' not to Tallulah but to the Norwegian-born actress Olga Lindo. Tallulah was devastated and later wrote in her autobiography: 'I had hysterics and fled down the stairs, sobbing as I had not sobbed since foiled as a child.'

In shock she wandered home and bumped into Mary Claire, a 'fine character actress' who had appeared with her in the play *Conchita*,[4] and who took her to a Lyons Corner House, almost certainly the one on Coventry Street by Leicester Square 200 yards from the Garrick Theatre on Charing Cross Road. The friendly face and a consoling cup of tea were to no avail and Tallulah made her way home to her serviced flat on Curzon Street (all the tenants in the building had access to a cook and a butler who would bring meals to your room). Bankhead later wrote, 'I went to sleep dramatising every detail of my suicide. London's shock! The curious and muted crowds at my door! The stern calm of the bobbies and the coroner! The headlines in the newspapers! Maugham stoned in the streets! The cables aquiver with news of the death of the American beauty who had conquered England.'

Above left: A smoking Tallulah Bankhead not long after arriving in London.

Above right: Tallulah Bankhead *c.* 1921.

There were no bobbies or coroners at the door the next morning, calm or otherwise, nor was there a public stoning of an eminent writer. In fact Tallulah woke up feeling 'marvellous'. Her telephone was ringing and it was Noël Coward who, fortuitously for the now out-of-work Bankhead, asked if she would appear in his new play *Fallen Angels* – a comedy that he had originally written two years earlier in 1923. His original lead was a very popular Canadian actress called Margaret 'Bunny' Bannerman and 'one of the kindest-hearted and least troublesome leading ladies I know', Coward would later write. Unfortunately she was close to having a nervous breakdown, and with only four days before the first night she had stood herself down, completely unable to remember her lines. Tallulah, despite being told by the precocious twenty-five-year-old playwright that she only had four days to learn her lines, told him she needed just four hours and would do it for £100 per week. With little choice, Coward accepted her price. He remembered the first rehearsal:

> Tallulah Bankhead came flying into the theatre. Her vitality has always been remarkable, but on that occasion it was little short of fantastic. She took that exceedingly long part at a run. She tore off her hat, flipped her furs into a corner, kissed Edna, Stanley, me and anyone else who happened to be in reach and, talking incessantly about *Rain*, which Maugham had just refused to allow her to play, she embarked on the first act. In two days she knew the whole part perfectly.[5]

At this point the Alabama-born Tallulah had been living in London for just over two years. She had arrived in England on the SS *Majestic* on 13 January 1923, just over two weeks before her twenty-first birthday. For some reason, despite his seniority and the fact that he had no idea who she was, the Chief Immigration Officer, the splendidly named Brodôme Edmund Reeve-Jones, made it his job to interview the beautiful twenty-year-old actress on her arrival at Southampton. She was little known in the UK and her career in the US had so far consisted of some small parts in a few silent films and a handful of appearances on stage in New York. Although her acting was sometimes praised, the plays themselves were all commercially and critically unsuccessful. Reeve-Jones noted down, 'She explained that her father was one of the American House of Representatives and had given her money to come over and see England, that she had no occupation and did not know how long she would stay or where.' Reeve-Jones then interviewed a steward from the ship and wrote: 'He confirmed my suspicion that she was not travelling on a liner for the first time and made male friends very quickly.'

Despite Brodôme's suspicions and concerns, Tallulah was allowed into the country and travelled to London by train, to be met at Paddington[6] by the theatre manager and impresario Charles B. Cochran. Known to his friends as 'Cockie', he was occasionally referred to as 'the English Ziegfeld', and while the American Florenz Ziegfeld Jr had his famous 'Ziegfeld Girls', Cochran had his own polite British equivalent: 'Cochran's Young Ladies', many of whom became huge stars. He was, or would be, responsible for discovering Gertrude Lawrence, Jessie Matthews, Evelyn Laye, Hermione Baddeley, Beatrice Lillie and many, many others.

Cochran had first met Tallulah a few weeks before in New York, at a party held by Frank Crowninshields, the editor of *Vanity Fair*, and he was immediately impressed, not least because of her long blonde hair ('unbanned, unwrapped, it fell to my knees'[7]) which she told him that she washed solely in Energine dry-cleaning fluid. Six weeks later, now back in the UK, he sent her a cable: 'POSSIBLE ENGAGEMENT WITH GERALD DU MAURIER IN ABOUT EIGHT WEEKS.' He soon followed this message with a letter:

My dear Tallulah,
This is the position.
Sir Gerald du Maurier is producing in about eight weeks' time a new play. The part-authoress [the actress Viola Tree, daughter of Sir Herbert Beerbohm Tree and niece of Max Beerbohm] tells me that there are two good women parts in it, one an American, the other an English girl. She tells me, and Sir Gerald confirms this, that the American is the better of the two parts. She is, I understand, somewhat of a siren and in one scene has to dance. She must be a lady, and altogether sounds like you. She is, in the play, supposed to be of surpassing beauty. I have told the part-authoress and Sir Gerald that I believe you are 'the goods'.

Gerald du Maurier.

Cochran promised to pay her expenses if she managed to get over to London. Tallulah cabled him that she would come immediately, but the impresario sent another telegram back: 'TERRIBLY SORRY, DU MAURIER'S PLANS CHANGED.' Tallulah returned with: 'I'M COMING ANYHOW!' to which he replied: 'DON'T, THERE'S A DEPRESSION HERE. IT'S VERY BAD.' Tallulah decided to pretend that she hadn't received his final missive, or that there was a depression, and sailed to England anyway.

After meeting Tallulah at the station, Cochran installed her at the Ritz hotel and then the next day took her to Wyndham's Theatre on Charing Cross Road to meet Sir Gerald du Maurier. The distinguished actor was performing in a matinee of *Bulldog Drummond*, a play that he had adapted with H. C. McNeile, the author of the original popular novel. Du Maurier, knighted the previous year, was the son of George du Maurier, the famous *Punch* artist and author of the best-selling novel *Trilby*, but also, of course, the father of author Daphne du Maurier. Not only that, his sister Sylvia Llewelyn Davies was the mother of the boys who were the inspiration for the Peter Pan stories by J. M. Barrie.

Success had come pretty easily to Gerald, although he had no formal training nor had he even been to drama school. He was seen as the most naturally gifted actor of his era, and incredibly influential. *The Times* later wrote of his career: 'His parentage assured him of engagements in the best of company to begin with; but it was his own talent that took advantage of them.' Du Maurier's initial popularity became assured because of his performances in two J. M. Barrie plays – as the Hon. Ernest Wooley in *The Admirable Crichton* and the two roles of George Darling and Captain Hook in *Peter Pan* at the Duke of York's Theatre in 1904. These successes were then followed by 'his exquisitely suave presentation' of *Raffles*. It cannot be coincidence that these plays with which he was associated are still remembered today by many.

Du Maurier's naturalistic, almost off-hand acting style made the mannered and melodramatic style of his predecessors – and, indeed, many of his contemporaries – suddenly seem terribly old-fashioned. Du Maurier performed as if he was just being himself, and the famed matinee idol's voice was quiet, conversational and understated. What seemed like an utter absence of technique needed huge amounts of rehearsal and he would practice smoking and drinking in front of mirrors for hours. 'Don't force it, don't be self-conscious,' he would say. 'Do what you generally do any day of your life when you come down into a room. Bite your nails, yawn, lie down on a sofa and read a book, do anything or nothing but don't look dramatically at the audience.'[8] Laurence Olivier once said, 'Brilliant actor though Gerald was, he had a most disastrous influence on my generation, because we really thought, looking at him, that it was easy. And for the first ten years of our lives in the theatre nobody could hear a word we said. We thought he was really being natural. Of course, he was a genius of a technician giving that appearance, that's all.'[9]

According to his daughter Daphne, he hated 'ardent lovemaking in the theatre': 'Must you kiss her as though you were having steak and onions for lunch? It may be what you feel but it's damned unattractive from the front row of the stalls. Can't you just say, 'I love you', and yawn, and light a cigarette and walk away?'[10] Cigarettes were forever associated with du Maurier's laid-back acting style, and in 1929, after being as blasé with his Inland Revenue paperwork as he was in making love on stage, he earned extra money by lending his name to a brand of cigarettes. 'The du Maurier filter tip gives a cool clean smoke with no loose bits in the mouth,' stated an advertisement of the time. Du Maurier, taking no notice of his own advertising and presumably preferring strands of tobacco left in his mouth, always smoked filterless cigarettes. These probably contributed to the cancer that killed him at the age of sixty-one. His cigarette name lives on, however, and to this day du Maurier cigarettes are still being manufactured in Canada by Imperial Tobacco.

Du Maurier, brilliant and skilful actor though he was, found it impossible to disguise his shock when, soon after his afternoon performance in *Bulldog Drummond*, Tallulah appeared in his dressing room. 'Here I am!' she said. 'But we cabled you not to come,' du Maurier replied, adding, 'Another girl has been engaged for the part. I'm terribly sorry. We're opening in a fortnight, you know.' 'Well,' replied Tallulah, 'I'm terribly sorry too, but I'm happy to be in England. It's been a great pleasure to meet you – perhaps she'll break a leg, or something!'[11]

Cochran knew du Maurier well, and was aware of his notorious roving eye (it takes one to know one, perhaps). The next day, after some thought, and admiring Tallulah's bravura, he suggested that she went to see the actor-manager again, this time dressed without headwear – 'I don't think he's aware of your unusual beauty. Your hat masks your extraordinary hair,' he told her. It's worth reiterating how profuse and effusive the admiration of Tallulah's hair was at that time. Janet Aitken, daughter of Max Beaverbrook, described it in her autobiography: 'I remember her hair more than anything else about

Gerald du Maurier with his daughters Jeanne and Daphne around the time when Daphne and Gerald met Tallulah for the first time in 1923.

Du Maurier cigarette advert from 1952. The cigarettes are still being made in Canada.

her. Not so much the colour of it, but the way it glowed and fell in gentle curves about her forehead and wide-set slumberous eyes.'[12]

Two days after the first visit, Tallulah and Cochran went to see Sir Gerald again, this time with her long, beautiful locks revealed. There were a few people in the room including Daphne, Gerald's fifteen-year-old daughter. Waiting until after the American actress had left, she turned to her father and said, 'Daddy, that's the most beautiful girl I ever saw in my life.' Not entirely disagreeing with this opinion, Gerald called Tallulah the next day and signed her for the part of Maxine in *The Dancers*. Tallulah was to be paid £30 per week and it was to preview in only two weeks.

Almost exactly a month after Tallulah had arrived in the country, *The Dancers*, billed as 'a melodrama in four parts', and written by du Maurier himself and the actress Viola Tree[13] (under the joint pseudonym Hubert Parson, presumably because the plot was more than preposterous), opened on 15 February 1923. The play was about two women, one Canadian and one English, who were both affected by 'dance mania' (post-war London was obsessed with the new jazz-dances). The Canadian (Tallulah) used her dancing talents to become a world famous ballerina while the rich aristocratic English girl (Audry Carten) in 'a moment's lapse' sleeps with her dance partner, becomes pregnant and subsequently takes her own life. The play was an immediate success and ran for thirty-four

Above left: Tallulah dressed in costume for Gerald du Maurier and Viola Tree's play *The Dancers* in 1923.

Above right: Tallulah in *The Dancers*.

weeks. Tallulah, who had taken the rehearsals so seriously she had given up smoking so as not to get breathless in the dancing scenes, was the clear attraction. The most famous scene in the play was one in which she performed an Indian dance (Tallulah likened it to an 'Alabama variation of Minnehaha!') costumed in feathers and jewels.

The public were disturbed and intrigued by Tallulah in equal measure. They loved her unique and exotic voice – the actor-writer Emlyn Williams once described it as 'steeped as deep in sex as the human voice can go without drowning' – and they loved her undoubted but unusual beauty. Tallulah, almost literally overnight, became the talk of London. Many male journalists, writing at the time, found it almost impossible to disguise their enthusiastic appreciation of her charms. Hannen Swaffer, after watching the première of *The Dancers*, wrote in the *Daily Express*, 'Tallulah is the essence of sophistication … she gives electric shocks! Sex oozes from her eyes! She is daring and friendly and rude and nice, and all at once!' While Reginald Arkell, the scriptwriter and comic novelist, wrote, 'Everybody knows that Tallulah is one of those girls who could lure a Scotch elder into any indiscretion. Positively! Her lips are as scarlet as a guardsman's coat, and her diamonds make the flashing signs of Piccadilly look like farthing dips. She plays "He loves me, he loves me not" with pearls that are as big as potatoes.'[14]

It wasn't just men, however, who were taken with Tallulah. Within a few weeks the American actress had developed a cult fan base of mostly teenage girls who copied the way she looked and dressed. Basil Dean, the producer who had wanted Tallulah for *Rain*, once described how her fans saw her: 'With her golden hair flying in the wind, husky voice, a soft Southern accent, and utter scorn of convention, she had become, almost overnight, the idol of all the up-and-coming working girls, who saw in her the embodiment of their dreams of a free life.'[15] The writer Arnold Bennett would later try to explain what Tallulah herself would call this 'mass lunacy':

> It begins on the previous afternoon. At 2 P.M., you see girls, girls, girls in seated queues at the pit and gallery door of the Tallulah theatre. They are a mysterious lot, these stalwarts of the cult ... They obstinately wait for a century or so, and then the doors are unbolted and there is a rush of frocks. This is the first of the ecstatical moments ... They seem quite nice girls, too. And when Tallulah comes out they will block her passage and murmur 'Tallulah'. Why is Miss Bankhead always called Tallulah? Nobody, except the privileged Hannen Swaffer, speaks of Marie, Gladys, Sybil, Evelyn.[16]

Lord Beaverbrook, the owner of the *Daily Express*, who often invited Tallulah to his parties during her eight years in London,[17] once said that 'there are only two people in the realm who could be identified by any costermonger on hearing their given name – Steve and Tallulah'. Beaverbrook was referring to Steve Donoghue, the great English flat-race jockey who to this day is the only rider to have won two triple crowns; however, with the exception of horse-racing fanatics, Donoghue has now been mostly forgotten. Tallulah Bankhead, on the other hand, and not only for the reason of her unusual name, has not.[18]

Noël Coward's *Fallen Angels* opened 21 April 1925 at the Globe Theatre situated on the corner of Shaftesbury Avenue and Rupert Street. It is now called the Gielgud Theatre and it was the young John Gielgud who replaced Noël Coward in his role in *The Vortex*, which allowed the brilliant actor-playwright to oversee the rehearsals of *Fallen Angels*. This meant that Coward had three of his plays running in the West End concurrently, and he later wrote of this time: 'With *Fallen Angels*, *On With the Dance*, and *The Vortex* all running at once, I was in an enviable position. Everyone but Somerset Maugham said that I was a second Somerset Maugham.'[19] The two women in *Fallen Angels* were played by Edna Best (now mostly remembered as the mother in Hitchcock's 1934 version of *The Man Who Knew Too Much*) and Tallulah. The second act of the play features almost nothing else but the two women getting more and more drunk on cocktails and champagne, while waiting for the return of their mutual former French lover.

The *Daily Mail* was disturbed that the 'long-drawn-out drunken scene won the loudest applause of the play,' and that 'Miss Bankhead's leer of triumph when she pronounced the word "psychology" without slurring the syllables was a little artistic triumph. It was received with loud laughter but it was not a healthy sort of laughter. Indeed there was scarcely a healthy laugh in the play … *Fallen Angels* offers only the flippancies of vice.' Joining in with the criticism, the *Daily Express* wrote: 'Drunkenness. Drunken women. Drunken young women. Drunken young married women both confessing to immoral relations with the same man. That is the bonne bouche of the new comedy by Mr Noël Coward.'[20] It wasn't just the drinking that worried the critics, it was the onstage admission that Edna and Tallulah's characters had both had pre-marital sex with the same man. Not only that, but during the absence of their passionless, golf-obsessed husbands, they both hoped to do so again. Indeed, an official in the Lord Chamberlain's office recommended that a licence for Coward's play should be refused on the grounds that the loose morals of the two main female characters 'would cause too great a scandal'. In the end the Lord Chamberlain (Lord Cromer) disagreed, saying: 'I take the view that the whole thing is so much unreal farcical comedy, that subject to a few modifications in the dialogue it can pass.'[21]

Noël Coward was pleased with his play along with the performances, and he singled out Tallulah, who in his opinion gave a 'brilliant and completely assured performance. It was a tour de force of vitality, magnetism and spontaneous combustion.'[22] He later described the first-night press notices as 'vituperative to the point of incoherence. No epithet was spared. It was described as vulgar, disgusting, shocking, nauseating, vile, obscene, degenerate, etc. etc. The idea of two gently nurtured young women playing a drinking scene together was apparently too degrading a spectacle for even the most hardened

Tallulah in costume for the play *The Creaking Chair* which opened at the Comedy Theatre in July 1924. It had terrible reviews but turned out to be a hit and ran for six months.

and worldly critics.'[23] It nearly always happens, of course, but the moralistic fuss and faux outrage in the newspapers over the 'drunken women' and 'decadence' only encouraged more people to see the play and it had a long run, eventually closing on 29 August 1925. During this last performance, Mrs Charles Hornibrook, a public morality campaigner, stood up during the second act and shouted: 'Ladies and Gentlemen, I wish to protest. This play should not go unchallenged–' At this point the orchestra struck up 'I Want to Be Happy' as the hapless Mrs Hornibrook was escorted out.

Twenty-four years later, in 1949, *Fallen Angels* was revived; this time Hermione Gingold and Hermione Baddeley (another Charles B. Cochran find) played the two women. Coward was in the audience and wrote, 'I have never yet in my long experience seen a more vulgar, silly, unfunny, disgraceful performance. Gingold at moments showed signs that she could be funny. Baddeley was disgusting. Afterwards I told them exactly what I thought.' Despite Coward's misgivings the production became another of his hits. He wrote in his diary, '*Fallen Angels* a terrific success. Livid.'[24]

On 2 August 1928, almost exactly three years after the initial Globe Theatre production of *Fallen Angels* had come to an end, the *Daily Express*'s 'Special Correspondent' wrote about the weather under the headline 'WHEN IT RAINS AT THE SEASIDE VISITORS TO

Tallulah Bankhead and Edna Best in *Fallen Angels*, which opened at the Globe Theatre in 1925.

BEXHILL STILL HAPPY'. It was 'windy and wet' in Bexhill-on-Sea, he wrote, but when he went for a stroll along the 'glistening pavement of the promenade', he was surprised to see it was crowded with 'people huddled happily in every imaginable piece of shelter. It seemed that people were happiest when things were most gloomy,' he concluded. On the front page of the same newspaper there was another innocent-sounding headline: 'JOLLIFICATION AT A THAMES RESORT'. The accompanying report, however, was slightly more sinister:

> A great sensation has been caused at Windsor by the news, which has just leaked out, that parents of at least half a dozen Eton boys were requested to remove their sons shortly before the end of term. The whole affair has been shrouded with the utmost secrecy by the college authorities. It appears that a party of boys decided they would enjoy an unauthorised evening outing on the Thames and accordingly they arranged a visit to a well-known restaurant at Bray – which is much frequented by members of society and the stage.

Although the article didn't name her, the rumours involved Tallulah Bankhead and they were serious enough for the Home Secretary

William Joynson-Hicks to request a report from MI5. Joynson-Hicks had a reputation for strict authoritarianism and during his long tenure as Home Secretary from 1924 to 1929 spent a lot of energy cracking down on aspects of the so-called 'Roaring Twenties'. He instructed the police to patrol public parks 'for violations of public decency' and established the Street Offences Committee, chaired by his wife, to crack down on prostitution. He also encouraged the police to charge dozens of nightclubs and casinos for gambling and sexual offences. Even the Bishop of Durham called him a 'dour fanatic' who proceeded against one cause after another with 'dervish-like fervour'. The senior Conservative politician was also heavily implicated in the banning of *The Well of Loneliness*, Radclyffe Hall's novel on a lesbian theme and in which he took a personal and prurient interest. Tallulah, who unusually for the time made no attempts to hide her bisexuality (albeit jokingly), was a friend of Radclyffe Hall and her partner Una, and they were often seen at First Night parties together at nightclubs such as Elsa Lanchester's Cave of Harmony Club in Charlotte Street.

The MI5 report, signed anonymously by 'FHM' and strewn with factual errors and rumours, was sent to Joynson-Hicks late in August 1928 and read:

The charge against Miss Tallulah Bankhead (an American aged 26) is quite broadly (a) that she is an extremely immoral woman and (b) that in consequence of her association with some Eton boys last term, the latter have had to leave Eton.

As regards (a) according to informant, she is both a Lesbian and immoral with men. Informant believes she comes from a respectable American family, her father, who was a senator, having turned her out of the house when she was young owing to immoral proclivities. It is also said she 'kept' a negress in America before she came to the country in 1925 and she 'keeps' a girl in London now. As regards her more natural proclivities, informant tells me that she bestows her favours 'generously' without payment. Informant added that her 'circle' is a centre of vice patronised by at least one of the most prominent sodomites in London. And that it was the considered opinion of the more respectable American actresses in this country that she was doing them a great deal of harm as people might be inclined to think that they were tarred with the same brush.

HOTEL DE PARIS BRAY
nr. Maidenhead

ENJOY THE DAY AT BRAY

DANCING
AND OTHER ATTRACTIONS

At week-ends, the bands from the Kit-Cat and Café de Paris play for "Thé Dansants" and at supper. The beautiful string orchestra plays during lunch and dinner. At supper, entertainment is provided by artistes selected from those appearing at the London establishments. There are two dance-floors, one under a magnificent tree on the lawn, the other in the restaurant. There is dancing every night, during the warm weather.

In addition to bathing and boating, for which every facility is provided, there are several hard tennis courts, a miniature golf course, beautiful walks in the gardens and around picturesque Bray, etc. Over 200 cars can be accommodated in the car-park.

PRIVATE SUIT

Amidst surroundings which can only b cribed as ideal, both as regards enviro and arrangements, the Hotel de Par a number of bedroom suites.

Each suite is fitted up as a separate possessing its own colour scheme and rative motif. Several of these suites sitting rooms and verandahs overlooki beautiful gardens. All have roomy bathrooms and each suite has its fir for use on a cool evening.

There is a telephone in every suite.

These suites should be reserved a possible in advance, as they are lim number and very much in demand.

A list of the suites with particular prices is on the reverse side of this pa

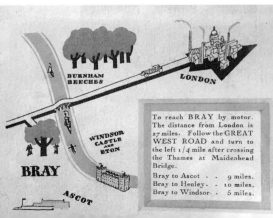

To reach BRAY by motor. The distance from London is 27 miles. Follow the GREAT WEST ROAD and turn to the left 1/4 mile after crossing the Thames at Maidenhead Bridge.

Bray to Ascot . . 9 miles.
Bray to Henley . . 10 miles.
Bray to Windsor . . 5 miles.

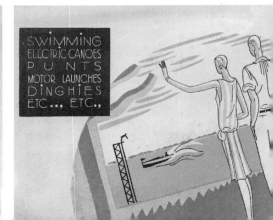

SWIMMING
ELECTRIC CANOES
PUNTS
MOTOR LAUNCHES
DINGHIES
ETC.., ETC.,

Above: Tallulah Bankhead back in London for the premiere of Alexander Korda's *The Private Life of Don Juan* at the London Pavilion in November 1934. She is accompanied by the bisexual model and future war heroine Toto Koopman. Tallulah was not long in London and was soon called back to New York, where she was to appear in *Dark Victory* on Broadway.

Opposite: Brochure of the Hotel de Paris in Bray, where Tallulah was purported to have consorted with Eton schoolboys in 1930.

As regards (b), There is no doubt that Tallulah Bankhead was seen at Eton frequently last term. I hear from another quarter that one or both of Sir M. Wilson's older sons used to motor down to Eton with her to see the third son who was then smuggled away from the afternoon under a rug in the car. It is said that this was the beginning of a T.B. Eton boys clique. FHM 29/8/28

In the end, FHM, lacking the evidence to throw Miss Bankhead out of Britain, pointed out that 'the headmaster is obviously not prepared to assist the Home Office – he wants to do everything possible to keep Eton out of the scandal'.[26] Years later Jeffry Amherst, fifth and last Earl of Amherst, journalist, airline executive and friend of both Noël Coward and Tallulah (whom he called 'Bellulah Blockhead'), said of her, 'She could have been a great star, but she could give a wonderful performance on Monday and a disgraceful performance on Tuesday. You never knew what the hell she would do.' He once recalled the incident in question: 'She took a cottage at Datchet, next to Eton. Eventually one of the authorities came to her and said, "We don't at all mind you taking some of the senior boys over for a smoke or a drink or a little sex on a Sunday afternoon. That doesn't upset me. What does upset me is you giving them cocaine before chapel."'[27]

After the run of *Fallen Angels* had finished, Tallulah stayed in London for a further six years acting in plays of varying success. As the decade was coming to an end she knew it was time to go back home to the US. She had no money and had always spent more than she earned. Viola Tree, the co-writer of Tallulah's first play in London, later wrote, 'When first I saw Tallulah at a rehearsal of *The Dancers* she was a pretty American, a raw and somewhat buxom girl. Now she's a slim, thoughtful, almost too vital woman. She earns a larger and larger salary and spends it all.'[28] Tallulah didn't disagree with Viola, and wrote in her autobiography: 'Professionally I had advanced from comparative obscurity to international recognition. Fiscally I had receded. I had a letter of credit for a thousand dollars on my arrival; on my departure I had less. I left a lot of debts behind me, a few income tax arrears. But I left a lot of friends behind me too. My eight years in London were the happiest and most exciting in my life.'

Suddenly, towards the end of 1930, there was a way to escape via an extraordinary offer from Paramount which began at $5,000 a week. This was the time when, with the recent coming of sound, Hollywood was signing up every attractive stage star it could find. The exotic Tallulah, they thought, with her husky seductive voice (an incompetent surgeon's clumsy tonsillectomy left it almost unnaturally deep), could well prove to be the next Garbo or the next Dietrich. 'Hollywood for me I'm afraid,' she said in a letter to her father, and in 1931, almost exactly eight years after she had arrived in England, she took the train down to Southampton and left for New York on the SS *Aquitania*. Before she left she read out a statement to the press that ended, 'I've never had a good part yet ...'

Tallulah leaving London for Hollywood on the boat train to Southampton, 7 January 1931.

9

The House of 'Cyn', Jimmy Greaves and the Rise and Fall of the Luncheon Voucher

France's most notorious brothel was the sophisticated Le Chabanais near the Louvre in Paris, renowned for famous visitors such as Cary Grant, Humphrey Bogart and Marlene Dietrich, who arrived on the arm of Erich Maria Remarque, the handsome author of *All Quiet on the Western Front*. The bedrooms were so splendid that one room, decorated in the Japanese style, won a design prize at the 1900 World Fair in Paris. In Germany the premier brothel was the infamous Salon Kitty, located at 11 Giesebrechtstrasse in Charlottenburg, a wealthy district of Berlin. It was run by Katharina Zammit, better known as Kitty Schmidt, whose house of ill repute is remembered for being taken over by the SS to spy on German dignitaries in the 1930s. One client was propaganda minister Joseph Goebbels, who enjoyed 'lesbian displays' at Kitty's, making an exception to what was usually considered a degenerate and 'anti-social' act in Nazi Germany. In America, men flocked to the infamous Mahogany Hall in New Orleans, housed on Basin Street beneath castle-like turrets. Jelly Roll Morton was the house pianist and E. J. Bellocq's surviving *Storyville* photographs of the bordello are evidence of the elegant furnishings, glittering chandeliers and Tiffany stained-glass windows. Britain's most infamous brothel, however, was situated in Streatham in an Edwardian house at 32 Ambleside Avenue. It was a stone's throw from the Streatham High Road, which, due to its 'run-down shop fronts, broken lighting, cramped and broken pavements and an ever-growing number of yellow Metropolitan police signs advertising violent crime', was once voted the worst street in Britain.[1]

The most celebrated British brothel was run by Britain's most celebrated madam, Cynthia Payne – once pronounced by Jeffrey Bernard in the *Spectator* as 'the greatest Englishwoman since Boadicea'.[2] She first became front-page news in 1978 when, after an anonymous tip-off, the police raided her 'respectable' net-curtained home and found a queue of fifty-three, mainly elderly, clients – elderly because pensioners received a generous £3 discount and men under forty were banned – 'All Jack-the-lads boasting about their prowess,'[3] she once maintained. The men, some of whom were dressed in lingerie, included vicars, lawyers and politicians, all patiently waiting to see the thirteen prostitutes on the premises. A sign in the kitchen read, 'My house is clean enough to be healthy ... and dirty enough to be happy.' The cleaning and decorating were usually done, often happily naked, by Slave Rodney and Slave Philip, both married men. To restore the clients' limited energy at the end of the 'parties', the men all received mugs of hot steaming Bovril, served by ex-squadron leader Robert

Cynthia at 32 Ambleside Avenue.

'Mitch' Mitchell Smith – Cynthia's devoted friend – who sported an RAF moustache but was often dressed as a French maid.

The notorious 'House of Cyn', as it came to be known, was celebrated neither for its luxurious surroundings – the interior was particularly chintzy, with antimacassars on the backs of the armchairs and flowery china ornaments and teacups on the shelves – nor the beauty of its women. The brothel's infamy came from the method of payment used: the luncheon voucher.

Cynthia hadn't always used luncheon vouchers. She originally used little plastic badges that she bought from the stationery chain Ryman. The clients paid an entrance fee and received a Ryman badge in return. The men would later give the badge to the women upstairs and they, in turn, would redeem them for cash from Cynthia as proof of services performed. This all worked like clockwork until some women started buying their own badges from Ryman's. Cynthia solved this problem when she came across an old box of out-of-date luncheon vouchers which were far harder to counterfeit. When the police raided her 1978 Christmas party, each of the men waiting on the stairs had a luncheon voucher in his pocket.[4]

Luncheon vouchers were once ubiquitous, especially in the 1960s and 1970s. Most restaurants, pubs and cafés, to show that they accepted them as payment, had a green LV sticker in the window. They were introduced as a tax concession by the Labour Government in 1946 (the same year a teenage Cynthia was expelled from her convent school for continually 'talking dirty' and generally being a 'bad influence') in the hope that they would encourage citizens to eat more healthily. In 1948 the tax relief was raised a few pence to three shillings (15p, but worth approximately £5 in 2017), which would have bought you a reasonable lunch back then.

Cynthia was born on Christmas Eve in 1932 in Bognor Regis, West Sussex. Her father was a strict, albeit often absent, man called Hamilton who worked as a hairdresser on Union-Castle liners.[5] Her mother, Betty, died of cancer when Cynthia was just ten, and she and her sister Melanie were brought up by a series of housekeepers. Cynthia's first job, in 1949, aged sixteen, was at a bus garage in Bognor, followed soon after by an attempt to follow her father's footsteps and become a hairdresser. She started training with some hairdressing friends of her father's in Aldershot, but because of her incessant swearing they insisted she saw a psychiatrist. After lying that she was pregnant and subsequently threatening to swallow some weedkiller, Cynthia was eventually disowned by her father.[6]

Above: 32 Ambleside Avenue in 2017, by Stephen Benton.

Right: Cynthia knitting in the garden of 32 Ambleside Avenue.

Jobs as a waitress and then a shop assistant in Brighton soon followed. At the age of seventeen she began an affair with a married man not much younger than her father called Terence, and this was the period of her life that featured in the 1987 movie *Wish You Were Here*, starring Emily Lloyd and written and directed by David Leland. Terence drifted from job to job and drank heavily every day: 'Even when there was nothing in the kitty he always found enough for whisky,' Cynthia later remembered.

It wasn't long before she moved to London, working at Swan and Edgar's department store on Piccadilly Circus while paying £3 a week for a flat in Hammersmith. Terence, without much else to do, followed Cynthia to the capital. Although he only stayed for a few days, Cynthia fell pregnant and eventually gave birth to her son Dominic. The following year, after the result of another affair, a second son was given up for adoption at not more than a few weeks old.

It was around this time that the luncheon voucher started to take off. The scheme initially had worked on an ad hoc basis, with each company printing their own vouchers and arranging for local cafes and restaurants to accept them. In 1954, the businessman John Hack realised that a standardised voucher, acceptable all over the UK, would be much more efficient for everyone concerned and

Emily Lloyd in a scene from *Wish You Were Here*, the second film of Cynthia's life to be released in 1987.

started the Luncheon Voucher Company, based in Saxone House on Regent Street. Establishments that were part of the scheme started to feature a green 'LV' logo in the window (as did Cynthia twenty years later). In 1957, an advert for the company boasted that 'two million vouchers were used every month at more than 4,000 catering establishments in London and the provinces'.

Many of the early voucher schemes seem to have been started by employers who thought their staff, through not getting a proper midday meal, were getting tired and inefficient in the afternoon. In 1961, the *Guardian* reported that young women in particular were too busy during their lunch hours to eat properly: 'Too often lunch-hour shopping swallowed whatever time had been set aside to buy food and whether stimulated by business efficiency or philanthropy, firms evolved the voucher system. In this way they were able to subsidise meals without the risk of the subsidy being diverted to other uses.'[7] In 1963 one Luncheon Voucher advertisement read, '"Good Afternoon," she said – and it was! Thanks to Luncheon Vouchers she'd eaten well that lunch-time. So she was attentive, looked alive, felt active. A good hot lunch had made all the difference between afternoon apathy and afternoon efficiency.'[8]

The *Guardian* was wrong, however, and the Luncheon Voucher subsidy *was* often diverted to other uses. The era of rationing had only just come to an end (meat and all food rationing came to an end in July 1954) so many people were unembarrassed to find a way around the system. In the summer of 1957, the footballer Jimmy Greaves turned professional at Chelsea (although he spent eight weeks working during June and July at a steel company to supplement his income). His wage was £3 plus £2 for accommodation, which went to his mother because he still lived at home. As he did reasonably well in his exams, one of his duties at Chelsea was to work in the club office for the club secretary, John Battersby, instead of working with the ground staff. At lunchtime the first-team players went to a 'posh establishment' called Anabel's, a tiny, in-the-know bistro at 356 Fulham Road, while the reserve team and youth players went to Charlie's, a steamy-windowed cafe where there was one spoon for stirring tea attached to a string on the counter. 'They served a smashing plate of bacon, eggs, sausages, beans and fried bread,' Greaves once remembered. 'It was the sort of daily meal to make Arsene Wenger pale![9]'

The players were given luncheon vouchers with a face value of 2/6*d* (12.5p) with which to pay for lunch. It was part of Greaves's job to issue the vouchers to the rest of the players, but he soon found out that no one really kept a tally on how many were in the office and how many were being issued. It wasn't long before he realised that the vouchers were valuable 'black market' currency. One of Chelsea's first-team players, John 'Snozzle' Sillett, approached Greaves with a scheme to make 'a few bob'. 'I'm not suggesting for one moment that you steal them,' John told him. 'Them luncheon vouchers are imprisoned in that office. I want you to help me liberate them.' Greaves knew that John and his

Jimmy Greaves as a Chelsea player in 1959.

Every business can now have a LUNCHEON VOUCHER SERVICE

Nearly 2,000,000 of our Vouchers are used every month in more than 4,000 catering establishments in London and the Provinces. Employees want them and the cost to you is negligible. We have a booklet fully explaining our Service, gladly sent on request.

WHEREVER LUNCHEON VOUCHERS ARE ACCEPTED—OURS ARE WELCOMED.

Luncheon Vouchers Limited

Luncheon Vouchers Limited, Saxone House, 74a Regent St., London, W.1. Telephone: REGent 5711

Luncheon Voucher advert from March 1958.

brother Peter, the Chelsea first-team full-back, traded the vouchers down at Charlie's 'at less than face value for fags'. John Battersby was a particularly heavy smoker and each morning he would give Greaves some money to buy some Senior Service cigarettes. The Sillett brothers, in return for some of this cash, would then give Jimmy the packets of Senior Service they had bought with the luncheon vouchers liberated from Battersby's desk drawer. Life at Stamford Bridge in those days, Greaves would later say, 'was like Harry Lime's Vienna'.[10]

Most knew that there was a Luncheon Voucher black market and there were often questions asked in the House of Commons. In 1960 Eric Fletcher, the Islington Central MP, asked Derick Heathcoat-Amory, the Chancellor of the Exchequer, whether he was 'aware that luncheon vouchers, issued by firms and subsequently claimed as tax relief, were frequently being used, not for the purpose of bona fide luncheons, but in exchange for groceries, cigarettes, and other commodities'. In response the Chancellor admitted that they had seen reports in the press about the misuse of luncheon vouchers but promised to 'keep the whole question of the taxability of luncheon vouchers under review'.[11] Even by 1960 the 3 shillings tax relief was seen by many as inadequate. A letter to *The Times* in August of that year claimed that it was 'meant to ensure that it would ensure a proper luncheon to young people starting in business or at the lower end of the salaries scale. Three shillings a day now only covers the cost of a couple of sandwiches and a beverage – the very type of luncheon previously scorned by medical experts for the maintenance of health.'[12]

When she was twenty-two, Cynthia Payne met an amusement arcade operator from Margate with whom she lived for five years. After her third traumatic and illegal abortion (the man refused to

Luncheon Voucher advert from 1963.

Sandwiches for sale in London in 1972. Note that all the prices are less than 15p.

use contraception), she left him and soon started the career that one day made her famous. Cynthia slipped into prostitution as a way of avoiding eviction from her flat when she was falling behind in the rent – 'I realised I could do "it" and make money at the same time,' she later said. 'It made me bloody determined. I was never going to go crawling for money again.'[13]

Cynthia spent two years working as a prostitute before realising she would make more money and have an easier life by opening her own brothel. She saved enough to buy a small terraced house in Eden Court Road in Streatham, and then a few years later, in 1974, bought the house in Ambleside Avenue called 'Cranmore'. To hide what was really going on at the house she told her neighbours that she held a lot of lunchtime conferences. This seemed feasible, as most of the cars that clients parked along the road were very expensive. 'We had a high-class clientele,' Cynthia remembered years later. 'No rowdy kids, no yobs, all well-dressed men in suits who knew how to respect a lady. It was like a vicar's tea party with sex thrown in – a lot of elderly, lonely people drinking sherry.'[14] She was proud that she provided for all sorts of men, and once said: 'Everyone can get lonely … We even used to have some of them coming along in wheelchairs, although not too many because they tended to block up the corridors.'[15]

By the mid-seventies, a time of high inflation, Luncheon Vouchers had become even less valuable. Another letter writer to *The Times* in 1976 complained of their value (readers of this newspaper seemed particularly careful with their money): 'I was horrified to find that the maximum untaxed limit on the value of luncheon vouchers imposed by the government of 15p only purchased a plain cheese sandwich. Meat was out of the question. Mr I. E. C Grant of Bookham in Surrey.'[16] The days of 'a couple of sandwiches and a beverage' at lunchtime were already long gone.

In 1980, two years after the police raid on Ambleside Avenue, the case went to court, with Payne eventually convicted for running 'the biggest disorderly house' in history. Judge David West-Russell noted, however, that Mrs Payne had appeared in court on four previous occasions, on similar charges and not only sent her to jail, he fined her a total of £1,950 and ordered her to pay costs of up to £2,000. A few days later a Commons motion criticising her imprisonment was signed by thirty MPs of all parties. They included Sam Silkin, a former Labour Attorney General, as well as Tony Benn. If anyone should be jailed, they reasoned, it should be her clients, who, of course, all remained nameless. A cartoon in the press at the time showed a vicar in bed with a prostitute, confronted by a policeman: 'I demand to see my solicitor,' said the vicar, 'who is in the next bedroom.'[17]

Although sentenced to eighteen months in prison, after an appeal she was released from Holloway after four. It was said she was driven away from prison in a Rolls-Royce driven by a former client to take her to a 'coming-out' party. Six years later, in 1987, *Personal Services*, the first film of her life, was released, starring Julie Walters and directed by former Python, Terry Jones. After the filming was completed, Payne organised a celebration party at Ambleside Avenue, and once again the police raided the house. At first, two plainclothes policemen gained access to the party, with one of them dressed as a woman, and then after a signal thirty more officers burst in to the property. 'I was not running a bawdy house,' she endlessly explained over the years,

Cynthia Payne and Julie Walters celebrating the completion of *Personal Services* in 1987.

'I was simply having a party.'[18] This time she was charged with nine counts of controlling prostitutes.

There was much laughter during the subsequent thirteen-day court case, and the judge warned the jurors that it was a criminal trial and not some kind of entertainment show. When, after five hours, the jury found her not guilty, the courtroom burst into spontaneous applause. Payne left the court clutching a Laughing Policeman doll, which she had kept as a mascot throughout the trial. 'This is a victory for common sense,' she said. 'But I have to admit all this has put me off having parties for a bit.'[19] Cynthia later sent Judge Brian Pryor QC a copy of her biography, *An English Madam*, with the inscription: 'I hope this book will broaden your rather sheltered life.'

No one was writing to the national papers any more about the Luncheon Voucher. They had become next to useless and the LV tax concession, still at 15p after almost sixty years, was abolished by the coalition government in 2013. Luncheon Vouchers do still exist, however, although no one knows who takes them.

Sadly, Cynthia Payne certainly doesn't, as she died aged eighty-two on 15 November 2015 while still living at Ambleside Avenue.[20] Britain's most notorious madam was always proud of how she treated her employees, and at the end of every afternoon shift she always provided something of which the glamorous women at Le Chabanais, Salon Kitty and the Mahogany Hall would have been more than envious: a poached egg on toast and a nice cup of tea. 'I'm not much of a cook, but I do a beautiful poached egg,' she once said.

Recipe for the Perfect Cynthia Payne Poached Egg
Cynthia Payne worked in a cafe in Whitfield Street (a road parallel and just west of Tottenham Court Road) when she was first pregnant. The owner, who looked after her when Cynthia felt she had few friends, showed her how to cook the perfect poached egg. Cynthia ended up cooking hundreds every day. 'When I started running brothels,' She once remembered, 'I made sure there were always plenty of eggs in the kitchen.'

Bring a pan half filled with salted water to a gentle simmer. Crack an egg first into a flowery china teacup (this is essential for a proper Cynthia Payne poached egg) and then create a gentle whirlpool in the pan to encourage the white to wrap around the yolk and avoid any feathering. A really soft poached egg will take about two minutes, while a soft to firm egg will take approximately four minutes – the exact time depends on the size, temperature and freshness of the egg. To check whether it is done, remove the egg with a slotted spoon and give a gentle push with a teaspoon. If it feels a little soft put it back for a minute or two. When it is ready place it on some kitchen paper to dry off and serve with hot buttered toast.

10

Cocaine, the 'Yellow Peril' and the Death of Billie Carleton

It was definitely a Saturday in September 1918, but no one could quite remember whether the party began on the evening of the 7th or a week later on the 14th. Odd, perhaps, considering that a few weeks later the night in question was described in court and in the press as 'squalid', 'deplorable' and even a 'disgrace to modern civilisation' – quite a charge considering the evening took place during the final weeks of the First World War. There was a reason, however, for the vagueness of the witnesses' memories – they had all spent most of the night in an opium-based stupor.

Early on that warm September evening six people arrived at a flat on Dover Street, 100 yards or so north of Piccadilly, where a thirty-seven-year-old theatrical dress designer called Reggie de Veulle lived with his wife Pauline. Five years his senior, she too was a designer and they both worked at Hockley's in Bond Street. At about nine o'clock a Scottish woman called Ada Ping You also came to the apartment, but she was shown into the drawing room while everyone else continued eating their supper. Ada, who with her Chinese husband Lo Ping You lived in a dilapidated house on the eastern end of Limehouse Causeway, sat in the middle of the room and began the initial preparations for the smoking of opium.

An hour later, after they had divested themselves of their clothing, and with the men now dressed in pyjamas and the women in chiffon and crepe de chine nightdresses, the de Veulles and their guests reclined on the many cushions and pillows placed around the room. In a circle around Ping You they watched with excited anticipation as she took a pea-sized ball of the dark opium paste and, with the end of a long needle, held it over the faint blue flame of a peanut-oil lamp until it started to swell and turn golden. The gooey mass was stretched into long strings several times before it was rolled back into its pea shape and pushed into the hole of the bowl of the opium pipe. At about eleven, just as the pipe began to be passed around, another woman arrived at the flat. This time it was an actress, well known at the time, called Billie Carleton, who had been staying with the de Veulles and had come straight from the Haymarket Theatre where she had been performing in a light comedy called *The Freedom of the Seas*. After disrobing as well, she joined the rest of the circle. It was later reported that the party remained, apparently in a comatose state, until about three o'clock on the following afternoon, Sunday.

Contemporary illustration of the Opium Party at Dover Street.

The location of the de Veulles' Dover Street flat in 2017.

Nine or ten weeks later on a Saturday morning in November, just twelve days after the end of the First World War, the Kensington branch of the Electrical Trades Union, without any warning, cut off the electricity supply to the Royal Albert Hall. Electric lighting had first been demonstrated at the venue forty-five years previously in 1873, and an outraged seat holder promptly wrote to *The Times* the next day complaining about 'this very ghastly and unpleasant innovation'.[1] Despite his worries, electric lights became a permanent fixture in 1888. Thirty years later the union had turned off the power supply in retaliation to the management refusing to allow the building to be used the following week for a Labour Party meeting addressed by George Lansbury. Mr Hilton Carter, the manager of the Albert Hall, said: 'When we get red flags stuck up over the crown that decorates the royal box, it is time something was done. I do not want a repetition of such scenes as were witnessed here last Thursday, when the whole place was alive with red flags.'[2]

Mr Carter knew that George Lansbury and his followers had held controversial meetings at the Albert Hall going back several years. On 26 April 1913 the left-wing former MP, who had resigned his Bow and Bromley seat in 1913 over women's suffrage (he lost to his Conservative opponent, who ran on the slogan 'No Petticoat Government'), addressed a Women's Social and Political Union (WSPU) rally at the venue. During his speech he openly defended suffragette violence: 'Let them burn and destroy property and do anything they will, and for every leader that is taken away, let a dozen step forward in their place'.[3] For these words Lansbury was charged with incitement and subsequently convicted and sentenced to three months' imprisonment. In 1917 Lansbury used the *Daily Herald*, under his editorship at the time, to praise the Russian Revolution, and at an Albert Hall rally on 18 March 1918 hailed the spirit and enthusiasm of 'this Russian movement', and urged his audience to 'be ready to die, if necessary, for our faith'.[4] Now eight months later the Electrical Union told Mr Carter that he should expect further action, and threatened to stop the huge and much publicised Allied Victory Ball from taking place the following Wednesday. Hilton Carter realised this would be a step too far and, with a recommending

George Lansbury postcard.

nudge from the government (due to the high number of society figures involved), he decided to lift the Labour meeting ban. Thus, fully lit, the magnificent Victory Ball went ahead.

On 27 November, with coloured bunting celebrating the end of the Great War still fluttering between lamp posts all over the capital, the Great Victory Ball was held to celebrate the recent Armistice. It was essentially a huge fancy-dress party, or as one newspaper put it 'a mad revel in which London relieved its emotions after four years of pent-up agony'.[5] The evening was also to celebrate women's achievement during the war, with all the proceeds going to the Nation's Fund for Nurses. The event was sponsored by the *Daily Sketch*, which agreed to pay all expenses and trumpeted:

> Today, women of the Allied nations take part in the festival of victory as a right. They have earned that right in hospitals at home and abroad; in the fields as labourers ploughing and garnering the grain; in the workshops turning out shells; in the towns doing men's work; in the homes suffering in silence.[6]

Thousands of people attended the ball, with the Albert Hall decorated throughout – this time not with red flags, but with blue and white in tribute to the nurses, who that evening mingled on the dance floor with guardsmen in scarlet dress uniforms. At one point, to the strains of Elgar's Pomp and Circumstance March No. 1 in D, a composition performed for the first time just seventeen years previously, a grand procession entered the hall led by Lady Diana Manners dressed as 'Britannia', wearing classical draperies with a plumed helmet and trident. Next to her was the Duchess of Westminster representing 'England' in white robes and the 'old red cross of St George on her bosom', while the Countess of Drogheda, one of the first female pilots, was, rather aptly, 'Air'.[7] Just before midnight, as the characters grouped together before the organ, 'Rule Britannia!' was played and the whole concourse of guests sang it in unison. Dancing then continued until the early hours.

An excited, vivacious Billie Carleton was at the ball and standing out from the crowd, not least because of her eye-catching dress designed by her friend and opium party host Reggie de Veulle. One newspaper described it as 'extraordinary and daring to the utmost, but so attractive and refined was her face that it never occurred to any one to be shocked. The costume consisted almost entirely of transparent black georgette[8] which revealed the flesh beneath to an extreme degree – to the limit in fact.'[9] Carleton was still performing in *The Freedom of the Seas*, which had been running since August, and she was currently fêted as the youngest leading actress in the West End. Although many contemporary reviewers spoke of her relatively modest talent and often noted her weak voice, she was pretty, with an impish smile, and was well-loved by the London theatre audiences. A few months earlier, *Tatler* magazine had reviewed one of her performances, saying that she had 'Cleverness, temperament and charm. Not enough of the first, and perhaps too much of the latter.'

Earlier that evening Carleton had received two visitors in her Haymarket Theatre dressing room. One was a middle-aged Italian officer, Jianni Bettini, who had been staying at the Savoy Hotel and had recently been taking her out occasionally. She had called him to visit her solely to show off – presumably without

Billie Carleton in 1918.

an objection on his part – her diaphanous Victory Ball costume. The other visitor, Carleton's personal maid May Booker, had, as asked, brought her mistress's Dorothy bag to the theatre, inside which was a little jewelled gold box. Carleton was no longer staying at the de Veulles' in Dover Street, but had moved just over half a mile away from the theatre to Savoy Court Mansions – an expensive serviced apartment block just behind the Savoy Hotel. Her new home was courtesy of another middle-aged gentleman friend called John Darlington Marsh – a rich Edwardian playboy whom she had known since she was about sixteen. He had kept her financially solvent ever since – very financially solvent. At one point, courtesy of Marsh, Carleton had £5,000 (the equivalent of about £250,000 as of 2017) in her bank account, despite never earning more than £25 per week.[10] Earlier that day, also courtesy of Marsh, she had redeemed from a pawnshop at the cost of £1,050 (although it was worth twice as much) some beautiful jewellery to wear for the ball.

Before setting off to the Albert Hall, Carleton had supper with another of her gentleman friends, a man called Frederick Stuart, a Knightsbridge doctor. Carleton, who had never known her father, relied heavily on men in her life, most of whom were twenty or thirty years her senior, although no one really knows how intimate these relationships were. Stuart, like Marsh, had known Carleton since she was fifteen or sixteen and was not only her physician but also, somewhat dubiously, looked after her financial affairs. Accompanying Carleton and Doctor Stuart that evening was her friend the actress Fay Compton (sister of Compton Mackenzie, author of *Whisky Galore* and co-founder of the SNP) who, despite being married to the actor and comedian Lauri de Frece – her second husband – was being escorted that evening by Lieutenant Barraud, a fellow actor and not long home from the front.

Carleton and Compton were close friends and a few months earlier had performed together in *Fair and Warmer*, a comedy by Avery Hopwood at the Prince of Wales Theatre, where Carleton played Tessie the maid to Fay Compton's 'flapper' character. After supper the foursome took a taxi (which had been paid for the whole day by the extravagant Carleton) to Kensington Gore and the ball at the Albert Hall. Carleton was reported by one newspaper to have 'thrown herself with somewhat feverish energy into the affair and danced again and again. It seemed that every man there wished to dance with her!'[11] At one point she met up with de Veulle, who was dressed in a Pierrot outfit which he had designed himself. Displeased that he had found himself at a 'dry' event, he told her that he was 'off to sniff some snow', and Carleton almost certainly followed suit. Another of her friends was at the ball – Irene Castle, a famous American dancer and currently a neighbour in the Savoy Court apartment block. With her late English husband Vernon, Irene had refined and popularised the foxtrot on Broadway and from about the time of their marriage in 1911 they were probably the most popular and influential dance partners in the world.[12] They were interesting characters and in many ways particularly modern in their outlook: they travelled with a black orchestra, had an openly lesbian manager, and the trendsetting Irene bobbed her hair a decade before the flapper look of the 1920s.

After the peak of their extraordinary celebrity, Vernon had joined the Royal Canadian Flying Corps in 1916 and served in France, but was killed in February 1918 after a flying accident in Fort Worth, Texas. Irene had recently arrived in England to appear in a film for the Red Cross, and was already a movie star of sorts (she would appear

Gay Victory Ball

"The Famous Victory Ball in the Early Morning Hours," as sketched by the well-known artist, Mr. Claud Shepperson, A. R. W. S.

Above: Billie Carleton and the Victory Ball by Claude Shepperson.

Right: Vernon and Irene Castle.

in more than a dozen films between 1917 and 1922). She was a guest of the American portrait painter and set designer Ben Ali Haggin and was dressed in a Persian boy outfit he had designed for her: 'If I do say it myself, I wore the most beautiful costume there. It was gorgeous. It cost two thousand dollars,' she later wrote to a friend, recalling that the ball was 'one of the most joyous and dazzling I'd ever seen'.[13] A newspaper reported that the Victory Ball 'grew into a wild night. The end of four years of the greatest slaughter in history demanded relief for overstrained nerves, an outlet for pent-up emotions.'[14]

At around three in the morning, when the Victory Ball was coming to a close, Carleton left the Albert Hall with her taxi full of friends. Fay Compton and her uniformed lieutenant were dropped off nearby on Hereford Square in Kensington, as was Doctor Stuart in Knightsbridge soon after. Continuing back to Savoy Court Mansions with Carleton was a cinema actor called Lionel Belcher, who was married but accompanied by his live-in lover, Olive Richardson. Belcher was also Reggie de Veulle's cocaine dealer and usually obtained the drug, along with heroin, from a Soho chemist in Lisle Street behind the Empire Theatre. When the taxi arrived at Savoy Mansions Carleton paid the

Belcher, Olive Richardson and Carleton eating breakfast.

Irene Castle in 1918.

taxi driver £3 for his day's work and, before they all squeezed into the tiny lift up to her apartment, she confirmed with the concierge that Irene was back from the ball. The American actress and dancer was still known as Mrs Vernon Castle, although she had secretly remarried earlier in the year, three months after Vernon's plane crash. Carleton ordered breakfast of bacon and eggs for everyone although before it arrived she went across to Irene's apartment to give her a close-up view of her jewellery and her beautiful translucent gown.

Years later Castle, wary of the press after they had given her a hard time when her secret and all-too-swift remarriage was uncovered, was very keen to extricate herself from any drug-taking rumours about that evening. She later wrote that she and Billie had done nothing but 'play dress-up' while Carleton told her how apprehensive she was about plans to go to Hollywood, to which Irene replied, 'You'll be wonderful there. They love blondes.' Using perhaps the wrong simile, at least as far as Carleton was concerned, the brief time the two dancing actresses spent together was once described as 'innocent as a teenager's pyjama party'.[15] After returning to her apartment,

Billie changed into a kimono, got into bed and, while eating her bacon and eggs, happily talked of her hopes and dreams, including the planned trips to America and Paris. At about six in the morning, Lionel and Olive's taxi arrived, and they turned off the lights as they left. Lionel Belcher would later say, 'We left Miss Carleton in bed, perfectly well and extremely bright!'[16]

Unfortunately there were no trips to California or France, and Billie Carleton's fame, such as it is, has more to do with the way she died than for any of her stage successes. The girl with too much charm and a daring costume was found dead in her bed that afternoon. On the dressing table next to her was a little jewelled gold box, half full of cocaine. Her maid had arrived at about 11.30 that morning and heard loud snores from her mistress's bedroom. She was used to Carleton's frequent late nights and left her alone. About four hours later, after getting no response, she found Carleton lying on her side seemingly sleeping. There were discarded clothes all over her bed and her face looked very pale.

Left: The Empire Theatre in 1915.

Below: Billie Carleton in *Watch Your Step* in 1915.

Booker tried to wake her mistress, but it was to no avail and she called Carleton's friend Doctor Stuart.

When Stuart arrived, he gave Carleton artificial respiration and injected her with brandy and strychnine, but it wasn't long before he had to pronounce her dead. Stuart then noticed some sachets of Veronal (a barbiturate used for sleeping[17]) in the bedroom and initially placed them in his pocket. The hotel manager noticed the sachets missing and Stuart, admitting that he had taken the Veronal, placed them back where he found them. The police surgeon soon arrived and noted that Carleton's pupils were widely dilated, there was a stain on the side of her mouth, 'as if of something trickling out', and the skin underneath the fingernails of the left hand was blue. The youngest leading actress in the West End had died aged just twenty-two.

Billie Carleton was the daughter of chorus singer Margaret Stewart, and was born on 4 September 1896 in Bernard Street in Bloomsbury – the road on which Russell Square Underground station opened ten years later. Christened Florence Leonora Stewart, she chose the name with which she became famous when she left school at fifteen to go on to the stage. It was the theatre impresario Charles B. Cochran who gave the nineteen-year-old Carleton her first big break in November 1915 when as an anonymous chorus girl in Irving Berlin's *Watch Your Step* at the Empire Theatre in Leicester Square he asked her to play Stella Sparkes, one of the leading roles. It's Carleton's voice on the London cast recording singing 'Show Us How to Do the Fox Trot' with George Graves.[18] *Watch Your Step* was actually Berlin's first complete musical, and he became the first Tin Pan Alley composer to move 'uptown' to Broadway when it opened at the New Amsterdam Theatre in December 1914 – a production, coincidentally, that starred Mr and Mrs Castle, with Irene playing the Stella Sparkes role.

Opposite the cast list in the *Watch Your Step* Empire Theatre programme, Reggie de Veulle's name appears in an advert for Elspeth Phelps. Before he moved to Hockley's, he had worked for the prestigious costumier based in Albemarle Street and had designed all of Carleton's gowns for the show. For a year or so previously Carleton had been supplementing her theatre wages by modelling de Veulle's confections of tulle and lace.

Through much of the run of *Watch Your Step* Cochran vastly increased business at the Empire by inviting Horatio Bottomley,

Horatio Bottomley
addressing a First World
War recruiting rally
in Trafalgar Square
September 1915.

editor of *John Bull* magazine and former Liberal MP, to deliver fifteen-minute 'patriotic addresses' at the end of the first act. During the war Bottomley, the self-appointed spokesman for the 'man on the street', addressed hundreds of public meetings throughout the country, often enjoying a percentage of the takings (he had resigned as MP for Hackney South in 1912 after declaring himself bankrupt). *John Bull* campaigned relentlessly against the 'Germhuns' and 'Austrihuns', but also British citizens with German-sounding surnames. The danger of 'the enemy within' was a persistent Bottomley theme, and after the sinking of RMS *Lusitania* a few months before he appeared at the Empire Theatre, he labelled the Germans as 'unnatural freaks' and called for their extermination.

Bottomley also reserved particular antipathy for Labour Party leaders, especially Keir Hardie and Ramsay MacDonald, but also for the *Daily Herald* editor George Lansbury (he even produced a poster that read: 'To the Tower with Lansbury'). There is no doubt, however, that his popular and populist rallies were particularly successful at either getting young men to their nearest Army recruitment office, or anyone else to invest their savings in war bonds. When Bottomley spoke at the Empire, his drawing power helped fill the theatre over and over again and did much to rescue the theatre's fading reputation.

Cochran later remembered Carleton's debut as a leading actress, writing: 'Despite her inexperience and her tiny voice, she pleased the audiences. A more beautiful creature has never fluttered upon a stage. She seemed scarcely human, so fragile was she.' During the run of *Watch Your Step*, however, he soon found out she 'was being influenced by some undesirable people and was going to opium parties'.[19] He fired her, but soon gave her another chance when she appeared in his production *Houp La!* at St Martin's Theatre. She made little impression and only appeared for one week before the production had to close.

Carleton was then taken under the wing of André Charlot, the chain-smoking French impresario who insisted that everyone called him 'Guv' and who never quite lost his Maurice Chevalier accent. He was infamous for pursuing the girls, of which there were dozens and dozens, whose names he put up in lights, but he was responsible for some of the best revues in London that were tasteful, lively and 'with it'.[20] Charlot put Carleton in a revue called *Some More Samples!* at the Vaudeville Theatre on the Strand. The Canadian actress and comedienne Beatrice Lillie, then twenty-one, was performing in the same show, and Charlot was driven mad by the constant laughing and joking by the two women. During one performance Lillie came on stage sporting an unrehearsed big false moustache wiggling under her nose. The audience giggled but Charlot didn't, and the following morning there was a note on the noticeboard by the stage door: 'BEATRICE LILLIE FINED FIVE SHILLINGS FOR TRYING TO BE FUNNY.' During one scene entitled 'The Nursery', the children were played by Carleton, Lillie and future star Gertrude Lawrence in her first West End appearance. Lillie would later recall that they would often run into the Strand to watch the Zeppelins, which she described as being 'like silver fish in the night sky, flying up above the Thames'.[21] The description was poetical, but when the German airships started dropping bombs it was the first time that Londoners realised they were no longer invulnerable to foreign-based wars.

At about the time Carleton was performing in *Watch Your Step*, the *Daily Mail* was noting that for many young women it was a changing world, especially in wartime London. The newspaper called them the 'Dining Out Girls' and was actually quite celebratory in tone about this modern, liberated woman who could be seen most nights 'dining out alone or with a friend in the moderate price restaurants in London. Formerly she would never have had her evening meal in town unless in the company of a man friend. But now, with money and without men, she is more and more beginning to dine out.'[22]

In her memoir *How We Lived Then – 1914–18*, Mrs C. S. Peel noticed how Soho was becoming a part of London where anyone, including single young women, might venture: 'Life was very gay,' said one young woman in Mrs Peel's book. 'It was only when someone you knew well or with whom you were in love was killed that you minded really dreadfully. Men used to come to dine and dance one night, and go out the next morning and be killed. And someone used to say, "Did you see poor Bobbie was killed?" It went on all the time, you see.'[23] These young single women, modern and independent, had started to be called 'flappers' in England (the word became popular in America a few years later in the twenties) and in August 1917, in a popular play called *The Boy* at the Adelphi, Carleton played an 'up-to-date flapper' called Joy Chatterton. *Tatler* described her as 'one of the most vivacious soubrettes on the musical-comedy stage, and has a droll method which is all her own'.[24] The slang word 'flapper' has several possible derivations or sources – a description of a young bird flapping its wings while learning to fly, an earlier use in northern England to mean 'teenage girl' (referring to hair not yet put up and whose plaited pigtail 'flapped' on her back) or an old English word meaning 'prostitute'.

Whether you were an independent woman or not, it was becoming far harder, courtesy of the government, to buy an alcoholic drink during the First World War. Before the notorious Defence of the Realm Act, 'affectionately' called DORA and enacted without debate four days into the war, Londoners could drink almost when they liked. Pubs would open at 5.30 in the morning and not close until nineteen hours later at half past midnight. The new opening hours (most of which lasted until 1988!) were from 12 noon to 2.40 p.m. and 6.30 p.m. to 10 p.m. The new law didn't stop there; it became illegal to buy a round and, in fact, a drink for anyone but yourself (the 'no treating order').

Initially the new law allowed restaurants and clubs to be open until 10.30 p.m. but this was soon brought forward to only

Jack May and Billie Carleton (both on the right) at Murray's Day Club in Maidenhead, 1916.

9.30 p.m. Subsequently the number of illegal nightclubs escalated profusely – by the end of 1915 there were 150 or so illegal clubs in Soho alone.[25] Mrs Peel wrote: 'The growth of the night club was an outstanding feature of war-time life. Such places had always existed but it was not until after war was declared that they were patronised by women and young girls of good reputation.'[26] Although drinking late into the evening was now illegal, the 'Beauty Sleep' order, as it was often called, never prevented the illicit sale of food and drink. Restaurants and nightclubs served spirits in coffee cups and champagne was disguised as lemonade. The order, however, undoubtedly encouraged other forms of illegality to proliferate – especially drugs. In January 1916 the *Evening News* columnist Quex spoke of 'dark stories' in 'West End Bohemia' and the prevalence of 'that exciting drug cocaine': 'It is so easy to take – just snuffed up the nose; and no-one seems to know why the girls who suffer from this body and soul racking habit find the drug so easy to obtain.'[27]

In 1916 it was well known to many of her associates that Carleton was taking drugs. One friend of hers said that the knowledge 'was rather public property'.[28] Carleton was probably introduced to cocaine and opium either by an American man called Jack May (his real name was Gerald Walter) or an odd character called Captain Ernest Schiff. May was the manager of Murray's Cabaret Club on Beak Street, which had opened just before the war and which was owned for most of its long life by Percival 'Pops' Murray, and subsequently by his son David (it was where Christine Keeler and Mandy Rice-Davies met while working there some forty years later). A customer during the First World War once claimed that 'cocaine was what people came to Jack May's club for. It was slipped to you in packets, very quickly, when you coughed up the loot.'[29]

In June 1915, Jack May is seen with an eighteen-year-old Billie Carleton in a photograph taken at Murray's Day Club in Maidenhead for *Tatler* magazine. May was also mentioned in a letter by the Eton-educated Captain Schiff who in December 1915 wrote to the Attorney General, Sir John Simon: 'A very bad fellow, Jack May, is the proprietor of Murray's Club in Beak Street – a quite amusing place. But for vice or money or both he induces girls to smoke opium in some foul place. He is an American and does a good deal of harm.'[30] Although the description was not inaccurate, the disingenuous Schiff wrote it to cover his tracks. As one biographer wrote of Schiff: 'It was rare a dope party was held in Soho that he failed to attend.'[31] Born of naturalised Austrian parents, Schiff was an habitual gambler, pimp and blackmailer and was said, despite a commission in the Royal Sussex Regiment, to have supported Germany during the war. He had the strange Teutonic habit of filing his fingernails to a point and *Empire News* once wrote that Schiff 'invariably took his soup in the noisy fashion in the "art" of which the Hun stands supreme'.[32] Captain Schiff and Horatio Bottomley, almost certainly, were no great friends.

The time was ripe for a moral panic, and in February 1916 cocaine was again mentioned in the newspapers when Horace Kingsley, an ex-soldier and ex-convict, and Rose Edwards, a London prostitute, were each given six months' hard labour for selling cocaine to Canadian soldiers at a military camp in Folkestone. The day after the verdict, the *Times*' medical correspondent came down hard on the drug: 'Cocaine is more deadly than bullets,' he wrote – an extraordinarily crass thing to write when in the preceding month alone about 10,000 British men had perished on the Western Front,[33] many by bullets. The ignorant stupidity continued when he added that 'most cocainomaniacs carry a revolver to protect themselves against imaginary enemies'.[34] A few days later an H. C. Ross wrote to the same newspaper about 'small silver matchboxes' he had seen in well-known West-End jewellers that were designed to be sent to friends and loved ones on the front and which contained three tubes filled with tablets of morphine hydrochloride, to be taken when severely wounded. The letter concluded, 'Morphiomania is a terrible malady.'[35] Which indeed it is, but possibly not of undue concern to a soldier who has just had his leg shot off.

The Times, ironically, had recently been carrying advertisements for preparations of morphine and cocaine by Harrods and Savory & Moore (Mayfair chemists and suppliers to King George V), describing them as a 'useful present for friends at the front'. In February 1916, both stores were found guilty of selling morphine and cocaine contrary to restrictions contained in the 1908 Poisons and Pharmacy Act. The prosecutor, Sir William Glyn-Jones, secretary of the Pharmaceutical Society and practising barrister, made a point of saying that it was an 'exceedingly dangerous thing for a drug like morphine to be in the hands of men on active service ... it might have the effect of making them sleep on duty, or other very serious results'. Both Harrods and Savory & Moore were fined, albeit nominal amounts.[36] In July 1916 Regulation 40B of the Defence of the Realm Act came into effect, which criminalised the possession or sale of opium or cocaine by anyone except licensed chemists, doctors and vets. Further domestic legislation followed after the war when the Treaty of Versailles contained a clause requiring signatories to introduce domestic drugs legislation. In Britain this evolved into the Dangerous Drugs Act 1920; this Act changed drug addiction to a penal offence, though up to then, within the medical profession, it had been treated as a disease.

Carleton's death, seemingly of cocaine, and the subsequent inquest and court cases often featured on the front pages until April 1919, and both *The Times* and the *Daily Express* used the case as an excuse to run an investigation into London's illicit drug trade. The long inquest at Westminster Coroner Court, presided over by the coroner Samuel Ingleby Oddie, began one week after the tragedy, and consisted of five sittings through December and into late January. Even though the inquest started at 2.30 p.m., crowds often convened outside the court from seven in the morning, eager to catch some of the highly publicised proceedings. It was often reported that well-known actresses were in the public gallery, but no names were mentioned. The first witness was Mrs Katherine Jolliffe, an aunt of Carleton's who had identified the body and confirmed that the deceased had no living parent when she died. She also identified to Mr Oddie the small, exquisitely jewelled gold box as belonging to Carleton.

Another early witness was May Booker, Carleton's maid, who confirmed that she had taken her mistress's gold box to the theatre. The coroner asked her, 'Was there any white powder in it?' 'No,' she replied. Booker then described the scene when she came to Savoy Court the next day and tried to wake Carleton, and Oddie asked if she had seen the little gold box in the bedroom. Booker replied: 'Yes, when I looked in the box there was some white powder. It was like sugar stuff. I had never seen powder like that before. I did not know my mistress took drugs.'[37] Next on the witness stand was Lionel Belcher, looking, as someone once said, far more handsome than his name would suggest. The actor had appeared recently with Mrs Patrick Campbell's *Mystery of the Thirteenth Chair* theatre company, and had a major role in the film *Yoke* the year before. The witness dodged and denied any insinuations that he or de Veulle were engaged in procuring prohibited drugs for Miss Carleton or anyone else. For an actor, Belcher was a bad liar and it was apparent to everyone in the court that he was avoiding the truth. Mr Oddie then adjourned the hearing until 12 December, when he empanelled a jury.

After the adjournment Belcher was questioned again, but this time, after a consultation with his solicitor and a voluntary visit to the police, his memory started to improve and he started telling something closer to the truth about his drug-taking habits. At one point Belcher nonchalantly admitted that he was 'more addicted to heroin than anything else' (heroin was not covered under DORA 40B) but also admitted selling cocaine to de Veulle at an inflated price – 'I don't look upon it as any more despicable than selling a bottle of whisky at an over-charged rate, after time'[38] – to which there was audible concurrence from the viewing galleries. The actor then spoke about procuring cocaine in Chinatown from a house on Limehouse Causeway, and said that a 'Chinaman named Lo Ping

Chinatown *circa* 1916.

You' supplied it. At the mention of Chinatown and Limehouse, the ears of the reporters pricked up.

Not that they really needed one, but this gave the newspapers an excuse to write about the encroaching so-called 'Yellow Peril' – a phrase credited to the Edwardian writer M. P. Shiel, who put Limehouse on the literary map in 1899 with his novel *The Yellow Danger*, about a Chinese gang that invades London. The scandal around Billie Carleton encouraged dozens of stories in the popular press over the next two or three years. In 1920 the *Evening News* headlined a story 'White Girls Hypnotised by Yellow Men', and wrote that it was the duty 'of every Englishman and Englishwoman to know the truth about the degradation of young white girls in this plague of the Metropolis – IT MUST BE STOPPED'.[39] The *Daily Express* at the same time had the front-page headline 'Yellow Peril in London' and wrote: 'A Chinese syndicate, backed by millions of money and powerful, if mysterious, influences, is at work in the East End of London. Its object is the propagation of vice.' White women, treated by the Chinese in ways that were left to the reader's imagination, were described as victims of this international drugs and gambling syndicate: 'White

Englishwomen seem to exert a remarkable fascination for them. But the white women who fall into the clutches of the "yellows" are not Londoners, but mainly come from provincial inland towns. They are without exception young and pretty, but in what manner they are attracted to the Chinese quarter of London has not been unravelled.'[40]

In reality the English 'yellow peril' was actually a small, relatively law-abiding Chinese community which had been based around the Limehouse docks area, probably from around the beginning of the nineteenth century. At the start of the twentieth century there were two separate communities in the area – the Chinese from Shanghai, who were based around Pennyfields and Ming Street (between the present Westferry and Poplar DLR stations) and the immigrants from Southern China and Canton, who lived around Gill Street and the Limehouse Causeway. By 1911 the whole area had started to be called Chinatown by the rest of London. An article in *The Times* in November 1913 wrote about how little was done to conceal the smell of opium around Limehouse: 'In the little shop, with its high deal counter and its piles of glittering empty tins stacked up behind, the air is heavy with fumes. You only have to lift a curtain to see an inner room to see the rites in progress.'[41]

Considering that there were rarely more than a few hundred Chinese people living around Limehouse before and after the First World War, the East End Chinatown had an extraordinarily bad reputation, even internationally. An overexcited *Washington Times* played on the exaggerated fear Americans had of their own Chinatowns and wrote that Carleton's friends took her to Limehouse 'to indulge in more fantastic and brutal orgies when the comparatively refined opium parties in West End flats were beginning to pall'. The newspaper continued:

Limehouse is perhaps the most grimly, gruesomely wicked quarter in the whole world. It is far to the east of the Strand, east of the Tower of London, lost in the purlieus of London's darkest east. The Causeway is the principal thoroughfare in this sink of iniquity, raised centuries ago above the mud flats of the Thames. Limehouse is the 'Chinatown' of London, but it contains among its swarming thousands specimens of many races besides the Chinese. It has become an Oriental quarter through the proximity of the vast East

India docks. Many opium smoking dens are kept in Limehouse by Chinamen. Their chief customers are Oriental sailors and dock labourers, commonly called Lascars in London parlance. With them, too are many sailors of other nationalities, together with an assortment of criminals, dock rats and dregs of society of both sexes. Here, too come persons from the higher strata of society, who have exhausted the pleasures of West End resorts and yearn for stranger and more brutal forms of dissipation.[42]

Sometimes it seemed that Limehouse was almost solely to blame for corroding the moral backbone of the entire British middle class. It wasn't just the fault of a slavering press with its lurid headlines of opium dens and traders in white slaves, however; there were also numerous writers, novelists and even filmmakers who helped exaggerate the danger and immorality of the area. H. V. Morton, the famous travel essayist and journalist, wrote about Limehouse in his book *The Nights of London*:

Still from *Broken Blossoms or The Yellow Man and the Girl* by D. W. Griffith, 1919.

The squalor of Limehouse is that strange squalor of the East which seems to conceal vicious splendour. There is an air of something unrevealed in those narrow streets of shuttered houses, each one of which appears to be hugging its own dreadful little secret... you might open a filthy door and find yourself in a palace sweet with joss-sticks, where queer things happen in a mist of smoke ... The silence grips you, almost persuading you that behind it is something which you are always on the verge of discovering; some mystery of vice or of beauty, or of terror and cruelty.[43]

The fact that the Chinese community liked to gamble and smoke opium was bad enough, but it was the fear of sexual contact between the races (which the drug taking of course only exacerbated) that frightened so many people. Thomas Burke, writing for an apprehensive suburban readership that lapped up his writings, even in the US, wrote a number of 'sordid and morbid' short stories and newspaper articles, owing much to Jack London, about the Limehouse Chinatown. One of his stories, from a collection entitled *Limehouse Nights* (which was banned for immorality by the national subscription libraries run by Boots and WH Smith), was called 'The Chink and the Child' and was made into a successful film entitled *Broken Blossoms, or the Yellow Man and the Girl* by D. W. Griffith that starred Lilian Gish. Another of the stories from *Limehouse Nights* was called 'Tai Fu and Pansy Greers' and was about a young white woman who submitted herself to a 'loathly, fat and old' Chinese man:

He was a connoisseur, and used his selected yen-shi (opium) and yen-hok (a needle used to cook the opium pellet) as an Englishman uses a Cabanas. The first slow inhalations brought him nothing, but, as he continued, there would come a sweet, purring warmth about the limbs ... She went to him that night at his house in the Causeway. He opened the door himself, and flung a low-lidded, wine-whipped glance about her that seemed to undress her where she stood, noting her fault and charm as one notes an animal. He did not love her; there was no sentiment in this business. Brute cunning and greed were in his brow, and lust was in his lips ... What he did to her in the blackness of that curtained room of his had best not be imagined. But she came away with bruised limbs and body, with torn hair, and a face paled to death.[44]

Sax Rohmer, born in the south London suburbs in 1883 as plain Arthur Ward, was another former journalist who used Limehouse myths as inspiration to write popular fiction. He wrote the incredibly successful *Fu Manchu* novels, about a depraved Chinese man whose evil empire's headquarters was based, improbably, in Limehouse:

Imagine a person, tall, lean and feline, high-shouldered, with a brow like Shakespeare and a face like Satan, a close-shaven skull, and long magnetic eyes of the true cat-green. Invest him with all the cruel cunning of an entire Eastern race, accumulated in one giant intellect ... Imagine that awful being and you have a mental picture of Dr Fu Manchu, the yellow peril incarnate in one man.[45]

Sax Rohmer's *Fu Manchu* stories went on to inspire over thirty films and television series throughout the following decades (even a brand of sweets, sold until the 1970s, was called Fu Man Chews). Rohmer, unashamedly cashing in on the Carleton scandal, also wrote a novel called *Dope*, in which a character called Rita Dresden was based on Billie Carleton. A silly socialite called Mollie Gretna in the same novel envies the Scottish wife of a Chinese drug dealer (based on Ada and Lo Ping You):

Oh! Mollie's eyes opened widely. 'I almost envy her! I have read that Chinamen tie their wives to beams in the roof and lash them with leather thongs. I could die for a man who lashed me with leather thongs. Englishmen are so ridiculously gentle to women.'[46]

On 20 December 1918 at Marlborough Street Police Court (presided over by seventy-one-year-old Frederick Mead, who had been called to the bar in 1869 and who was as Victorian in his outlook as his Dickensian side-whiskers[47]) Ada Ping You was the first to be sentenced during the legal aftermath of Carleton's death. While Billie Carleton's inquest was still ongoing, Ping You was charged, under Regulation 40B of DORA, with possession and supplying opium and cocaine to the late actress, and also for preparing opium at Mr and

Mrs de Veulle's Dover Street flat. Of the two charges Ping You pleaded guilty only to the latter. Mr Muskett, for the prosecution, said that he wanted to present the facts in as colourless a manner as possible and was determined to avoid any unnecessary sensationalism. He took no notice of himself, however, and immediately called the story 'sordid', 'squalid' and 'deplorable' and thought everyone would agree that it was 'a disgrace to modern civilisation'.[48] In his closing statement, Frederick Mead, who was not known for his leniency, said that Ping You played a leading part in the 'disgraceful orgy' and that she was 'the high priestess at these unholy rites'.[49] He gave Ada Ping You the harshest sentence possible – five months of hard labour. She was already ill when she was sentenced, and, after a tough stint at Holloway Prison, died of tuberculosis in 1920.

Marek Kohn, in his book *Dope Girls*, says of Ada Ping You that 'while there had been a tradition of tolerance towards opium use by the introverted Chinese community as long as it didn't affect the indigenous population, a woman crossing the East–West divide to bring the foreign drugs to Mayfair was quite a different story'.[50] The tolerance to the Chinese community was shown in another court where Ada's husband Mr Ping You (arrested at the same time as his wife at their Limehouse residence where a small amount of opium was found) was fined just £10.

During the inquest, the influence of Carleton's middle-aged male 'friends' had over her was acknowledged but little criticised – except in the case of Reggie de Veulle, the man with the effete name, effete manner and effete job. He faced nothing less than a continual character assassination. One newspaper described him as 'a strange, sallow, very well dressed, effeminate little man, who hovered about her [Carleton] with deadly persistence',[51] while the *Daily Telegraph* wrote of his 'effeminate face and mincing little smile'.[52] Reginald de Veulle was the son of a former British vice-consul and French mother and was born in France but brought up in Jersey.

Lionel Belcher's counsel, Cecil Hayes, was particularly keen to deflect any blame from his client and direct it towards de Veulle. 'How long have you been engaged in the gentle art of designing ladies' dresses?' he asked, and then followed with, 'I put it to you that while your youth lasted you often made curious friendships with older men?' De Veulle responded, 'Has that anything to do with this case at all?' Mr Hayes continued: 'I believe these curious friendships that you made with older men were sometimes very paying, were they not?' De Veulle pretended not to understand the question, but Hayes was not to be deflected from his line of questioning. 'Were some friendships with men much older than you very remunerative for you?' De Veulle admitted to the court that he had once been given money as a young man by William Cronshaw, by whom he had been employed as a 'gentleman's secretary'.[53] Before the First World War de Veulle had had been involved in a homosexual blackmail case and William Cronshaw, to allay suspicions, had paid de Veulle to leave the country. Reggie travelled to America where he found jobs acting and performing. He was fortunate perhaps that Mr Hayes, Belcher's counsel, hadn't access to American newspapers. One gossip column in the *Chicago Tribune* described de Veulle as a guest of honour at a supper party where he had showed off his 'naughty wiggly dance in *The Queen of the Moulin Rouge* (a musical he had been touring in) and who had recently been "pinched" for so doing'.[54]

Malvina Longfellow, a twenty-nine-year-old American actress, who had lived in London after marrying a British officer, was also called as a witness. The photographer E. O. Hoppé, who was happy to consider himself a connoisseur of this sort of thing, once called her one of the most beautiful women in the world, and she had recently played Lady Hamilton in the film *Nelson*. Longfellow testified that she knew of Carleton's addiction to drugs and had tried to persuade her to stop using them. Longfellow also told the court she had asked de Veulle to stop supplying Carleton with drugs, and had told him on the night of Armistice Day that there 'would be trouble' if he went on doing so.

Fay Compton, Billie's close friend, was also called and told the court that although she knew Billie took drugs and had tried to dissuade her, she had never taken them herself. In the summing up the coroner began, 'We are approaching the conclusion of this somewhat disgusting case and I am sure we are all very glad to have got to the end of it.' Evaluating the evidence, it was obvious that he considered de Veulle had supplied the fatal cocaine. Subsequently it took the jury barely fifteen minutes to find that Billie Carleton had died of a cocaine overdose 'supplied to her by de Veulle in a culpable and negligent manner', and found him guilty of manslaughter. A very pale de Veulle, after giving his wife a hug, was taken into custody.[55]

The trial reached the Old Bailey in March where Reggie de Veulle was up against two charges – manslaughter but also conspiracy (with Ada Ping You) to supply cocaine. The prosecutor was sixty-one-year-old Sir Richard Muir, a man described as 'grim and remorseless' and famed for his thoroughness and diligence, so much so that when the murderer Dr Crippen learned that he was to face the daunting Muir, he said despairingly, 'It is most unfortunate that he is against me. I wish it had been anyone else but him. I fear the worst.'[56]

The trial went over the same ground as the inquest, and at the end the judge, Mr Justice Salter, more or less directed the jury to find de Veulle guilty of manslaughter. After just fifty minutes, however, the jury returned with a surprising 'not guilty' verdict. For once it seemed Muir had lost a case. De Veulle's wife Pauline screamed out and collapsed and there was faint applause heard from the public benches. After the weekend, however, de Veulle pleaded guilty to the conspiracy charge and Salter addressed him, saying:

> You persistently procured quantities of this drug to satisfy the craving of yourself and another. It is perfectly clear that you well knew you were doing what was wrong. Traffic in this deadly drug is a most pernicious thing. It leads to sordid, depraved, and disgusting practices. There is evidence in this case that following the practice of this habit are disease, depravity, crime, insanity, despair, and death.

Salter sentenced de Veulle to eight months in prison, mitigated, because of his clean record and poor health, in that it came without hard labour. The judge then said, 'It was a strange thing to reflect that until quite lately these drugs could be bought by all and sundry like so much grocery. I earnestly hope that it may never be the case again.'[57] During his summing up, Salter had directed the jury that the medical evidence was that Carleton had recently administered to herself a considerable dose of cocaine, and that all the indications were, without being conclusive, consistent with death by cocaine. Mr Huntly Jenkins, for the defence, however, was almost certainly more accurate in his description of how Billie Carleton came to die. He described to the court her tiring day – a matinee in the afternoon, an evening performance, and then the Victory Ball, after which she sat up with Lionel Belcher and Miss Richardson until six in the morning. It was unlikely, Mr Jenkins told the jury, that she would have then taken cocaine and it was more plausible for her to have taken a dose of Veronal (sachets of the drug were in her bedroom, initially taken away by Doctor Stuart who presumably had prescribed them, but brought back when they were noticed missing) to try and sleep.

Almost exactly a year before Carleton's death, the novelist Ivy Compton Burnett's younger sisters Stephanie Primrose and Catherine (nicknamed 'Baby' and 'Topsy'), died in a suicide pact, clinging together in the bed they always shared. They had taken Veronal behind the locked door of their bedroom in a flat in St John's Wood on Christmas Day, 1917. It was almost certain that if Carleton had taken drugs after Belcher and his girlfriend had left her apartment, she would have taken something not to keep her awake, but to help her sleep. If she did, unfortunately she never woke up again, and Marek Kohn, who in his book *Dope Girls* covers Carleton's death in exact detail, puts forward the case that the manner of Carleton's death suggests opiates or barbiturates rather than a stimulant like cocaine, and that she probably entered a deep coma and choked on fluid secretion or even her tongue.[58]

The Carleton case made drugs a long-running concern, not only in the British press but in literature, theatre and cinema. Philip Hoar, in his biography of Noël Coward, lists three plays with drug themes that were performed in the West End the year after Carleton's death – *Dope* by Frank Price, *Drug Fiends* by Owen Jones and *The Girl Who Took Drugs* (aka *Soiled*) by Aimée Grattan-Clyndes.[59] In 1923 Agatha Christie, in one of her first short stories that featured Hercule Poirot, wrote 'The Affair at the Victory Ball' in which the Belgian detective and Captain Hastings investigate a society mystery about a young woman who had been found dead of a cocaine overdose. In 1924, Noël Coward, who later wrote in his autobiography that he was 'pleasant but not intimate friends' with Carleton, used the tragic death as inspiration for *The Vortex*, the play that made him famous and which featured a cocaine-taking protagonist.

Lionel Belcher's promising cinema career was more or less ruined by his involvement in the Carleton affair. His notoriety, however, meant that the movie *Yoke*, adapted from a 1907 novel that had been suppressed on the grounds of obscenity (a woman has pre-marital sex and doesn't get punished for it), was re-released, not least because of the subject matter – the story of a young man weaned from drugs by a lover's dedication. After the court case, Belcher's wife Gladys, displeased that it was announced in court that he was openly living with Olive Richardson in a flat on Great Portland Street, eventually divorced him. In 1924 Belcher was imprisoned for fourteen days for thrashing his second wife with a cane in the street. The dubious Dr Stuart was fined in 1929 for signing prescriptions for morphine and heroin without entering them in the register (he claimed his actions were due to overwork). As a result his authority to possess or supply raw opium, coca leaves and Indian hemp was withdrawn.

After prison, Reggie de Veulle continued to work as a dress designer in London, and worked with Elspeth Phelps again when she became head designer at Paquin. When Irene Castle came to perform at the Embassy Club for a few weeks in 1923, it was reported that de Veulle designed her dresses, which were described as having very full skirts although the 'waistlines were all normal because Mrs Castle says the low waistline is not becoming to her'. Subsequently de Veulle moved back to Paris for a few years, but died in Islington in 1956.

Five days after the Allied Victory Ball and two days after Billie Carleton was buried in an Epsom cemetery (courtesy of her generous friend John Darlington Marsh, who lived in Epsom[60]), the representatives of the Electrical Trades Union joined the huge Labour Party meeting at the Royal Albert Hall which, despite the doubts of the manager Hilton Carter, went ahead. The famous dance floor was filled this time not with a 'broken, swirling scene of various colours', but with a predominance of red in a vast meeting of 10,000 men and women who covered every inch of the hall, including every single box. The meeting, which demanded a League of Nations, disarmament, and self-determination of Ireland, was addressed by George Lansbury, who throughout had the huge crowd in the palm of his hand. The first speaker, however, was Mr Muir, the leader of the Electrical Trades Union, who shouted, 'Just as the electricians took the soul out of the Albert Hall, so we mean to take the soul out of capitalism.' The entire audience rose to their feet and cheered and cheered and then sang 'For He's a Jolly Good Fellow', again and again and again.[61]

Dennis Eadie and Billie Carleton in *Freedom of the Seas* at the Haymarket Theatre. Carleton's last role.

AFTERNOON TEA.

A SPECIAL SERVICE OF TEA IS SERVED AT MATINÉES in all the Saloons and in the Auditorium.

To facilitate service visitors are kindly requested to ORDER IN ADVANCE.

AIR RAID WARNINGS.

Arrangements have been made for warning of a threatened air raid to be communicated by the Military Authorities to this Theatre.

On receipt of any such warning the audience will be informed with a view to enable persons who may wish to proceed home, or to secure better shelter, to do so.

The warning will be communicated as early as possible before any actual attack can take place. There will, therefore, be no cause for alarm or undue haste. Also to give any Naval and Military Officers whose duty requires them to go to their posts, the opportunity of immediately leaving the Theatre for this purpose.

Those who decide to leave are warned not to loiter about the streets, and if bombardment or gunfire commences before they reach home they should at once take cover.

The tiers and the main portion of the ceiling of the Theatre being constructed of steel and concrete, danger from falling shrapnel is remote, but those who desire more shelter than the Auditorium affords would find it in the Corridors, Bars, Staircases, etc., as follows:—

In the **Upper Circle** and **Gallery**, the staircase corridors on each side, the two staircases leading to the street, and the Refreshment Bar at the back of the Upper Circle.

In the **Dress Circle**, the corridors on either side, the small stairways at the ends of these, and the two staircases leading to the main entrance. A few could be accommodated in the Ladies' Cloak-Room and the Refreshment Bar.

In the **Stalls**, the "Exit" Corridor on the right-hand side of the Stalls facing the Stage, the Corridor and the Refreshment Bar under the Stalls, and the Ladies' Cloak Room.

In the **Pit**, the Refreshment Bar, the stairway leading to it, and the corridors leading to the street.

All the positions indicated are entirely covered with steel and concrete.

This page: Freedom of the Seas programme.

EVERY EVENING AT 8. (DOORS OPEN 7.45.)

MATINEES—EVERY WEDNESDAY & SATURDAY AT 2.30. (DOORS OPEN 2.)

In conjunction with VEDRENNE and EADIE,
FREDERICK HARRISON presents

The Freedom of the Seas

A Play in Three Acts by
WALTER HACKETT.

The Characters are in the Order of their Appearance.

George Smith	DENNIS EADIE
Horatio Gamp	VINCENT STERNROYD
Daniel Harcourt	E. HOLMAN CLARK
Stanley Bolton	TOM REYNOLDS
Phyllis Harcourt	BILLIE CARLETON
Harry Jackson	RANDLE AYRTON
Nils Bergstrom	JAMES CAREW
Ginger Brown	CHARLES GROVES
O'Hara	HENRY SCATCHARD
Adoniram Wallace	SYDNEY VALENTINE
Jenny Weathersbee	MARION LORNE

ACT I. ... Offices of Harcourt & Harcourt, in Lincoln's Inn Fields, 1815

ACTS II. & III. ... On Board the Tramp Steamer, "Marion May," 1918
53° 25' N. Lat.: 11° 20' W. Long.

Stage Director ... WILFRED EATON

The Scene for Act I. has been painted by ALFRED CRAVEN.
The Scene for Acts II. and III. by JOSEPH and PHIL HARKER.

Special Electrical Apparatus lent by the LONDON TELEGRAPH TRAINING COLLEGE, LTD., Earl's Court.

Programme of Music.

1.	(a) SPANISH DANCE	Albenia
	(b) VALSE	Sibelius
	(c) MEDITATION	Massenet
	(d) HAUTIER	Darewski
2.	(a) VALSE ("Lilac Domino")	Cuvillier
	(b) "Where Corals Lie"	Elgar
3.	(a) SONG ("Round the Map")	Finch
	(b) "Chanties"	Arr. by N. O'Neill
	THE NATIONAL ANTHEM.	

Musical Director - - - NORMAN O'NEILL.

Stage Manager } For VEDRENNE and EADIE { E. H. BROOKE.
Acting Manager } { DOUGLAS LOWE.

THE BOX OFFICE (W. H. LEVERTON) is open daily from 10 to 10.
Telephone—Regent 9930, 6031 and 6032.

Private Boxes, £2 12s. 6d. (Tax, 7/6) and £3 3s. (Tax, 9/-). Orchestra Stalls, 10s. 6d. (Tax, 1/6). Balcony Stalls, 8s. 6d. (Tax, 1/-). Upper Circle, 2s. 6d. (Tax, 6d). Pit, 2s. 6d. (Tax, 6d.). Gallery, 1s. (Tax, 3d.).

MATINEES:
EVERY WEDNESDAY AND SATURDAY AT 2.30.

Nearest Underground Stations—PICCADILLY CIRCUS, TRAFALGAR SQUARE, LEICESTER SQUARE and CHARING CROSS.

Piccadilly Circus Station is in The Haymarket, a few yards from the Theatre; the others are within a few minutes' walk.

Ladies are earnestly requested to remove Hats, Bonnets, or any kind of head dress.

This request being made for the benefit of the audience, the Management trust that it will appeal to everyone, and that Ladies will kindly assist in having it carried out.

General Manager - - - HORACE WATSON.

The Refreshment Bars are open as usual during the performance, but alcoholic liquors cannot be served after 2.30 in the afternoon or after 9.30 in the evening.

"SMOKING IS NOT PERMITTED IN THE AUDITORIUM." *Extract from the rules made by the Lord Chamberlain.*

Recipe for the 'Hanky-Panky' Cocktail

Ada Coleman is perhaps the most famous female bartender of all time. Nicknamed 'Coley', she became head bartender at the American Bar at the Savoy in 1903. During her time there she invented a cocktail called the Hanky Panky, which at that time in England meant not so much 'sexual goings-on' but 'magic' or 'witchcraft'. In an interview with the *Daily Express* in 1925, Coleman recounted how the drink had been named after she had made it for one of her regulars, the comedy actor and musician Charles Hawtrey:

> The late Charles Hawtrey ... was one of the best judges of cocktails that I knew. Some years ago, when he was overworking, he used to come into the bar and say, 'Coley, I am tired. Give me something with a bit of punch in it.' It was for him that I spent hours experimenting until I had invented a new cocktail. The next time he came in, I told him I had a new drink for him. He sipped it, and, draining the glass, he said, 'By Jove! That is the real hanky-panky!' And Hanky-Panky it has been called ever since.[62]

The drink, made with gin, sweet vermouth, and Fernet-Branca, with a rind of orange marinating in the mix, is still on the menu at the Savoy. Who knows but Billie Carleton during her short time at Savoy Court Mansions may have dropped in and had a Hanky Panky, perhaps with Irene Castle.

In a cocktail shaker over ice pour:

One measure of Italian Vermouth
One measure of dry gin
2 dashes Fernet-Branca

Strain into a (4 oz) cocktail glass.
Garnish with a twist of orange peel.

11

Judy Garland, Johnnie Ray and the Talk of the Town at the Hippodrome

At the Register Office in the Chelsea Old Town Hall on the King's Road, Judy Garland, wearing a blue chiffon mini dress, with a draped neck and ostrich feather sleeves, married a gay ex-discotheque manager and part-time jazz pianist called Mickey Devinko, better known to his friends and associates as Mickey Deans. After the brief marriage ceremony, held at midday on 15 March 1969, and which was actually the forty-six-year-old's fifth, Garland said: 'This is it. For the first time in my life, I am really happy. Finally, I am loved.' Not that loved, it seemed, because despite the long celebrity guest list none of Judy's famous friends made it to the reception. It was held at Quaglino's, the large and expensive restaurant opened forty years previously in 1929 and situated in Bury Street just south of Piccadilly.

Several hundred people were invited, albeit at very short notice, and only a few made it to the function. 'I can't understand it,' Judy was reported to have said in the next day's *Sunday Express*, 'they all said they'd come.'[1] Even her daughter Liza Minnelli, who had turned twenty-three just three days before, had called her mother to say, 'I can't make it Mamma but I promise I'll come to your next one!'

The large formal room hired for the reception was a mistake and only accentuated the lack of guests. Glasses of champagne remained un-drunk and most of an ostentatious three-tiered cake stayed uneaten. The cake had been given to Garland six weeks previously at the end of her five-week Talk of the Town engagement. Nobody had remembered to take it out of the deep-freeze in time, however,

Mickey Deans, Judy Garland and Johnnie Ray at Judy and Mickey's wedding at Chelsea Register Office on 15 March 1969.

and it was almost impossible to cut and eat. A young actor friend of Mickey's called Allan Warren was asked to be the wedding photographer and has described what happened:

Mickey phoned and said, 'Am not looking to stay, as I'm staying at Claridge's, but have you got a camera?' At the time I was in Alan Bennett's *Forty Years On* and oddly enough had just bought one. He offered me twenty pounds for me to take some photographs of the reception. He was usually stone broke. So I laughed and said, 'Sure, who're you marrying?' He said, 'Judy Garland so I can pay you.' I had never taken any pictures before, but I said I would do it.

When I got to Quaglino's, there was a small band playing, a huge amount of press and a little group of people sitting with him in the opposite corner. One was Judy, the other Johnnie Ray and a third was a girl beside them in a wheelchair, who was never introduced.

Cutting the frozen wedding cake at the reception at Quaglino's.

I took a few snaps including some of Judy and Mickey dancing. Then Mickey told me to dance with Judy as there was nobody else apart from Johnnie. She seemed very frail and very skinny. When we waltzed I could feel the bones of her spine sticking out. She also seemed very dazed as if on drugs, her eyes glazed over and she seemed very uptight. We danced in time to a one-armed trumpet player playing 'Somewhere Over the Rainbow'. Afterwards I left as had to get to do the play. Mickey never paid me of course![2]

One journalist wrote that the reception was 'the saddest and most pathetic party he had ever attended' but Judy and Mickey at least looked as if they were having a good time. They later sat on the edge of a small stage and together sang the Al Jolson song 'You Made Me Love You'. Jolson had always been an important influence for Judy. Three months after she had signed her MGM contract in 1935, at the age of thirteen and not yet a big star, she appeared on the Al Jolson radio show. Her father, courtesy of nurses who held a radio up to his ear listened to her sing 'Zing! Went the Strings of my Heart' shortly before he died in hospital of spinal meningitis. Sixteen years later, in 1951, she sang a Jolson medley during her four-week stint at the London Palladium – her first live performances in Britain (and first anywhere for thirteen years) and for which she received £7142 a week.

It's not strictly true that there were none of Judy's celebrity friends at the wedding: Mickey Deans' best man was Johnnie Ray, the American singer, famous for his ability to cry on stage and who had had several big hits in the UK, including 'Such a Night' and 'Just Walkin' in the Rain'. Ray had recently been touring the country and in four days he was due to perform with Judy on a Scandinavian tour that Deans had organised, anxious to make his new wife some money. Garland was severely in debt and when she returned to London at the end of 1968 some newspapers reported that she was immediately served with a writ from Harrods, who said that she owed them £145 15s 2d, a bill outstanding from October 1964.

A few weeks before the wedding, on the evening of 19 January 1969, Garland appeared on ATV's popular *The London Palladium Show*. No one knew but it was to be the American star's last ever performance on television anywhere in the world, and it went wrong from the very start. Garland was introduced by the compère Jimmy Tarbuck but the orchestra had to play for two very long minutes before she appeared on stage. Richard Stott in the *Daily Mirror* wrote:

> Singer Judy Garland appeared to be ill last night ... Towards the end of the act 46-year-old Judy, who is starring at the Talk of the Town in the West End of London, seemed to have trouble pronouncing the words of towns in a song about Britain. She bent down and asked the orchestra conductor how the words of the song went! At the end of the spot, she threw her arms round Tarbuck and he helped her on to the Palladium 'roundabout'.[3]

A spokesman from ATV said the next day: 'She has been suffering from an attack of the flu.' Two days later, and still complaining of feeling unwell, Garland was welcomed up on stage by Johnnie Ray, who that night was top of the bill at Caesar's Palace. Alas it was not the famous Las Vegas casino but a cabaret/nightclub (sometimes spelt C'esars) situated 20 miles or so from central London in Luton, not far from junction 11 of the M1. Remembered these days mostly

Judy performing in the UK in 1951.

for his nicknames, such as 'the Nabob of Sob' and the 'Prince of Wails', the frail, almost emaciated, partly deaf American singer was still a relatively big star in Britain in 1969.

Bob Stanley in his history of British pop music *Yeah, Yeah, Yeah* describes the Oregon-born singer as 'arguably the most

significant modern pop forbear',[4] and during most of the 1950s
Johnnie Ray was huge. Eight or nine years before the Beatles
achieved anything similar, Ray was the first star in Britain to
make girls in the audience feel the need to scream continually
throughout the concert (this can be heard on his 1954 album *Live
at the London Palladium*). In September 1955 London's *Evening
Standard* wrote that for the first time since London Airport
(renamed Heathrow twelve years later in 1967) was opened just
after the war, crash barriers had to be installed outside the arrivals
hall to keep back the 'teenage Johnnie fans'. It reported that girls
were 'screaming, sobbing, waving their arms and they pressed
against the barriers as the singer, wearing his deaf-aid, a sports
coat and open-necked shirt, was escorted from the Stratocruiser
by a police superintendent'. On the same flight an utterly confused
Australian minister for External Affairs, who had seen nothing like
it, asked, 'Who is this entertainer?'[5] Four years later, in 1959, the
Guardian was still reporting that Ray's 'emotional impact on his
predominantly girlish audience was staggering' and that 'amorous
contortions with the microphone brought forth shrieks of delight
and thunderous clapping and stamping'.[6]

The manager of C'esars, the large Luton club that featured a
twenty-lane bowling alley on the first floor, was George Savva,
a man who did absolutely nothing to discourage the use of his
nickname 'Mr Show-Business'. In the late 1960s Savva had enough
contacts to bring over not only Johnnie Ray but other transatlantic
stars such as Jack Jones, Johnny Mathis and Frankie Laine. It was
fair to say, however, that some of the big stars found the venue less
than glamorous. Tom Jones tells a story of how Shirley Bassey once
summoned Savva to her dressing room during a break in rehearsals
and said: 'Are you the manager of this shit-house'? Savva nodded,
to which the Welsh singer informed him that she'd refuse to perform
unless the dressing room was completely redecorated and a chaise
longue found.[7]

It was at about this time when C'esars, which had up to then
relied on chicken-in-a-basket and similar meals, started to feature a
more sophisticated, upmarket fare. The nightclub/restaurant started
serving new dishes, printed in French on a menu that, according to
Savva, 'beckoned the diner seductively'. They included:

Beef Bourgoine (*sic*), Cock eu Vin (*sic*), Canard a la Orange (*sic*), and lastly, and presumably after the useless translator had given up, Venison in Cherry.[8]

Supplied by Alverston Kitchens as frozen bricks, the great advantage of these new-fangled factory foods to large club/restaurants was their almost total elimination of expensive experienced chefs. The meals came in one-portion polythene bags, which were then simply placed in boiling water for about fifteen minutes before they were snipped open, emptied onto a plate and served. Although the frozen boil-in-the-bag meals were far cheaper to produce, Savva later wrote that although he knew it was wrong, 'my greed got the better of me and I placed a £1 surcharge on the dishes'.[9]

Meanwhile up on stage at C'esars in January 1969, Ray was dressed in a black tuxedo and at about 11.15 p.m. surprised and excited the audience by welcoming Judy Garland up on to the Luton nightclub's stage. She was wearing a very short white mini-dress with white leather boots, and to the audience looked far more fragile and thin than they remembered. Eighteen years before, in 1951, the newspapers talked of Garland's weight and the *Manchester Guardian*, reviewing her successful concerts at the Palladium, described her as 'a well-built girl in a lot of black chiffon'. The *Daily Mail* agreed, writing that her dress 'did little to hide her almost matronly new girth',[10] while the *Sunday Dispatch* just simply went with the description, 'plump and perspiring'.[11] Judy told *The Times* at the time that it was quite simple: 'Fat I'm happy, and thin, I'm miserable.' Garland had been taking drugs since she was in her early teens, essentially to keep her weight down – Louis B. Mayer, the owner of MGM, called her 'that fat kid' (not to mention 'my little hunchback' – you can understand why she had trouble with self-esteem all her life) and was constantly troubled by what he saw as her weight problem. Studio doctors prescribed the new wonder drug Benzedrine, and subsequently the more sophisticated offshoots Dexedrine and Dexamyl. Back then drugs like these seemed like miracles of science and were almost as common as aspirin.

Despite the comments about her weight, the first night at the Palladium in 1951 was an absolute triumph. Even after she tripped and landed on her backside after the fourth song (the audience howled with laughter at her unfortunate mishap) the appreciation at the end of the show was extraordinary. Before she had even finished singing 'Somewhere over the Rainbow', her last song, the audience was so loud and effusive that Val Parnell, the managing director of the Palladium, and someone who had seen a few, described it as the biggest ovation he had ever seen or heard.

Eighteen years later at C'esars the American stars sang the song 'Am I Blue' as a duet, at the end of which the crowd leapt to their feet and gave the two stars a five-minute standing ovation. George Savva, however, described it as the most awful performance of the song he had ever heard and said that the ageing superstars sang not only out of tune but out of sync. Something must have worked because he added, 'It was also one of the most moving nights of my life.'[12]

Not long after finishing the duet, Judy Garland was back in her black limo which, via the ten-year-old M1 motorway, drove her to her nightly show at the Talk of the Town at the Hippodrome on Charing Cross Road. She had been booked for five weeks from the very end of 1968 and her first show, on 30 December, with Zsa Zsa Gabor, Ginger Rogers, David Frost and Danny La Rue[13] in attendance, was a huge success. With echoes of her Palladium triumph, Bernard Delfont described the audience roaring their approval like 'a football crowd at a cup-final'.[14] For that first night Garland wore a bronze sequinned trouser suit, originally designed for the movie *Valley of the Dolls* and first worn in 1967. In Jacqueline Susann's original book the character Neely O'Hara, whose talent was blunted by self-destructive alcoholism and a dependency on prescription drugs, was purportedly based on Garland. The American singer had been utterly addicted to Seconal (the drug that would eventually kill her) off and on since the 1950s. Seconal, a barbiturate derivative medicine, became widely misused in the sixties and had nicknames such as 'reds', 'red-devils' or 'seccies'. Another common name for the pills, especially in California, was 'dolls' and thus responsible for the punning title of Jacqueline Susann's novel – 'Valley of the Dolls'. Judy was actually cast in the film, not as O'Hara but to play the character Helen Lawson. Not long into the filming Garland, not helped by the drug that gave the novel and movie its name, missed several days of rehearsals and was fired in April 1967.

The Stage magazine reviewed Garland's performance at the Talk of the Town in January 1969: 'There are few artists who create an emotionalism – almost amounting to hysteria – minutes before they actually set foot onstage. Of these, probably the greatest is Judy.'[15] Tony Palmer of the *Observer* also wrote about her latest comeback, 'Her survival gives her power and sex-appeal. She generates the hysteria that homosexuals, for instance, find it easy to identify with, and necessary to idolise – "We love you, Judy," shout the audience. "I love you, too," comes the response.'[16] The reviewer in *Variety* published a week later was perhaps more prescient: 'Make no mistake, the Garland magic, warmth, and heart are as irresistible as ever. Nagging question is how long can Judy Garland keep it up? How long does she want to? Audience affection and goodwill are there, but there can be a limit to how long folks will watch a well-loved champ gamble with her talent.'[17]

Three weeks later the champ was gambling with reckless abandon and her performances were rapidly going downhill, with the audiences' affection and goodwill soon dissipating. After the duet with Johnnie Ray, Garland had left C'esars about 11.30 p.m. which, unfortunately, was exactly the time Garland was meant to be appearing on stage (Robert Nesbitt, the producer, had already put back her nightly show by half an hour because of her continued lateness). The crowd, despite being informed that Garland was on her way and that dancing would continue, were very restless. Judy eventually arrived at the Talk of Town at 12.50 a.m. and Lonnie Donegan, who was kept as reserve for these occasions, was stood down. Fifteen minutes later Burt Rhodes, the musical director, began the overture with Judy, microphone in hand, waiting behind the curtain. The angry audience had not been told why the American singer's show had been delayed and their impatient noise was heard in the dressing room.

When she emerged on stage singing 'I Belong to London', which on previous nights had always gone down well, she could barely be heard over the drunken booing and slow hand-claps. The stage was strewn with cigarette boxes and pieces of bread, and Garland had to kick her way through the litter. When she began her next song, 'The Man that Got Away', the audience's catcalls continued. At one point a red-haired man got up on stage from one of the nearby tables and grabbed Judy in one hand and the microphone in another and shouted – 'Miss Garland! Your behaviour is disgraceful! If you can't make it on time, why bother to turn up at all?'[18] At that moment a thrown wine glass smashed almost at Judy's feet, at which she burst into tears and staggered off stage. Andrew Lloyd-Webber was in the audience during Judy's short performance that night and it inspired him to write, a few years later, 'Don't Cry For Me, Argentina'.[19]

The impresario Bernard Delfont had opened the Talk of the Town in the autumn of 1958. Just before it opened, the *Financial Times*, armed with some obscure facts, wrote: 'London's first theatre-restaurant will seat 700 people and provide employment for some 400. It has approximately one and a third miles of Wilton carpet and over 1,000 square yards of linoleum. Air conditioning supplies 34 tons of fresh air per hour.'[20] Despite what the press release said, the first 'theatre-restaurant' was not the Talk of the Town. Delfont had originally got the idea from the pre-war theatre-restaurants of Paris and Berlin, but the first in London was at the Casino on the corner of Old Compton Street and Greek Street, where Josephine Baker and her notorious banana dance made her London debut. Opened in 1930 and originally called Prince Edward's Theatre (it has since returned to its original name), it became the London Casino in 1935. The idea of combining a cabaret show with a dinner package was an attempt to avoid paying an entertainment tax, insisting to an unimpressed Inland Revenue that customers were paying for the meal while the show was thrown in for free. The Inland Revenue, as is usually the case, won the dispute and the theatre soon abandoned the idea.

Bernard Delfont had been born Boruch Winogradsky in Tokamak in the Ukraine in 1909 but from a young age had been brought up above a shop on Brick Lane. His brothers Lew and Leslie adjusted their original surname to Grade, while Bernard took his name from the Delfont Brothers, a forgotten dance act he had once been part of. Delfont 'struggled, worked and starved'[21] as a professional dancer until the age of thirty, when he became an agent. Eleven years later he became a theatrical manager and didn't look back.

Bernard Delfont and Charles Forte at the Talk of the Town around 1960.

Kitchen at the Talk of the Town restaurant in 1958.

The Talk of the Town at night in 1958, the year it opened.

After the war Delfont was still mulling over the idea of a theatre-restaurant. At the Pigalle, a nightclub on Piccadilly with 300 seats, he started incorporating a show into a full evening's entertainment, with dancing at eight and then a midnight supper. It proved exceedingly popular and was where both Sammy Davis Jnr and Tony Bennett made their UK debuts. Delfont thought this could be repeated but on a larger scale, similar to the London Casino shows, and when the lease of the Hippodrome on the corner of Charing Cross Road came up he made every attempt to acquire it. As the theatre was in need of extensive renovation, the lease was relatively cheap but, as Delfont wanted to turn it into a huge restaurant, it needed to be totally reconstructed anyway.

At that time the London Hippodrome was not yet sixty years old. Designed by Frank Matcham for Moss Empires, it was built for £250,000 as a 'hippodrome' for circus and variety performances and originally opened in 1900. The first show at the theatre was a music-hall revue entitled 'Giddy Ostend' with Little Tich and (in one of his first roles) Charlie Chaplin. In 1909, it was reconstructed by Matcham as a music-hall and variety theatre, and it was here that Tchaikovsky's *Swan Lake* received its English première by the Ballets Russes in 1910. Nine years later the same venue hosted the Original Dixieland Jazz Band – the first official jazz gig in the UK. In 1948 a twelve-year-old Julie Andrews made her West-End stage debut at the Hippodrome. From 1949 to 1951 it became a slightly tacky London equivalent of the Folies Bergère but subsequently became neglected and run-down.

For his Hippodrome project Delfont brought in Robert Nesbitt, an experienced director of glamorous stage spectaculars in London and Las Vegas, who thought the restaurant/nightclub idea would need at least £350,000 capital (approximately £8.5 million in 2017). Despite his successful career Delfont was in no position to raise this sort of money but an old acquaintance of his, Charles Forte, whose company at the time was the largest privately owned catering business in Britain, became interested. Forte had recently bought the Cafe Royal on Piccadilly and was interested in developing the whole area around Piccadilly and Leicester Square.

Opposite top: The interior of the Talk of the Town at the Hippodrome in 1958.
Opposite bottom: The stage at the Talk of the Town in September 1958.

The Hippodrome in 1911.

At the time it was a location still relatively run-down and seedy and which was expected by most to be completely redeveloped. Forte offered to take over the whole catering side of Delfont's enterprise but also would stump up the necessary money for the entire project. The deal, however, would give Delfont 30 per cent of the profits.

To achieve the relative intimacy of a restaurant in what was essentially a large theatre, the gallery was closed off with a false ceiling and the dress circle became a mezzanine dining area with stairs on each side leading down to the dance floor and the main part of the restaurant. The stage was reconstructed to allow for such technical wizardry as a lift sunk into a 11-metre well, capable of introducing into the action a prop as weighty as a vintage Rolls-Royce.

Delfont's Talk of the Town opened 28 September 1958 featuring, twice nightly at 8.45 p.m. and 11.30 p.m., a Robert Nesbitt revue entitled *The Whole Town's Talking* with Valerie Walsh, Steve Arlen, Maggie Fitzgibbon and Jean Muir. Two years later the entertainment policy was changed with a revue earlier in the evening, but with a cabaret performance by a star guest at 11 p.m. The first star to appear was Eartha Kitt (making use of the Rolls-Royce appearing from nowhere) and followed two weeks later by Max Bygraves. The Rotherhithe-born comedian had been on the same bill as Judy Garland when she performed at the Palladium in 1951 – 'A new suit but not enough new jokes,' wrote the *Daily Mail* at the time.[22]

By the time Judy Garland came to perform at the Talk of the Town at the end of 1969, the entertainment policy was still the same, with the famous star appearing late in the evening. Garland had been preceded by the singers Joe Brown, Englebert Humperdinck and Frank Ifield and would be followed by Lonnie Donegan, Sandie Shaw and the Baron Knights in 1970.

By the end of January and three weeks into the engagement, Bernard Delfont realised that Garland was now unwell and unable, realistically, to continue with her booking. 'I'm sorry, Judy. I can't let you go on unless you let me have a doctor's certificate to say you are fit,' he ended up telling her. A headline the next day said 'Delfont Bans Judy Garland', but he knew that he was now dealing with a very sick woman 'brought low by twenty years of drink and drugs'.[23] Much to Delfont's surprise, however, her doctor, John Traherne, confirmed unequivocally that Judy Garland was able to perform the rest of the engagement, which, after a weekend off to try and shake off her flu-like symptoms, she did.

The timekeeping didn't improve, and on most nights Delfont noticed that whatever was left from the pre-show meal usually ended up on the stage. By now Garland was taking a cocktail of drugs just to keep going. She hardly ate at all and, unsurprisingly, was nearly always unwell. Mickey Deans later wrote about this time: 'During the last two weeks of the Talk of the Town engagement, when she was physically so drained by the flu, she took enormous amounts of Ritalin in order to perform and large doses of Seconal to lull her to sleep. When she suffered from a kind of malaise of spirit, the combination of Ritalin and Seconal taken together produced an instant high. Judy, of course, took Ups early in the evening before a performance and more, if she were sagging physically, during the performance. The drug killed her appetite, made her sick to her stomach and increased her pulse rate. She sometimes took another drug when she felt her heart was beating too fast.'[24]

The last of Garland's Talk of the Town performances took place on 1 February 1969. She left the club at 2 a.m., and when she signed a fan's magazine outside the stage door she first covered the eyes, and then her mouth on the cover photo with her hand and said, 'See? The mouth smiles ... but the eyes do not.' Not long after her final performance, Garland and Mickey Deans moved from the Ritz hotel into a small mews house on a Chelsea cul-de-sac called Cadogan Lane. Judy had already lived in Chelsea for a short while late in 1960 when she lived in a house owned by Sir Carol Reed in King's Row. Her children, Joey and Lorna, went to Lady Eden's School in Kensington and 'Liza was enrolled at a tutorial school on Victoria Street'.

The Cadogan Lane house was later described by Mickey Deans as a 'modest little mews house with six cosy, intimate rooms. A white stucco house with a yellow front door and a cement flower box that ran its length.'[25] The front door of the house opened directly into a living room that had white walls, grey carpeting, and a sofa and chairs upholstered in black and white ticking. The dining room had red walls, a round table under a skylight and a matching 'buffet and sideboard'. The main bedroom had a chest of drawers, two small chairs, a dressing table and two large wardrobes. Judy and Mickey added lamps coloured sheets and a bright blue 'chintz' bedspread. The bedroom alongside, which became Judy's dressing room, was painted a warm pink with a green Tiffany lamp and rose-coloured carpeting. Across the hall from the bedroom was a 'large sallow-green' tiled bathroom that had a window through which you could see the skylight of the kitchen. On the turn of the staircase was a large rubber tree in a tub.

After their March wedding, Garland and Deans flew to Majorca for a brief honeymoon, but quickly transferred to Paris where they stayed at the Georges V hotel. Three days after the wedding, they flew to Stockholm for the short Scandinavian tour with Johnnie Ray. Her last public appearance in London was on 18 June 1969, when she was picked up at 9 p.m. by her neighbours Gina Dangerfield and Richard Harris (an interior designer and not the actor) and taken to Bromley for the opening of Jackie Trent and Tony Hatch's 'grand opening' of their new menswear shop.

Four days later, on Saturday 22 June, just three months after their wedding, Judy and Mickey had been watching a BBC documentary on the royal family but as both felt unwell they went to bed early. At around 10.40 a.m. the next morning the phone rang for Garland. Deans got up and found the bathroom door locked. He climbed out on to the roof and looked through the window and saw Garland motionless on the toilet with her head slumped forward and her hands on her knees. Climbing into the bathroom, he found her skin was discoloured and dried blood had dribbled from her mouth and nose. She had been dead for about eight hours. A bottle containing twenty-five barbiturate pills was later found by her bedside half-empty, and another bottle of 100 was still unopened. It was twelve days after her forty-seventh birthday.

Judy Garland's death report.

DEPARTMENT OF STATE
FOREIGN SERVICE OF THE UNITED STATES OF AMERICA

Form FS-192
11-19-51

REPORT OF THE DEATH OF AN AMERICAN CITIZEN

American Embassy, London, England, July 7, 1969
(Place and date)

Name in full Judy Garland DE VINKO Occupation Entertainer

Native of Minnesota Born in Minnesota on June 10, 1922 Last known address

in the United States 111 East 88th Street, New York

Date of death June 21 1969 Age 47 years
(Month) (Day) (Hour) (Minute) (Year) (As nearly as can be ascertained)

Place of death 4 Cadogan Lane, Chelsea, London, England
(Number and street) or (Hospital or hotel) (City) (Country)

Cause of death Certified by G. Thurston, Coroner for Inner West London, at inquest held on June 25, 1969, to other authority for statement Barbiturate poisoning (quinalbarbitone), incautious overdose, accidental.

Disposition of the remains Transported by air to the United States on June 25, 1969.

Local law as to disinterring remains —

Disposition of the effects Michael De Vinko, husband

Person or official responsible for custody of effects and accounting therefor Michael De Vinko

Informed by telegram:

NAME	ADDRESS	RELATIONSHIP	DATE SENT

Copy of this report sent to:

NAME	ADDRESS	RELATIONSHIP	DATE SENT
Liza Minelli Allen	300 E. 57th St., New York	Daughter	7/7/69
Michael De Vinko	111 E. 88th St., New York	Husband	7/7/69

Traveling or residing abroad with relatives or friends as follows:

NAME	ADDRESS	RELATIONSHIP
Michael De Vinko	4 Cadogan Lane, Chelsea, London, England	Husband

Other known relatives (not given above):

NAME	ADDRESS	RELATIONSHIP
Lorna Luft	1212 Manning Avenue,	Daughter
Joseph Luft	Beverly Hills, California	Son

This information and data concerning an inventory of the effects, accounts, etc., have been placed under File 234 in the correspondence of this office.

Remarks: U.S. Passport No. H057990 issued 1/11/67 at Boston canceled and returned to husband. Details of death confirmed by Certified Copy of Entry of Death No. 20 issued in Sub-District of Chelsea First, Royal Borough of Kensington and Chelsea, London, showing death registered on 6/25/69.
(Continue on reverse if necessary.)

[SEAL]
No fee prescribed.

(Signature on all copies) Ralph H. Cadeaux

Consul of the United States of America.

Judy Garland's former house at 4 Cadogan Lane in Chelsea, 2017.

The Chelsea Coroner, Gavin Thurston, wrote, 'This is a clear picture of someone who had been habituated to barbiturates in the form of Seconal for a very long period of time, and who on the night of 22/23 June perhaps in a state of confusion from a previous dose (although this is pure speculation) took more barbiturate than her body could tolerate.' Garland two years earlier had spoken of Marilyn Monroe's death and predicted her own: 'You take a couple of sleeping pills,' she had explained, 'and you wake up in twenty minutes and forget you've taken them. So you take a couple more, and the next thing you know you've taken too many.'[26]

Ironically, considering the effort she put into keeping her weight down for most of her life, Garland was probably less than 70 pounds when she died. She was so thin that when her body, covered in only a blanket, was removed from the Cadogan Lane mews house it was said she was carried out draped over someone's arm like a folded coat. Deans took Garland's remains to New York City on 26 June, where an estimated 20,000 people lined up to pay their respects at the Frank E. Campbell Funeral Chapel in Manhattan. The funeral the next day was paid for by Frank Sinatra (Garland was $4 million in debt when she died) and the eulogy was read by James Mason. Her *Wizard of Oz* co-star, Ray Bolger, commented at the funeral, 'She just plain wore out.'[27]

A few weeks after the funeral Allan Warren, actor and occasional wedding photographer, met Mickey for lunch at his New York apartment:

> He never got off either of the two telephones he was talking on, for nearly two hours. The room was piled high with Judy Garland memorabilia that he was auctioning off. When he did get off the phone he shouted over the desk, 'Did you bring the negatives from England?' I said 'no' – he was furious as he said he could have sold them. I never did get lunch, or ever see him again.[28]

Johnnie Ray, a gay man who was never in a position to acknowledge, publicly, his sexuality, suffered from alcoholism throughout his life. After he was hospitalised with tuberculosis in

1960 he stopped drinking and for a few years was in a long-term relationship with his manager Bill Franklin, a man thirteen years his junior. In 1969, not long after his friend Judy had died, an American doctor told Ray he was now well enough to enjoy the odd glass of wine. It was bad advice; the heavy drinking resumed and he never really recovered. Ray died of liver failure in 1990 and is buried in Hopewell, Oregon.

Five years after Garland's death, Johnnie Ray was still performing 'Am I Blue', the song he sang with Garland on stage at C'esars in Luton, as a sort of 'duet'. Barry Coleman of the *Guardian* reviewed a 1974 Johnnie Ray concert in Chorley: 'The spotlight on the absent, not to say dead, Judy's stool seemed a bit much. But that, as sure as hell, is showbiz.'[29]

Johnnie Ray at Judy's wedding, by Allan Warren.

12

An Absolute Sirocco, Old Boy! Quo Vadis, Evelyn Laye, and the Story of Soho Girl Jessie Matthews

Late in 1927, Noël Coward was so upset that he made plans to leave the country. After a run of golden successes, the twenty-nine-year-old writer had just suffered two humiliating flops, the last of which was *Sirocco*, a play he had originally written in New York in 1921. The opening night at the Daly's Theatre was nothing less than a catastrophe. The trouble started during the initial love scene between Ivor Novello, perhaps a little camp for the Italian ladies' man he was meant to be playing, and a beautiful but inexperienced Canadian actress called Frances 'Bunny' Doble. Novello, the composer of popular melodies such as the wartime song 'Keep the Home Fires Burning', was at the time the only British male film star close to true stardom, and had recently appeared in Hitchcock's film *The Lodger*. He was not an odd choice for the lead in Coward's play. In the film *The Call of the Blood* in 1920, Novello's first acting role of any kind, he was praised not only for his performance but for being the only cast member to be convincingly Italian.[1] Noël once said of Novello, 'The two most beautiful things in the world are Ivor's profile and my mind.'[2]

When Novello and Doble started kissing, however, there was no chemistry at all, and the audience began to make loud sucking sounds. When the couple started to roll on the floor together, supposedly in the throes of passion, the gallery broke into fits of laughter. The last act was 'chaos from beginning to end with the gallery, upper circle and pit hooting and yelling' while people in the dress-circle were shushing loudly. Ridicule turned to pandemonium and when the curtain fell amongst 'a bedlam of sound' Coward's mother Violet, who was slightly deaf, turned to him in the darkness and said wistfully: 'Is it a failure?'

Meanwhile Basil Dean, the producer, had been dining in a nearby restaurant during the performance (as was his first-night custom) and hadn't heard the uproar. He also was slightly deaf, and when he arrived at the theatre he misheard the jeers for cheers, and signalled to the stage manager to raise and lower the curtains as if the play had gone well. Coward hissed in his ear, 'Wipe that smile off your face, dear – this is it!'[3] A bewildered Frances Doble then began a curtain-call speech she had prepared in the hope of the play's success: 'Ladies and Gentlemen, tonight is the happiest night of my life ...' At that point both Coward and Novello started giggling, which inflamed the audience even more. When Coward left the theatre, ignoring the warning not to leave by the stage door, a crowd was still waiting and were so angry they spat on him as he pushed through the angry throng. 'The next day I had to send my evening coat to the cleaners,' he later wrote. Essentially *Sirocco* was a weak play and neither of the principal actors had enough stage presence for this not to matter. In theatrical circles the word 'Sirocco' quickly became a synonym for disaster: 'How did the opening night go?' 'An absolute Sirocco, old boy!'

Frances Doble's career survived, albeit relatively briefly, and she went on to appear in Basil Dean's films *The Constant Nymph* and *Nine till Six*, but also the film version of Coward's *The Vortex* (as did Ivor Novello). In 1929 she married Anthony Lindsay Hogg, and when Basil Dean once described 'her mixture of bland self-confidence and intellectual stupidity' as 'vastly irritating' he may have had a point – she became enamoured with Franco and Hitler in the 1930s. In 1937, while in Spain and now divorced after a marriage that had lasted just four years, Doble had an affair with the spy Kim Philby (ten years her junior) who was working as the *Times* correspondent attached to Franco's headquarters. By now he was already spying for the Soviet Union, and he described the aristocratic former actress as 'a royalist of the most right-wing kind'. Living in Saragossa with her gave him cover but also access

Frances Doble and Ivor Novello in Coward's play *Sirocco*.

to Franco's inner circle. Doble was not unattractive, of course, and he later wrote, 'I would be lying if I said I started the affair only for the sake of my work.'[4]

After the *Sirocco* debacle the theatre impresario C. B. Cochran soothed Coward by saying that only he had the talent to write the new revue he had commissioned. Cochran knew that after the two recent failures Coward, as a working partner, would be more malleable, at least for a short while. The subsequent rehearsals for *This Year of Grace*, at this point still known as *Cochran's Revue of 1928*, took place in the Poland Rooms on Poland Street in Soho. Noël Coward once described the 'dusty and dreary' room: '[It contained] a tinny piano, too many chairs, a few mottled looking glasses, sometimes a practice bar and always a pervasive smell of last week's cooking. Here rows of chorus girls in practice dress beat out laboriously the rhythms dictated by the dance producer. The chairs all round the room are festooned with handbags, hats, coats, sandwiches, apples, oranges, shoes, stockings and bits of fur. It is all very depressing, especially at night in the harsh glare of unshaded electric bulbs.'[5]

Above: Berwick Street market in 1928.

Left: Jessie Matthews aged sixteen in Cochran's *Music Box Revue* at the Palace Theatre in 1923.

According to Jessie Matthews, the young female lead in the revue, Coward was an exacting and strict director. At one point during the rehearsals Matthews, still only twenty years old, started to rehearse Coward's song 'A Room With A View' – the title of which was a direct and shameless steal from the E. M. Forster novel and had come to the playwright while convalescing on a Honolulu beach. Years later Matthews described meeting Coward for the first time as he entered the rehearsal room: 'He walked in, tall and elegantly dressed and immediately terrified me. He was obviously everything I was not. Highly sophisticated, articulate and completely sure of himself.'[6] An anxious Matthews kept on 'over-elocuting' one line from the song over and over again – 'High above the mountains and sea,' she sang. Soon Coward could stand it no more. 'How do you spell "mountain", Jessie?' 'M-o-u-n-t-a-i-n,' she answered. 'How do you pronounce it, dear?' 'Mountin.' 'Then for God's sake sing "Mountin" and not "moun-TANE",' he barked. It is said that Coward's own clipped accent came about in childhood when he had to enunciate his words clearly and precisely for his deaf mother Violet.

Today, except for the oldest amongst us, and the blue plaque on the wall of the Blue Posts pub on the corner of Berwick Street and Broadwick Street, the stage and film star Jessie Matthews has almost been forgotten. Once, however, she was one of the most famous women in the country. In 1936 it was reported that in Britain she was more popular than Shirley Temple, Bing Crosby and Gary Cooper,[7] and during the 1930s she was always voted one of Britain's favourite film-stars. Sixth of sixteen children (only eleven survived), Jessie was born on 11 March 1907 in a small, cramped and overcrowded flat above a butcher's shop in Soho's Berwick Street. Her father was a costermonger in the market for which the street is, just about, still famous. His stall was always outside the Blue Posts pub and sold oranges, apples and pears arranged in pyramids. At Christmas, with the market lit by yellow paraffin flares, he had a toy stall selling wooden soldiers, spinning tops and skipping ropes. The family weren't long at Berwick Street (the butcher wanted his flat back for his recently married son) but after a brief sojourn in Camden, they returned to Soho and lived in a small flat at number 9 William and Mary Yard on the north-west side of Little Pulteney Street. The yard contained stables and sheds that overnight stored the stalls and vans from the nearby Berwick Street market. They also housed the horses used by the local tradesmen to transport their stock from Covent Garden each morning.

Adjacent to William and Mary Yard was the Electric Cinema Theatre, which was opened in 1908 by the French-born chemist Felix Haté at 6 Ingestre Place and was Soho's first cinema.[8] It was popular with locals, especially the English, Swedish, French and Jewish children, who, for the price of a penny (far cheaper than

Blue Posts pub on Berwick Street with plaque, 2017.

Butchers shop at 94 Berwick Street. Jessie Matthews was born in the flat directly above.

elsewhere in the West End), watched an hour-long programme of films accompanied by an electric automatic piano. Like many early cinemas, the Electric was a conversion, in this case from a ground-floor residence and an adjoining stable. Leslie Wood, in his 1937 book *The Romance of the Movies*, claimed that the cinema's 'screen was erected over the manger, some of the horse stalls still being there'.[9] In 1910, when an inspector from the London County Council (LCC) visited the cinema, he found part of the auditorium to be 'a stable yard which had been roughly roofed in with boarding'. There were more boards on the floor, and the seating consisted of plain wooden benches with space for about 180 people, plus standing room for forty more. The projection box, situated above the entrance from Ingestre Place, was constructed out of wood and sheet metal. 'Altogether,' noted the inspector, 'the interior is somewhat crude.'[10]

Jessie Matthews was one of a class of sixty at the Pulteney LCC School for Girls on Peter Street, just around the corner from the cinema and William and Mary Yard. During a childhood she once described succinctly as 'three or four in a bed, bread and scrape for supper some nights, and a swipe from Dad if we got in his way',[11] she started to train as a dancer. When she was ten her mother bought her the cheapest available ballet shoes from the theatrical shoe shop on the corner of Dean Street and Old Compton Street, and not long after Jessie performed in a show called *Bluebell in Fairyland* at the Metropolitan on the Edgware Road. The following year, as principal child dancer and billed as 'Little Jessie Matthews', she danced in *Dick Whittington* at the Kennington Theatre. As a teenager, with intensive elocution lessons from her sister Rosie to remove her natural cockney accent, she auditioned for one of André Charlot's famous revues. Three decades later he still remembered that day:

> Girl after girl had stepped forward, sung and said her little pieces, answered a few questions, and stepped back again. And suddenly one of them walked out of line to the front of the stage, leaned over, and said to me 'What do you mean by keeping us waiting all this time? I want my lunch.' I gasped. That I should be so addressed in my own theatre by a mere child, not yet fifteen, was beyond belief. Her eyes flashed and she stamped her little feet. 'What a little spitfire,' I said to myself.[12]

Two years later she became one of C. B. Cochran's high-kicking 'Young Ladies' and performed in the chorus of *Music Box Revue* in 1923. Within three years the saucer-eyed little spitfire[13] was the lead in *Charlot's 1926 Revue* – the *Daily Chronicle* said of her performance: 'A triumph that would have turned the head of many an actress who has been 20 years on the stage'.[14]

Above: Noel Coward and C. B. Cochran.

Right: Jessie Matthews and Sonnie Hale in Coward's *This Year of Grace*.

Jessie Matthews' co-star in *This Year of Grace* was to be the short and bespectacled comic actor Sonnie Hale – well known at the time not only for his comedic abilities on stage but also for being married, somewhat incongruously as far as looks were concerned, to the beautiful and popular West End actress Evelyn Laye. Laye was a big star when they married in 1926, and she was earning more than £100 (approximately £5500 in 2017) a week and drove her own Lagonda car around town. Her parents disapproved of Hale and her mother told the bride-to-be on the actual wedding morning, 'I hope you know what you're doing,' before saying gently but firmly, 'Daddy and I won't be coming on to the reception.'[15] Hale was once described as looking like 'some dim young man just starting on an obscure career in the City',[16] but although he wasn't blessed with too much inherent talent, he was one of the best revue comic actors around and worked ceaselessly to perfect his singing, dancing and acting.

This Year of Grace was not the first show in which Hale and Matthews had appeared together. They were both in Cochran's previous revue called *One Dam Thing After Another*, which had opened earlier in the year at the London Pavilion. The music was by Richard Rodgers and Lorenz Hart, and the big hit of the show was Matthews, introducing the song 'My Heart Stood Still' to the world. During one of the rehearsals Cochran heard the song for the first time,[17] and although he liked it said, 'We've got to have a verse. Where's the verse?' Jessie Matthews later described what happened next:

> Larry Hart, who was sitting in the stalls with his hat on the back of his head, the inevitable cigar sticking out of his mouth, jumped up and rushed down the aisle and onto the stage. 'You wanna verse? You wanna verse, right?' He pulled an envelope out of his pocket and leaning against the proscenium started to scribble. 'How's this?' He turned to me. 'How do you like this, babe?' He handed me the envelope. 'Think you can read my writing?'[18]

Hart had quickly knocked off a verse about 'hating boys' and 'loveless joys' which was how the song remained, and it became Jessie Matthew's signature tune for the rest of her life. Hart was sometimes accused of being unnecessarily complex in his rhyming. The songwriter Arthur Schwartz told a story of his lyricist partner Howard Dietz, who had accused Hart of over-rhyming, saying, 'Larry Hart can rhyme anything – and does.' Schwartz didn't agree and in defence of Hart recalled something Hart said to him while the two were walking down Broadway: 'They said all I could do was triple rhyme. Now just take a look at this lyric. "I took one look at you, that's all I meant to do, and then my heart stood still." I could have said, "I took one look at you, I threw a book at you …" but I didn't!'[19]

One Dam Thing After Another was yet another Cochran success. St John Ervine, the Irish critic and writer, reviewed the production in the *Observer* and picked out the song 'My Heart Stood Still' and Miss Jessie Matthews for particular praise: 'A young girl who is clearly destined to be a very brilliant revue actress … she has grace and charm and variety and an irresistible air of jolly youth that makes her fascinating to watch.' It was not all kind words for the show, however: Mr Ervine, the man who had stood next to the suffragette Emily Davison at Epsom racecourse before she ran out to fall under the king's horse, had a problem with legs, specifically women's legs: 'Eight women out of ten have hideous legs,' he wrote, 'skirts were properly invented to hide them. But Mr Cochran insists on letting us see the whole bare leg, with all the bony cavities about the knee lit up by limelight. How much longer must we wait for women to realise that their legs are nearly the ugliest things in nature?'[20]

Three weeks after *One Dam Thing* had opened in London, the Prince of Wales was at a dance at the Royal Western Yacht Club in Plymouth and asked the rotund American bandleader, Teddy Brown (on leave from the Café de Paris), to play 'My Heart Stood Still'. Brown had never heard of it and so the prince hummed and sang the tune until the band could play the melody. The following day the *Evening News* headlined the story: 'The Prince dictates a foxtrot.' The royal publicity soon meant long queues of people, both at the London Pavilion and the music shops to buy sheet music and records of 'My Heart Stood Still'. It became a big hit and the most popular song since 'Tea for Two' in 1922.

A few months later, and not long before the opening night of *This Year of Grace*, Evelyn Laye held a small supper party for her close friends at Soho's Gargoyle Club – a recently opened private members' club on the upper floors of 69 Dean Street (at the corner with Meard Street). Owned by the aristocratic socialite David Tennant, there was a ballroom, a bar, coffee room and drawing room with some of the interiors by Henri Matisse. It was reached by a rickety lift so small it was said that strangers became intimate friends by the time it reached the top floor. Laye's guests that evening included the film actors Ruby Miller and a boyish twenty-four-year-old called Frank Lawton. Slightly late, and after a *This Year of Grace* rehearsal, Laye's husband Sonnie Hale turned-up at the club accompanied by his charming co-star.

The Gargoyle Club was not a stone's throw from the street where Jessie Matthews was born and brought up, but in some respects it was a million miles away. It was actually around this time that the old Electric Cinema Theatre was being demolished, as was the whole area around William and Mary Yard, including Jessie's childhood home. In its place was built Rex Garage, which eventually opened in 1929. At the time it was described as 'probably the largest and best-equipped building for the service of the motor-car that has yet appeared in this congested city',[21] and it was intended to serve the West End, especially 'Theatreland', to which increasing numbers were coming by car. Originally there were vehicle-turntables in the centre of each floor with a chauffeurs' canteen, café and kitchen on the first floor. On the ground floor there was a garage and shop, with petrol pumps in the forecourt. The building still stands and is now the Brewer Street NCP car park. It costs £15 an hour to park there and is a listed building as one of the earliest surviving ramped multi-storey car parks to be built in the country.

Evelyn Laye greeted Jessie warmly when she arrived at the Gargoyle, and although the two women had met at various theatrical parties they did not know each other well. Born Elsie Evelyn Lay, and from a young age known informally as 'Boo', Laye was six years older than Matthews and had been born in Russell Square in Bloomsbury. Her parents were both respected actors and her father had become a theatre manager, and also a musician and composer. While Jessie was still at Pulteney School, Evelyn made her first stage appearance in August 1915 at the Theatre Royal in Brighton as Nang-Ping in *Mr. Wu*. Sitting opposite each other at the

NCP car park on Brewer Street, formerly Rex Garage and now a listed building.

Gargoyle, it must have been noticed by many that the two actresses contrasted both in looks and in temperament. The blue-eyed blonde Laye was tall, cool and sophisticated, but maybe slightly aloof, whereas Matthews, although not classically beautiful, had a sexual attractiveness and zest for life that a lot of people found utterly beguiling. One of those people, unfortunately, was Evelyn's husband Sonnie Hale. There was a reason the *Sunday Times* theatre critic James Agate had once described Matthews as 'the rogue in porcelain'.

Matthews was also married, but in her case to a womanising, debt-ridden actor called Henry Lytton Jnr. He had a famous name, but only because of his father, who was the popular Gilbert and Sullivan comedian Sir Henry Lytton Snr. Although the couple were now all but estranged, Matthews had married Lytton to seek stability in a life that must have become extraordinarily unreal when she quickly shot to stardom. The young actress from the wrong part of Soho thought the famous theatrical family could offer her a form of stability in her life, but the security she sought crumbled after just a few months.

Lytton, an insecure man, had not only been sleeping with chorus girls behind Matthews' back (he'd actually been having an affair with one girl from the very week they had been married), but he had become increasingly envious of her growing success. In fact he was envious of anybody's success and for the rest of his life found it impossible to emerge from the shadow of his eminent father. Lytton Snr didn't help by disinheriting his son from his will (he died in 1936), as he disapproved of not only his son's theatrical career (what there was of it) but also his marriage.[22] Lytton Jnr ended his show business days as a ringmaster at Blackpool Tower Circus alongside Charlie Cairoli. He died in the same town aged just fifty-nine.

In 1928, early in the new year, Evelyn Laye travelled to Manchester where *This Year of Grace* was previewing. When she arrived at the theatre she caught her husband and Matthews holding hands. On seeing her, the co-stars quickly and expeditiously moved away from each other and Laye, pretending to joke, asked whether they were in love with each other. They nervously laughed and assured her that the idea was absurd and foolish. It was, as Sonnie pointed out, less than a month to only their second anniversary. Jessie and

Evelyn Laye in *One Heavenly Night*, directed by George Fitzmaurice, 1931.

Sonnie were lying. They had already been lovers for several weeks. At a rehearsal, after they had sung 'A Room with a View' together, Sonnie had whispered in her ear, 'Let's make it come true.' The next day he took Matthews to the romantic French restaurant called Moulin d'Or on Church Street in Marylebone.

The following month, in February 1928, Frank Lawton, the handsome actor at the Gargoyle, suddenly became, according to Laye, 'the most talked-about actor in London'. He was playing a young public schoolboy suspected of having a love affair with his housemaster's wife in the play *Young Woodley*. The *Manchester Guardian* wrote that Lawton 'acted with a quiet intensity that became in the most genuine sense beautiful to watch'.[23] Produced by Basil Dean at the Savoy Theatre on the Strand, it had been written three years previously by John Van Druten, but had initially been banned by the Lord Chamberlain because of its controversial subject matter and a negative depiction of public school life. Van Druten would go on to write, among many other successful plays, *I Am a Camera* based on Christopher Isherwood's short stories which would later form the basis of the musical *Cabaret*. When *I Am a Camera* opened on Broadway in 1951, the drama critic Walter Kerr wrote a famous three-word review: 'Me No Leica.'[24] Two years after the London stage production, Lawton went on to appear in the film version of *Young Woodley* with Madeleine Carroll, but it was notable for its staginess and was unpopular with critics and audiences alike.

This Year of Grace opened to rave reviews both for Jessie and, to his great relief, the writer Noël Coward (it resurrected his career). The *Sunday Express* ranked Jessie Matthews and Evelyn Laye, together with Cicely Courtneidge, as 'the three brightest female stars of our English light musical stage'.[25] This would have rankled with Laye, who saw herself as London's reigning stage beauty, and this only got worse when the song 'A Room with a View' became a huge hit that summer. A few weeks later, Evelyn Laye found passionate and rather explicitly detailed love letters, written in an ill-educated childish scrawl, from Jessie to Sonnie. After confronting her husband with them, he admitted his love for Matthews.

Laye at the time was performing at the Daly's Theatre (in Cranbourn Street just off Leicester Square and demolished in 1937) in a show called *Lilac Time*, an English version of *Das Dreimäderlhaus* (*House of the Three Girls*), a Viennese pastiche operetta with music by Franz Schubert. A depressed Laye had started to shrink away from her friends and even her colleagues in *Lilac Time*: 'I was either tortured by jealousy or helpless self-pity,' she once wrote. 'I never knew when I might be crying. I could be walking along a street and suddenly find them streaming down my face.'[26] She started eating alone before her performances and often went to a little Italian restaurant at 27 Dean Street called Quo Vadis. The owner, Peppino Leoni, had no idea who she was, and she appreciated that 'the little Italian restaurateur with the round face and kindly eyes' showed no surprise when night after night she'd ask for a wall table for one. Years later Laye would remember these solo dining experiences and later quoted, in an appreciative epilogue to Leoni's biography, 'The best number for a dinner party is two – myself and a dam' good head-waiter.'[27]

One night, before a show, Laye came to a decision at Quo Vadis. There was no choice but to leave her cheating husband. She started crying uncontrollably while Leoni stood wordlessly by her side occasionally topping up her champagne glass. He had been

Evelyn Laye in promotional material for *Evensong* (1934).

watching the time and put his hand on her shoulder and pointed to the clock when it was time for her to leave for the theatre. 'You have been my guest,' he said when she went to pay, and then put her in a cab for the 300–400-yard journey to Daly's. A few days later, Laye moved out of the Hale home in Linden Gardens and moved into a small, poky flat on South Audley Street in Mayfair.

When Leoni opened Quo Vadis in 1926, it occupied solely the ground floor of 27 Dean Street, not far from the corner of Bateman Street. It had just seven tables and the first day's takings was 12s 6d. The name of the restaurant was chosen after Leoni saw a billboard in Leicester Square advertising the silent film of the same name. In Latin it means 'Where are you going?' (or, as Evelyn Laye preferred, 'Whither Goest Thou?') and as the new restaurateur was unable to tell if the restaurant would bankrupt or enrich him, he thought the name apt. Of course, and probably more importantly, it also had connotations of a sumptuous Roman feast.

In the same month that Jessie Matthews was born, Peppino Leoni arrived in London from Cannero, near Lake Maggiore in

Italy, aged just fifteen. Living in lodgings on Whitfield Street, his first job at 5 shillings a week was at a Swiss cafe that offered English fare, but with continental service – a 'chop, a steak, or plate of meat for 1s 6d to 2s'. In the summer of 1914, he became the manager of Gallina's Rendezvous in Dean Street (where the Groucho Club is now) run by Peter Gallina. After the war, Leoni became the head waiter at the Savoy, and then a few years later he started Quo Vadis.

During the 1920s and 1930s 'Little Italy', as Soho was often called, was permeated by fascism. The Italian fascists even had a headquarters – the first to be organised outside Italy – based in Noël Street, the road that crosses Berwick Street and Poland Street just south and parallel to Oxford Street. In 1924, the food critic known as 'Diner-Out' praised a man called Luca Martini as the 'ruling spirit' of the Rendezvous on Dean Street (where Leoni had once worked), writing that if anything, 'shouldn't please you send for Martini, and watch him in his best "Fascistic" manner put things right'.[28] While Robin Douglas, in his book *Well, Let's Eat* published in 1933, wrote that Gennaro's on Old Compton Street had 'Lasagne alla Mussolini' on its Saturday evening menu.[29]

Quo Vadis, not least because of Laye's initial patronage, became extremely popular, and in 1935 Leoni opened the top two floors of the building. Eventually, the restaurant expanded to three buildings in the street, including no. 28, which had once been tenanted by Karl Marx between 1851 and 1856. In his autobiography, the splendidly named *I Shall Die on the Carpet*, Leoni tells a story that when workmen were decorating the new acquisition, the foreman came up to him and said, 'Guv, there's a lot of junk upstairs in the top attic. What shall I do with it?' 'What kind of junk?' Leoni asked. 'Oh, mostly exercise books, full of scribblings in some foreign language ...' Later that day Leoni's architect, Alistair MacDonald, son of Ramsay MacDonald, told him that Karl Marx had apparently lived in the attic. 'Karl Marx! *Madonna mia*, what a fool I've been!' Leoni exclaimed. But by then it was too late and the rubbish had been taken to a wharf, compressed, loaded onto barges and dumped in the North Sea. Leading up to the Second World War, the food at the restaurant was described by reviewers as 'International' or

Stanley Baker and Luciana Paluzzi at Quo Vadis in 1958. They were appearing in the film *Sea Fury* together that year.

'Franco-Italian' and would not be seen as authentic Italian food today. In 1938 the *Wine and Food* journalist Christopher Dilke described the food served at Quo Vadis often being a '"surprise": the sole is served with bananas, the pigeon with pineapple'.[30]

Early in 1929, Noël Coward came to see Laye who was still very low about Sonnie and Jessie, and offered her a new play that he had written and C. B. Cochran would be producing. 'I'm calling it *Bitter Sweet*,' he explained eagerly, 'and Cocky wants you to play the lead.' Laye knew that the writer and producer had worked together on *This Year of Grace* and spun around on her dressing room chair and howled, 'You can tell him I'd rather scrub floors than work for *him* again. Sonnie met Jessie in one of his shows, they were together in one last year and they're together in the new one now. Cocky knows about them, so go on, tell him!'[31] Unused to people saying 'no', a rather shocked Coward gave Laye a perplexed, exasperated look and then walked out of the room, taking his manuscript with him.

Noël Coward's *Bitter Sweet* opened later that summer with an American actress and singer, Peggy Wood,[32] in the leading role (thirty-five years later in 1965 she played the Abbess in *The Sound of Music*, singing 'Climb Every Mountain'). Another actor in the production was twenty-seven-year-old Alan William Napier-Clavering, better known as Alan Napier, who, after a decade in West End theatres and a long film career, became best known to most people for portraying Alfred Pennyworth, the butler in the 1960s *Batman* television series. After the opening in Manchester (a Cochran tradition), the *Manchester Guardian* wrote that there was nothing to stop the show doing well: 'If a wealth of light melody, a spice of wit, and much beauty of setting can assure it, Mr Coward need have no misgivings'.[33]

Laye, meanwhile, was appearing in popular productions such as *Blue Eyes*, composed by Jerome Kern, and *The New Moon* by Sigmund Romberg at the Theatre Royal in Drury Lane. Determined to start afresh, she moved to a new and spacious luxury flat in St John's Wood that she furnished with specially designed furniture and curtains of pure silk. She had a chauffeur, a maid and a housekeeper at the apartment, and a dresser and secretary at the theatre. She ordered expensive frocks and gowns from Norman Hartnell, and, feeling rich and reckless, she started dabbling in stocks and shares.

When Laye heard Cochran was sending another company to perform *Bitter Sweet* in New York, she swallowed her pride and asked for an audition with Coward. It was agreed and she insisted she sang the whole score with the playwright watching from the stalls at the Scala theatre on Charlotte Street. During her entire performance he paced up and down the aisle, and when she finished he came round to the stage and said, 'It's good, darling.' He then kissed her and said in a matter-of-fact voice, 'Now I'm going to get some lunch,' and disappeared. Elsie April, Cochran's musical director, was also present and said, 'There'd have been no lunch for him, or for you, if he hadn't liked it.'[34] The role of Sari was hers, and she took April to Leoni's to celebrate. There was a reason, however, why Laye decided to audition for a part that she initially had turned down: she needed the money. During an interval a few days before, she had got a call from her stockbroker: 'Boo, I've got to tell you, I've lost all of it. I put the lot on what I thought was a good speculation. It's crashed.' He had just lost her £10,000 (approximately £600,000 in 2017).[35]

When *Bitter Sweet* opened on Broadway, after effusive preview reviews, it was so popular the police had to cordon off Sixth Avenue. Coward told his mother that the production was 'the most triumphant success I've ever seen. When she made her entrance in the last act in the white dress they clapped and cheered for two solid minutes and when I came on at the end they went raving mad.' After telling her that Laye was 'weeing down her leg with excitement', Coward complimented his mother: 'How right you were with Evelyn – she certainly does knock spots off the wretched Peggy!'[36] While Evelyn Laye was receiving acclaim in New York, the *Daily Mail*'s headline on 22 November 1929 was: 'Miss Jessie Matthews' divorce suit. Discretion in her favour. Sonnie Hale named.'[37] The following summer in the Probate, Divorce and Admiralty Division of the High Court of Justice on the Strand, Evelyn Laye's divorce petition came before Sir Maurice Hill – a judge who was close to retirement and particularly averse, in an almost prehistoric fashion, to divorce. Evelyn Laye, with her deposition taken earlier, was away filming *One Heavenly Night* in Hollywood. Against all advice Matthews was present in the courtroom, but soon realised her mistake when her private letters to Sonnie were read out in open court:

My Darling, I want you and need you badly, all of you, and for a very long time. I am lying here, waiting for you to possess me.

The dear little boobs, which you love so much, are waiting for you also.[38]

During the reading of one particularly embarrassing letter Matthews fainted and had to be helped outside. Whether it was an act or not, it garnered no sympathy from Sir Maurice Hill, who once described his legal work as 'having one foot in the sea and one foot in the sewer'.[39] Perhaps the judge's mood can be blamed on his being an England cricket fan – it was that very day at Headingley in Leeds that Don Bradman scored a 100 before lunch, 219 by tea and ended the day with 309 not out – but whatever the reason, his final comments, written down with glee by the watching reporters, were spoken with brutal severity:

It is quite clear that the husband admits himself to be a cad, and nobody will quarrel with that, and the woman Matthews writes letters which show her to be a person of an odious mind.[40]

Later that year, Jessie and Sonnie appeared in another Cochran musical, *Ever Green*, again with music written by Rodgers and Hart. It premiered on 3 December 1930 and was the first show at the newly renovated Adelphi Theatre. It was an expensive production – Cochran had agreed to pay Matthews a remarkable £250 a week and just before the curtain went up on the first night told her, 'I've spent tens of thousands of pounds on this show. So now it's all up to you!'[41] The production was notable for using London's first revolving stage during the song 'Dancing on the Ceiling' when the two stars danced around a huge chandelier that was standing up from the floor, simulating the ceiling. The song, rejected from a Broadway musical earlier that year, became one of Jessie Matthews' signature tunes, although it was banned for a while by BBC radio because the word 'bed' was used twice in the verse and once in the refrain. The staging of it was not without struggle, and Matthews, still upset with her ongoing marital difficulties, later wrote:

Dancing on the Ceiling was the big song and dance number in the show, and the way those men mauled it about! 'She's too

Jessie Matthews and Sonnie Hale from *There Goes the Bride*, released in 1932.

coy' said Benn Levy (who wrote the book); 'she isn't coy enough' said Rodgers. 'Sweeter and lighter' said Hart. 'I don't like it' said Cochran. I looked down at these four men so busy manipulating me. I felt like a puppet with tangled strings. Some demon took hold of me. What was I to them? Nothing but some image they had in their minds, an object, a bloody blueprint to scrawl their ideas on. I was sick and tired of letting four old men mess me about. What the hell did they know about love? How did they know how a girl in love really feels?[42]

Despite the public criticism over Evelyn Laye's divorce, for which Matthews was almost entirely blamed, *Ever Green* easily became her biggest stage success and was the greatest of all the Cochran musicals.

In January 1931, Sonnie Hale and Jessie Matthews married at Hampstead Register Office, and he was to have a major influence on her career during much of the decade. Their marriage wasn't always a happy one and almost immediately there were problems. The Hales, a big theatrical family, never accepted Jessie like they had Evelyn. Robert Hale, a Scottish comedian, had told her in 1928 after meeting her for the first time, 'Don't let on to the old lady that we've met, will you?' The 'old lady' was Belle Reynolds, an Irish actress who had failed to hide her dislike of Jessie right from the start – likewise Sonnie's sister Binnie, who was also a big star at the time after appearing in *No No Nanette* in 1925 at the Palace Theatre. Binnie, responsible for making the song 'Spread a Little Happiness' popular, would perform Evelyn Laye impressions on the piano if Jessie ever came to visit. Behind her back, however, Binnie's impressions of Jessie were of a 'cockney guttersnipe affecting ladylike airs and graces'.[43]

Two months after the wedding ceremony, Jessie's first major film, *Out of the Blue*, was released. The *Daily Mirror* called it a 'charming and amusing trifle' and said Jessie Matthews 'was good in the leading role' but the newspaper was being kind. The film was atrocious and she looked frightened out her wits in front of the camera. Despite Sonnie Hale's conviction that 'the future was in the film industry', he and Jessie were bitterly disappointed with the movie. Michael Balcon, then in charge at Gainsborough and later to run the famous Ealing Studios, initially felt that Jessie 'was a dead loss as far as films are concerned',[44] but after seeing some early rushes of her next film he signed her to a two-year contract.

Her next film, released in the autumn of 1932, was *There Goes the Bride*, directed by Albert de Courville (although Balcon was working her so hard, Matthews had completed the films *The Man from Toronto*, *The Midshipman* and the excellent *The Good Companions* before its premiere), and Jessie received a delighted reception. *The Observer* wrote: 'What really matters is the discovery of Jessie Matthews. Miss

Jessie Matthews in
1931.

Matthews is a revue actress, who doesn't know much yet about film angles, tricks, and paces but she is going to be the biggest star name we have in their country before she is through. Her pert little face photographs irresistibly.'[45] The *Daily Mail* was similarly unrestrained in its praise: 'Miss Matthews is personality and a portent. Her arrival is a revolution. I feel certain she will be a sensation.'[46] The ramifications over the divorce scandal, however, were still affecting Jessie's life and she was not allowed to meet King George V and Queen Mary with the rest of the cast at *The Good Companions* premiere.

These films were followed by a series of stylish and escapist musicals, the most popular of which was the filmed version of her stage success *Evergreen*,[47] directed by Victor Saville in 1934. Just as the shooting of *Evergreen* was coming to an end, Evelyn Laye returned from Hollywood. *One Heavenly Night* was unsuccessful in America and she had come back to star in *Princess Charming* for Gaumont-British in Shepherd's Bush. One day she came to the same studio as Jessie. Lionel Burleigh, a costume designer, often recounted a story of how he once took a lift at the studio with Evelyn Laye on one side and Jessie on the other, both looking resolutely ahead and not saying a word. When the lift reached the dressing room floor, neither wanted to leave it first. Finally they all moved forward simultaneously like 'an automaton chorus line from *The Chocolate Soldier*'.[48]

On 7 June, *Evergreen* opened at the beautiful New Gallery cinema at 121 Regent Street (later, and for forty years, a Seventh-Day Adventist church, then Habitat and now Burberry's flagship store) and completely captivated the critics, including C. A. Lejeune in the *Observer*: 'Jessie Matthews grows so much in stature in every part she tackles that our directors might safely dispense with their production numbers and leave it to her to pull them through. Her movement and poise in this new picture of Victor Saville's is enchanting.'[49] The *Daily Mirror* concurred, saying, 'Jessie Matthews gives the finest performance of her screen career in *Evergreen*,' but continued, 'Her performance is more remarkable as during the whole six weeks the picture was being made, Miss Matthews was ill, and had to stop work repeatedly to recover her strength.'[50] This was the first time it came to public knowledge that all was not well in Jessie Matthews' life. During the production of *Evergreen*, Jessie had continually collapsed and had been close to a complete nervous breakdown.

Griffith Jones and Jessie Matthews in the film *First a Girl*, released in 1935.

In America, however, the film also got great reviews. In New York the film opened at the Radio City Music Hall, and *Variety* almost yelled from the very high rooftops their appreciation of the girl from Soho: 'The most sensational discovery in years. Princess Personality herself. She can sing. She can dance. She can act. She can look. She has charm, youth, beauty and a million dollars of magnetism. This is not a prediction, this is a promise. Jessie Matthews will be one of the biggest box-office bets in America within the next six months.'[51] But that was it. What seemed a certain Hollywood career never happened. As Victor Saville, who directed most of her best films, admitted: 'The big problem was to find a dancer capable of partnering Jessie. We never did.'[52] Saville thought that Fred Astaire would have been the perfect partner. The thirty-five-year-old American performer was in London at the time, dancing with Claire Luce at the Palace Theatre in *The Gay Divorce* (his first stage musical without his sister Adele, who had married Lord Charles Cavendish the previous year). RKO, however, had him under contract and refused to release him. Jessie carried the next few films almost by herself, and indeed often danced alone.

The two-year contract she had signed with Michael Balcon in 1932 was now coming to an end, and she horrified him by saying that she wanted a year's break from the business. A month after the *Evergreen* premiere, she went to Ilford to open a fete in aid of the People's Dispensary for Sick Animals, but at the entrance she suddenly collapsed and fell to the ground unconscious. Two weeks later the bad news turned to good news when it was reported that Miss Jessie Matthews was to have a baby. Sonnie was quoted in the newspapers: 'We have always wanted a baby. Jessie is very fit and happy.'[53]

On 7 December 1934, Evelyn Laye married again, this time to the *Young Woodley* actor Frank Lawton, who had been at the late supper at the Gargoyle Club where Laye and Matthews had first met. The couple were to remain happily married until Lawton's death in 1969, and Evelyn continued to work in the theatre until well into her nineties. Just eleven days after Laye's marriage, on 18 December and after a fall in her garden, Jessie and Sonnie's son was delivered two months early. He was named after his father and his grandfather, but after just four hours John Robert Hale-Monro the third died.

Despite this awful setback, and with her mental health still in the balance, Jessie was at the peak of her popularity, and in 1935 her film *First a Girl* was released. Based on Reinhold Schunzel's *Viktor und Viktoria*, Jessie played a young woman acting as a male musical artist famous for his female impersonations. Men dressing as women, and women as men, has long had a part in British theatrical history but the *Observer* critic C. A. Lejeune was not impressed: 'I have a violent physical animus against men dressed up as women and women dressed up as men. It distresses me to see Jessie Matthews and Sonnie Hale, both of whom I admire enormously, reduced to this sort of undergraduate antic.'[54]

Another film, *It's Love Again*, came out the following year and again received more enthusiastic reviews, including one from Graham Greene: 'For once it is possible to praise an English "musical" above an American. Victor Saville has directed *It's Love Again* with speed, efficiency and a real sense of the absurd.' Not long after the film's release and following a salary dispute, Victor Saville, who had directed all Jessie's best films, left Gaumont-British. On Jessie's insistence her husband Sonnie took over the directing role in her films, despite his inexperience. The critical reception for the three Jessie Matthews vehicles directed by Sonnie were noticeably less fulsome. Graham Greene wrote of *Gangway* in 1937: 'Miss Jessie Matthews has only been properly directed by Mr. Victor Saville. Mr Sonnie Hale, whatever his qualities as a comedian, is a pitiably amateurish director and as a writer hardly distinguished.'[55]

Early in 1939, with the Gaumont-British contract coming to an end, Jessie and Sonnie decided to put on a lavish stage musical starring themselves. The provincial tour of *I Can Take It* was particularly successful, and everyone was looking forward to the show opening in London at the Coliseum. The planned opening night on 11 September 1939 turned out to be a week after war with Germany was announced. It was awful timing. All the theatres in the capital were initially closed and the production was cancelled. The couple had invested in the production and lost heavily.

Just over six months later, in April 1940, John Boswell in the *Daily Mirror* wrote of the Italian fascists in Soho:

England has always tolerated everything with a mild smile. Suffering everything gladly. London alone shelters more than eleven thousand of them. Italians by birth. Fascists by breeding. So now, every Italian colony in Great Britain and America is a seething cauldron of smoking Italian politics. Black Fascism. Hot as hell. Even the peaceful, law-abiding proprietor of the back-street coffee-shop bounces into a fine patriotic frenzy at the sound of Mussolini's name ... We ought to smoke out our Fascist wasp-nests.[56]

Two months later, Italy declared war on Britain. Churchill, not long Prime Minister, ordered that all London's Italian males between the ages of sixteen and seventy were to be rounded up and interned, telling the police to 'collar the lot'. Even though he had lived in London for over three decades, Peppino Leoni was no exception. The restaurateur with the kindly face remembered years later that while he was walking to his cell, he felt a 'sudden hatred for the police, for the British government which had issued the instructions for my internment and for all forms of authority. I had starved for thirty-three years in England with no political or police blemish on my record I had been scooped up without proper consideration.'[57] He was taken first to the Lingfield racecourse in Surrey, subsequently to a disused cotton mill in Bury, and finally to makeshift barracks on the Isle of Man. At his interrogation he refused to say that he was forced into fascism and would not lie. In his statement he said, 'The King is a Fascist, Mussolini is a Fascist, most of the Italian people are Fascists. I am a patriotic Italian. Therefore I am a Fascist.'[58] In his autobiography, however, he insisted that while he had been to the Fascist Club, 'it was only for ten minutes'. He was also impressed that his tax return was sent, without being forwarded, direct to his internment camp. 'That would have never have happened in Italy,' he wrote.[59]

In the summer of 1941, Matthews was given a contract for a Broadway musical called *The Lady Comes Across*. In August, she flew via Lisbon on a Pan American Boeing 314 'Clipper' flying boat over to America. The B-314, in overnight sleeper configuration, accommodated forty passengers in seven luxurious compartments, including a fourteen-seat dining room and a private 'honeymoon suite' at the tail end of the plane. Accompanying her on the fifteen-hour flight was the actress Bebe Daniels but also Rose Kennedy, the wife of the US Ambassador and mother of the future president. Jessie took with her a collection of bomb splinters and air-raid souvenirs, which she planned to auction for British war charities over in America.

The rehearsals of *The Lady Comes Across* were first delayed, and then fraught with difficulties. Whole sections of the musical were totally rewritten, and the show, again with awful timing, opened for previews in Boston in the very week the Japanese bombed Pearl Harbour in December 1941. In an interview with Elliot Norton of the *Boston Post*, an uptight Matthews said: 'If you walk by a candy store you don't even notice. If I do, I am almost nauseated by the smell. It is so long since we have had enough candy, or even sugar, in England. Recently I had to ride for miles on a bicycle even to get an egg.'[60] A month later Jessie collapsed and was taken to the Columbia Presbyterian Medical Centre in New York. Sonnie Hale was appearing in pantomime in Newcastle and told the press: 'I would like to be able to go straight out there, but it would throw too many people out of work, so I am carrying on, but it won't be so easy to play a comic part when one is so worried.'[61]

Matthews was diagnosed with chronic paranoid schizophrenia, and the hospital reported to her doctor in England that she was 'on the brink of madness'. *The Lady Comes Across*, with Evelyn Wyckoff as a last-minute replacement, opened on 9 January 1942. The *New York Daily News* critic, Burns Mantle, a year before he retired, was particularly dismissive: '"Cold" Porter, I'd say.'[62] The show closed after just three performances. By now a very ill Jessie became even more distraught. At one point she was in a straitjacket and had to be force-fed. Victor Saville later stated, 'Before the illness it was well on the cards that I could sell her to Louis B. Mayer. But after the breakdown it was hopeless. Nobody wanted to know.'[63]

When Jessie returned to Britain, she found out that Hale had fallen in love with the nanny who had been employed to look after their adopted daughter, Catherine. A year later they were divorced. Jessie Matthews never returned to the popularity of her pre-war years. Her style of dancing and singing appeared old-fashioned, which wasn't helped by the cut-glass accent from her teenage elocution lessons. At the age of fifty-six she emerged from more than a decade in the show business wilderness when she took on the role of radio's *Mrs Dale*, the paragon of middle-class respectability. In 1970 she was awarded an OBE, but by now she had become slightly more rotund and matronly than in her lithe days as an actress and dancer during the twenties and thirties. It is a fate that comes to most, but after watching Jessie at a charity gala, Evelyn Laye, who had never quite forgiven her, and who retained her slim, gracile figure throughout her life, was as waspish as her waist and said: 'Oh look, the dear little boobs have become apple dumplings.'[64]

In 1995, fourteen years after Jessie died of cancer aged seventy-four, a plaque was erected to her on the wall of the Blue Post pub on Berwick Street – the road where she was born. The stallholders suspended their familiar cries and the street went quiet when Andrew Lloyd Webber unveiled the blue plaque.

After the war, Peppino Leoni arrived back at Dean Street to find that his customers had gone and his premises had been turned into an Indian restaurant. The place was a mess and there was bomb damage to a wall at no. 27. Slowly the restaurant became recognisable again and he had the facia repainted to say Leoni's Quo Vadis. A few feet above ground level a special display panel was created that announced, '*Hic sunt Leones*' (Here are lions). The restaurant reopened on 31 December 1946 to a world of food shortages and rationing even more severe than during the war. Eventually Quo Vadis became more popular than ever, and famous for its elegant silver service, celebrity guests, and most of all the charming manners of its host.

The restaurant is still there, as it has been for over ninety years, in one incarnation or other (including the ill-fated Damien Hirst/ Marco Pierre White Cool Britannia collaboration of the 1990s), in the same place at 26–29 Dean Street in Soho.

Quo Vadis in 2017.

Recipe for a Supreme 'Sophia Loren'
One of the 'established dishes and perennial favourites' served at
Quo Vadis in its Peppino Leoni heyday.

Cut the white meat from the breast of a chicken and beat out one
piece as an escalope, but do not flatten too much. Lay on top a
piece of Bel Paese cheese, a slice of Jambon de Parme and one or
two slices of truffle. Lay on top another piece of chicken, this time
rather more flattened. Turn over the prepared complete portion,
flour, egg and breadcrumb on the one side and fry in butter until
nicely brown. Garnish on top with small artichoke hearts (the
tinned variety may be used) and surround with Sauce Madère and
Beurre Noisette. Serve.

Quo Vadis, Dean Street, in 1965.

Selected Bibliography

Aitken Kidd, Janet, *The Beaverbrook Girl* (Great Britain, Collins, 1987)

Bloch, Michael, *Closet Queens* (Great Britain, Little, Brown, 2015)

Boothby, Lord, *My Yesterday, Your Tomorrow* (London, Hutchinson & Co., 1962)

Boothby, Robert, *Boothby: Recollections of a Rebel* (Great Britain, Hutchinson, 1978)

Bret, David, *Tallulah Bankhead – A Scandalous Life* (London, Robson Books, 1996)

Brian, Dennis, *Tallulah Darling – A Biography of Tallulah Bankhead* (New York, Macmillan, 1972)

Canning, Paul, *British Policy Towards Ireland, 1921–1941* (Oxford, Oxford University Press, 1985)

Castle, Charles, *The Duchess Who Dared* (London, Sidgwick & Jackson, 1994)

Clarke, Gerald, *Get Happy – The Life of Judy Garland* (Great Britain, Random House, 2000)

Clayton, Tim & Craig, Phil, *Finest Hour* (Great Britain, Hodder and Stoughton, 1999)

Cotes, Peter, *Sincerely Dickie* (London, Robert Hale Limited, 1989)

Coward, Noël, *Autobiography* (Great Britain, Methuen, 1986)

Dean, Basil, *Mind's Eye – An Autobiography 1888-1927* (London, Hutchinson & Co., 1970)

Dean, Basil, *Mind's Eye – An Autobiography 1927-1972* (London, Hutchinson & Co., 1973)

Deans, Mickey & Pinchot, Ann, *Judy Garland Weep No More, My Lady* (Great Britain, W. H. Allen, 1972)

Donaldson, Frances, *P. G. Wodehouse, the Authorized Biography* (Great Britain, George Weidenfeld & Nicolson, 1982)

Du Maurier, Daphne, *Gerald: A Portrait* (Great Britain, Virago, 2004)

Duchess of Argyll, Margaret, *Forget Not* (London, W. H. Allen & Co., 1975)

Feigel, Lara, *The Love-charm of Bombs* (Great Britain, Bloomsbury, 2013)

Fisher, John, *A Funny Way to be a Hero* (Great Britain, TBS, 1973)

Foster, R. F., *Modern Ireland 1600 – 1972* (London, Allen Lane, 1988)

Gardiner, Juliet, *The Blitz – The British Under Attack* (Great Britain, HarperPress, 2010)

Gardiner, Juliet, *The Thirties – An Intimate History* (London, HarperPress, 2010)

Glinert, Ed, *The London Compendium* (London, Penguin Books, 2003)

Glinert, Ed, *West End Chronicles* (London, Penguin, 2008)

Golden, Eve, *The Brief, Madcap Life of Kay Kendall*, (USA, University Press of Kentucky, 2002)

Golden, Eve, *Vernon and Irene Castle's Ragtime Revolution* (USA, University Press of Kentucky, 2007)

Greaves, Jimmy, *Greavsie: The Autobiography* (Great Britain, Sphere, 2004)

Greene, Graham, *Ways of Escape* (London, The Bodley Head, 1980)

Harding, James, *Cochran – A Biography* (London, Methuen, 1988)

Harding, James, *Gerald du Maurier – A Biography* (Great Britain, Hodder & Stoughton, 1989)

Hoare, Philip, *Noël Coward – A Biography* (London, Sinclair-Stevenson, 1995)

Hudd, Roy & Hindin, Philip, *Roy Hudd's Cavalcade of Variety Acts* (Great Britain, Robson Books, 1997)

Israel, Lee, *Miss Tallulah Bankhead* (London, W. H. Allen, 1972)

Jivani, Alkarim, *It's Not Unusual, A History of Lesbian and Gay Britain in the Twentieth Century* (London, Michael O'Mara Books, 1997)

Kohn, Marek, *Dope Girls – The Birth of the British Drug Underground* (Great Britain, Lawrence & Wishart, 1992)

Kynaston, David, *Austerity Britain 1945-51* (Great Britain, Bloomsbury, 2007)

Lavery, Bryony, *Tallulah Bankhead* (Bath, Absolute Press, 1999)

Laye, Evelyn, *Boo to my Friends* (Great Britain, Hurst & Blackett, 1958)

Leon, Ruth & Morley, Sheridan, *Judy Garland, Beyond the Rainbow* (Great Britain, Pavilion, 1999)

Leoni, Peppino, *I Shall Die on the Carpet* (London, Leslie Frewin, 1966)

Lillie, Beatrice, *Every Other Inch a Lady* (London and New York, W. H. Allen, 1972)

Lord, Graham, *John Mortimer, The Devil's Advocate* (London, Orion, 2005)

Macintyre, Ben, *For Your Eyes Only – Ian Fleming and James Bond* (London, Bloomsbury Publishing, 2008)

Maguire, Kevin & Parris, Matthew, *Great Parliamentary Scandals: Five Centuries of Calumny, Smear and Innuendo* (Great Britain, Robson Books, 2004)

Matthews, Jessie, *Over My Shoulder – An Autobiography* (London, W. H. Allen, 1974)

McCann, Graham, *Bounder! The Biography of Terry-Thomas* (Great Britain, Aurum Press, 2008)

McCrum, Robert, *Wodehouse, a Life* (London, Penguin Group, 2004)

McLagan, Graeme, *Bent Coppers* (London, Orion, 2003)

McLellan, Diana, *Sappho Goes to Hollywood* (New York, St Martin's Griffin, 2001)

McWhirter, Norris, *Ross* (London, Churchill Press, 1976)

Meyrick, Kate, *Secrets of the 43 Club* (London, Parkgate Publications, 1994)

Morley, Sheridan & Payn, Graham (edited by), *The Noël Coward Diaries* (Great Britain, George Weidenfeld & Nicolson, 1982)

Morley, Sheridan, *Spread a Little Happiness – The First Hundred Years of the British Musical* (Great Britain, Thames & Hudson, 1987)

Murphy, Robert, *Realism and Tinsel – Cinema and Society in Britain 1939-49* (London, Routledge, 1989)

Neville, Richard, *Hippie Hippie Shake* (London, Bloomsbury, 1995)

Nixon, Barbara, *Raiders Overhead, A Diary of the London Blitz* (London, Scholar Press, 1980)

Pallett, Ray *They Called Him Al: The Musical Life of Al Bowlly* (Great Britain, BearManor Media, 2010)

Pearson, John, *Notorious – the Immortal Legend of the Kray Twins* (Great Britain, Arrow, 2011)

Pim, Keiron, Jumpin' *Jack Flash – David Litvinoff and the Rock 'n' Roll Underworld* (London, Vintage, 2017)

Ratcliffe, Sophie (edited), *P. G. Wodehouse, A Life in Letters* (United Kingdom, Hutchinson, 2011)

Rhodes James, Robert, *Boothby – A Portrait* (Great Britain, John Curtis / Hodder & Stoughton, 1991)

Richards, Jeffrey, *The Age of the Dream Palace, Cinema and Society in Britain 1930-1939* (London, Routledge & Began Paul, 1984)

Savva, George, *For Whom the Stars Come Out at Night* (Crickhowell, Boulevard Publishing, 2003)

Schechter, Scott, *Judy Garland – The Day-by-Day Chronicle of a Legend* (New York, First Cooper Square Press, 2002)

Shepherd, John, *George Lansbury: At the Heart of Old Labour* (USA, Oxford University Press, 2004)

Sherry, Norman, *The Life of Graham Greene, Volume Two: 1939-1955* (United Kingdom, Jonathan Cape, 1994)

Sitwell, William, *Eggs or Anarchy: The Remarkable Story of the Man Tasked with the Impossible: To Feed a Nation at War* (Great Britain, Simon & Schuster, 1917)

Smith, Lorna, *Judy with Love* (Great Britain, Robert Hale & Company, 1975)

Stanley, Bob, *Yeah, Yeah, Yeah – The Story of Modern Pop* (Great Britain, Faber & Faber, 2014)

Taylor, A. J. P., *English History 1914-1945* (Great Britain, Oxford University Press, 1965)

Thornton, Michael, *Jessie Matthews – A Biography* (London, HarperCollins, 1974)

Tunney, Kieran, *Tallulah, Darling of the Gods* (England, Martin Secker & Warburg, 1972)

Walkowitz, Judith, *Nights Out: Life in Cosmopolitan London* (London, Yale University Press, 2012)

Wheen, Francis, *Tom Driberg – His Life and Indiscretions* (London, Chatto & Windus, 1992)

White, Jerry, *London in the 20th Century* (London, Vintage, 2008)

Ziegler, Philip, *London at War 1939–1945* (Great Britain, Sinclair-Stevenson, 1995)

Notes

1 The Headless Polaroids, Mrs Sweeny, Mussolini and P. G. Wodehouse

1 *Daily Express*, 11 February 2004, p. 26
2 H. Montgomery Hyde, *Tangled Web: Sex Scandals in British Politics and Society*
3 Margaret Duchess of Argyll, *Forget Not*
4 Charles Castle, *Duchess who Dared*, p. 10
5 Ibid., p. 19
6 Margaret, Duchess of Argyll, *Forget Not*, p. 49
7 Stephen Gundle, *Glamour – A History*, p. 142
8 Charles Castle, *Duchess who Dared*, p. 16
9 Margaret, Duchess of Argyll, *Forget Not*
10 *Daily Express*, 24 September 1931, p. 15
11 *Daily Telegraph*, 3 Saturday May 1997
12 Anne Edwards, *Throne of Gold: The Lives of the Aga Khans*
13 *Los Angeles Times*, 2 September 1951
14 Ross McKibbin, *Classes and Cultures: England 1918–1951*, p. 29
15 *Daily Express*, 10 March 1932, p. 11
16 Paul Spicer, *The Temptress: The Scandalous Life of Alice, Countess de Janzé*
17 Judith R. Walkowitz, *Nights Out – Life in Cosmopolitan London*, p. 239
18 Charles Castle, *Duchess who Dared*, p. 23
19 http://www.ourwarwickshire.org.uk/
20 *Daily Mirror*, 17 February 1933, p. 7
21 *The Times*, 22 February 1933, p. 17
22 Margaret, Duchess of Argyll, *Forget Not*
23 The part is usually Reno Sweeney, although in this initial London production the part was changed to Reno La Grange, to suit Aubert's French background.

24 Juliet Gardiner, *The Thirties*, p. 669
25 P. G. Wodehouse, *A Life in Letters*, p. 245
26 Margaret, Duchess of Argyll, *Forget Not*, p. 78
27 *Daily Express*, 28 June 1941, p. 2
28 *The Mirror*, 28 June 1941, p. 1
29 P.G Wodehouse, *Performing Flea*, p. 115
30 *The Manchester Guardian*, 1 October 1922, p. 8
31 *Ibid.*, 9 December 1922, p. 10
32 Peter Neville, *Mussolini*, p. 98
33 Ed Glinert, *West End Chronicles*, p. 81
34 *The collected works of Mahatma Gandhi: (13 October 1931 – 8 February 1932), Volume 54*
35 Gareth Griffith, *Socialism and Superior Brains: The Political Thought of George Bernard Shaw*, p. 253
36 Mary Soames, *Winston and Clementine: The Personal Letters of the Churchills*, p. 298
37 Judith R. Walkowitz, *Nights Out: Life in Cosmopolitan London*, pp. 273–74
38 Sophie Ratcliffe (ed.), *PG Wodehouse: A Life in Letters*, p. 161
39 Sophie Ratcliffe (ed.), *PG Wodehouse: A Life in Letters*, p. 507
40 Margaret, Duchess of Argyll, *Forget Not*, p. 117
41 https://themitfordsociety.wordpress.com/
42 Margaret, Duchess of Argyll, *Forget Not*, p. 117
43 *The Independent*, 31 July 1993
44 *The Sydney Morning Herald*, 12 May 1963, p. 9
45 https://themitfordsociety.wordpress.com
46 Juliet Gardiner, *The Thirties*, p. 627
47 Charles Castle, *Duchess who Dared*, p. 111
48 *Daily Mail*, 28 December 2013

2 Scott's Restaurant, the Balcombe Street Gang and the Second Blitz of London

 1 *The Independent*, Saturday 23 May 1998 – Gerry Adams actually formed part of the guard of honour alongside members of the African National Congress at Nelson Mandela's farewell memorial service in Pretoria, December 2013.
 2 *Irish Examiner* 17 October 2009
 3 http://www.u-35.com/crew/lott.htm
 4 *LIFE* magazine 16 September 1939, p. 22
 5 *Ibid.*, cover and p. 79
 6 *Irish Independent*, 18 September 2009
 7 *Irish Examiner* 17 October 2009
 8 Nigel West (ed.), *The Guy Liddell Diaries, Volume I: 1939–1942*
 9 Paul Canning, *British Policy Towards Ireland, 1921–1941*, p. 246
10 Arthur Jacob Marder, *Winston is Back: Churchill at the Admiralty, 1939–40*, p. 18
11 Randolph Spencer Churchill, Martin Gilbert, *Winston S. Churchill, Volume 6*, p. 68
12 Royal Submarine Museum via http://www.u-35.com/mountbatten/

13 John Carey, *William Golding: The Man who Wrote Lord of the Flies*
14 *Illustrated London News*, 27 February 1988, p. 55
15 When *Colonel Sun* was published in 1968, it was indeed in the GLC and Westminster Council's plans to raze most of this area to the ground.
16 Sally Beauman writing for *New York* magazine believed that Amis's *Colonel Sun* 'has all the obvious ingredients for success' including 'an exotic troubled international setting, a beautiful girl, frequent imbibings, and even more frequent killings; and, most imperative, a villain. Yet the book drags and becomes a bore.' Beauman complains that the story lacks suspense and that Bond is far too gloomy: 'He's more like Ingmar Bergman's creations than Ian Fleming's hero.' Beauman attributes the novel's failure to the 'differing characters of the authors'. Sally Beauman, *Of Brooding Bondage*, p. 60
17 *Guardian*, 24 October 1975, p. 6
18 *Ibid.*, 19 November 1975, p. 1
19 *Ibid.*, 5 November 1975, p. 13
20 Norris McWhirter, *Ross*, p. 1
21 *The Observer*, 30 November 1975, p. 1
22 *Daily Express*, 28 November 1975
23 *Ibid.*, 9 December 1975
24 *Daily Mirror*, 8 December 1975
25 Christopher Hibbert, Ben Weinreb, *The London Encyclopaedia*, p. 34
26 *Guardian*, 10 February 1977, p. 11
27 *The Palm Beach Post*, 11 February 1977, p. 3
28 *New York Times*, 25 February 1990
29 Mountbatten Archives, Hartley Library, University of Southampton
30 http://www.u-35.com/crew/stamer.htm
31 Mountbatten Archives, Hartley Library, University of Southampton
32 *Daily Telegraph*, 19 May 2015
33 *Ibid.*
34 *New York Times*, 25 February 1990
35 *The Irish Times*, 1 March 1996
36 *Ibid.*, 15 May 1998

3 The Trial of Schoolkids OZ, the Downfall of the 'Dirty Squad'

 1 *The Observer*, 22 June 1969, p. 12
 2 Adam Geczy, *Art: Histories, Theories and Exceptions*, p. 141
 3 *The Observer*, 22 June 1969, p. 12
 4 Clive James, *The Metropolitan Critic*, p. 210
 5 *The Observer*, 8 February 1970, p. 2
 6 Barry Miles, *The Beatles Diary Volume 1: The Beatles Year*
 7 Lennon quickly became disillusioned by Janov. As former Apple Corps executive director Peter Brown wrote in his book *The Love You Make: An Insider's Story of the Beatles*, Lennon felt that Janov – like the Maharishi a few years earlier – had other motives: 'One day Janov appeared at a therapy session with two 16mm cameras. John wouldn't even consider having his session recorded. 'I'm not going to be filmed,' John said, 'especially not

rolling around on the floor screaming.' According to John, Janov started to berate them. 'Some people are so big they won't be filmed,' Janov said. Janov said that it was coincidental that he was filming the session, and it had nothing to do with John and Yoko's fame. 'Who are you kidding, Mr. Janov?' John said. '[You] just happen to be filming the session with John and Yoko in it.' Lennon would later dismiss primal therapy as a passing fad.

8 National Archives DPP 2/4798
9 National Archives DPP 2/4798
10 *The Daily Telegraph*, 26 January 2001
11 Vivian's mother was Grace Berger, at the time Chair of the National Council for Civil Liberties.
12 Jonathon Green, *Days in the Life*, p. 387
13 *Guardian*, 23 December 2000, p. 3
14 Richard Neville, *Hippie Hippie Shake*, p. 276
15 *The Independent*, 7 January 1999
16 *Financial Times*, 30 October 2015
17 Graham Lord, *John Mortimer: The Devil's Advocate*, p. 152
18 *Ibid.*, p. 154
19 Marsha Rowe, *Introduction to the Spare Rib Reader*
20 *Daily Mail*, 12 November 2011
21 Graham Lord, *John Mortimer: The Devil's Advocate*, p. 156
22 It was John Passmore Widgery, Lord Widgery who produced the rushed 'Bloody Sunday' report which took the side of the British Army but is now widely discredited. The historian Max Hastings has described the Widgery report as 'a shameless cover-up'.
23 *felixdennis.com*
24 *Daily Mail*, 17 November 1955
25 Steve Chibnall (ed.), *Law-and-Order News: An Analysis of Crime Reporting in the British Press*, p. 163
26 *The Independent*, 28 January 1999
27 *Daily Telegraph*, 1 October 2010
28 Ed Glinert, *West End Chronicles*, p. 216
29 *The Independent*, 28 January 1999
30 Paul Willitts, *Members Only – The life and Times of Paul Raymond*, pp. 93–94
31 *Ibid.*
32 *The Observer*, 15 August 1971, p. 9
33 Paul Willitts, *Members Only – The life and Times of Paul Raymond*, p. 182
34 The Telegraph, *Bonker, Bounder, Beggarman, Thief: A Compendium of Rogues, Villains and Scandals*
35 Barry Miles, *London Calling: A Countercultural History of London since 1945*
36 Dominic Sandbrook, *Seasons in the Sun: The Battle for Britain, 1974–1979*
37 Graeme McLagan, *Bent Coppers*
38 Michael Gillard, Laurie Flynn, *Untouchables: Dirty cops, bent justice and racism in Scotland Yard*

4 *Captain Sears, the Nazi Wreath at the Cenotaph and the Hitler Paint-throwing Incident at Madame Tussaud's*

1 *Daily Express*, 31 January 1933, p. 1
2 *The Times*, 31 January 1933, p. 9
3 The apostrophe in the name has now been dropped. Merlin Entertainments decided that since Madame Tussaud no longer actually owns the franchise there's no need for the possessive-indicating apostrophe.
4 Northumberland Street used to house a workhouse which came into use in 1752. It was demolished in 1965. A number of writers used to live on the street. In 1835, the novelist Anthony Trollope lived in lodgings at No. 22. He was just starting his career with the General Post Office and complained that he never had the money to pay his rent. English novelist Rose Macauley, later author of *The Towers of Trebizond*, lived at No. 7–8 for most of the 1930s.
5 *The Times*, 15 May 1933, p. 9
6 *Ibid.*
7 *The Manchester Guardian*, 9 December 1922, p. 10
8 Mosley's ideas on economics were similar to the ideas of the famous theorist John Maynard Keynes. Mosley and Keynes often met during Mosley's time at the Labour Party to discuss economic ideas. However, Mosley's Memorandum pre-dated even Keynes himself. Keynes did not advocate Mosley's level of deficit spending until he wrote *The General Theory of Employment, Interest and Money* in 1936.
9 A. J. P. Taylor, *English History 1914–1945*, p. 285
10 *New Statesman*, 14 April 2006
11 *The Manchester Guardian*, 21 April 1933, p. 13
12 *Evening Standard*, 12 May 1933
13 His birth records suggest that he would have been thirty-eight at the start of the war.
14 *Evening Standard*, 12 May 1933
15 *Ibid.*
16 Hugh P. Cecil and Peter Liddle, *At the Eleventh Hour*, p. 353
17 Norma S. Davis, *A Lark Ascends: Florence Kate Upton, Artist and Illustrator*
18 *Journal of the Society for Psychical Research*, p. 273
19 *Ibid.*, p. 5
20 Arthur Conan Doyle, *The Case for Spirit Photography*, p. 44
21 *Daily Sketch*, 15 November 1924
22 Arthur Conan Doyle, *The Case for Spirit Photography*, p. 60
23 John Evans (ed.), *Journeying Boy: The Diaries of the Young Benjamin Britten 1928–1938*, p. 140
24 *Spectator*, 11 May 1933, p. 4
25 *Spectator*, 12 January 1974, p. 21
26 Airey Neave, *Nuremberg*, p. 103

5 The Charming Lord Boothby, His Friend Ronnie Kray and the Humble Woolton Pie

1 Matthew Parris and Kevin MacGuire, *Great Parliamentary Scandals: Five Centuries of Calumny, Smear and Innuendo*, p. 116
2 *Guardian*, 17 July 1986, p. 1
3 A. N. Wilson, *Our Times*
4 *Oxford Dictionary of Biography*, Boothby, Robert John Graham, Baron Boothby
5 Leslie Mitchell, *Maurice Bowra: A Life*, p. 210
6 *Daily Express*, 28 May 2016, p. 37
7 Robert Boothby, *Boothby: Recollections of a Rebel*, p. 169
8 *Daily Mirror*, 19 July 1940, p. 1
9 *Daily Express*, 19 July 1940, p. 5
10 William Sitwell, *Eggs or Anarchy: The Remarkable Story of the Man Tasked with the Impossible: To Feed a Nation at War*
11 Amy Helen Bell, *London Was Ours: Diaries and Memoirs of the London Blitz*, p. 74
12 Matthew Parris & Kevin MacGuire, *Great Parliamentary Scandals: Five Centuries of Calumny, Smear and Innuendo*, p. 120
13 William Sitwell, *Eggs or Anarchy: The Remarkable Story of the Man Tasked with the Impossible: To Feed a Nation at War.*
14 John Pearson, *Notorious: The Immortal Legend of the Kray Twins*, p. 103
15 Sarah Macmillan never imagined that anyone else might be her father until 1947, at the age of seventeen, when she was dancing in a nightclub with Colin Tennant. His original partner, jealous with drunken rage, broke up the dance saying, 'What do you think you're doing with Colin? You're only illegitimate anyhow, you're Boothby's daughter.' Sarah died an alcoholic (known in her mother's family as 'the Cavendish disease') just twenty-three years later at the age of forty.
16 Robert Rhodes James, *Boothby: A Portrait*, p. 120
17 John Pearson, *Notorious: The Immortal Legend of the Kray Twins*, p. 103
18 Robert Rhodes James, *Boothby: A Portrait*, p. 123
19 *The Independent*, 23 February 1994
20 Robert Boothby, *Boothby: Recollections of a Rebel*, pp. 24–25
21 Robert Boothby, *Boothby: Recollections of a Rebel*, p. 107
22 *Lord Boothby Speech House of Lords Debate, 24 May 1965 vol 266 cc 654–712*
23 *The Observer*, 27 April 1997
24 *Hansard, HL Deb 24 May 1965 vol. 266 cc654–712*
25 *Hansard, HL Deb 21 July 1967 vol. 285 cc522–6*
26 *Daily Express*, 28 July 1959, p. 5
27 *Daily Express*, 7 May 1963, p. 4
28 Keiron Pim, *Jumpin' Jack Flash*, p. 85
29 Francis Wheen, *Tom Driberg: His Life and Indiscretions*, p. 350

30 John Pearson, *The Cult of Violence*

31 Kingsley Amis, *Memoirs*, p. 311

32 Francis Wheen, *Tom Driberg: His Life and Indiscretions*, p. 352 and from interviews with Driberg and Boothby by Susan Crosland, December 1970

33 *Hansard, HL Deb 11 February 1965 vol 263 cc271–3*

34 Robert Rhodes James, *Boothby: A Portrait*, p. 454

35 *Guardian*, 24 June 1997, p. 19

6 *The Prince of Wales Theatre and the De-Mob Suit – Starring Sid Field and Featuring Dickie Henderson, Kay Kendall, Terry-Thomas and the Ross Sisters*

1 Roy Hudd and Philip Hindin, *Roy Hudd's Cavalcade of Variety Acts*, p. 79

2 Dickie Henderson and Peter Cotes, *Sincerely Dickie*, p. 31

3 Philip Hoare, *Noël Coward: A Biography*, p. 242

4 Alister Satchell, *Running the Gauntlet: How Three Giant Liners Carried a Million Men to War, 1942–1945*, p. 236

5 Dickie Henderson and Peter Cotes, *Sincerely Dickie*, p. 33

6 *Ibid.*, p. 40

7 The derivation of 'The Full Monty' isn't truly known but the Burton tailor story is as good as any other, if only for this book.

8 Anthony Powell, *The Military Philosophers*, pp. 241–42

9 Dennis Rooke and Alan D'Egville, *Call Me Mister!*, p. 11

10 *Guardian*, 31 July 1971, p. 9

11 Humphrey Carpenter, *Spike Milligan: The Biography*, p. 44.

12 Judith Walkowitz, *Lights Out: Life in Cosmopolitan London*, p. 273

13 *The Times*, 17 August 1974, p. 7

14 J. B. Priestley, *Sid Field, Particular Pleasures*, p. 162

15 John Fisher, *John Fisher Presents A Funny Way to be a Hero*, p. 152

16 Eve Golden, *The Brief, Madcap Life of Kay Kendall*, p. 33

17 *Ibid.*, p. 35

18 *Observer*, 22 September 1946, p. 2

19 *Daily Express*, 3 September 1945

20 In 1939 Field had featured in an inauspicious comedy entitled *That's the Ticket* which remained almost unnoticed, so much so that many critics in 1946 wrote that *London Town* was Field's first film. He also made another relatively unsuccessful film, *The Cardboard Cavalier*, in 1948 – an historical romp with Field as a Cromwellian barrow-boy helping to restore Charles II to the throne.

21 Eve Golden, *The Brief, Madcap Life of Kay Kendall*, p. 34

22 *Ibid.*, p. 36

23 The National Archives reference T275/137

24 David Thomson, *Film Studies: Kay Kendall, the lost heroine of screwball comedy*

25 *Hope Star*, 15 September 1942, p. 4

26 *New York Times*, 14 April 1944

27 Dickie Henderson and Peter Cotes, *Sincerely Dickie*, p. 48

28 Graham McCann, *Bounder!*, p. 10

29 *Ibid.*, p. 19

30 *Ibid.*, p. 20

31 *Ibid.*, p. 24

32 David J. Cox, Kim Stevenson, Candida Harris and Judith Rowbotham, *Public Indecency in England 1857–1960: A Serious and Growing Evil*, p. 112

33 Terry-Thomas, *Terry-Thomas tells Tall Tales: An Autobiography*, p. 18

34 Roy Hudd and Philip Hindin, *Roy Hudd's Cavalcade of Variety Acts*, p. 179

35 Terry-Thomas, *Terry-Thomas tells Tall Tales: An Autobiography*, p. 91

36 *Daily Express*, 2 August 2007, p. 33.

37 David Kynaston, *Austerity Britain*, p. 264

38 *Ibid.*, p. 386

39 Hal Burton (ed.), *Great Acting*, p. 28

7 *A Hungry Graham Greene on the Night of 'The Wednesday', and the Death of Al Bowlly*

1 Ray Pallett, *They Called Him Al: The Musical Life of Al Bowlly*

2 *Ibid.*, foreword

3 http://www.memorylane.org.uk, *Al Bowlly's Last Theatre Date*

4 *The Ludington Daily News*, 3 February 1976, p. 9

5 Juliet Gardiner, *The Blitz*, p. 341

6 *Ibid.*, p. 331

7 Barbara Nixon, *Raiders Overhead*, p. 109

8 *Ibid.*

9 Lara Feigel, *The Love Charm of Bombs*, p. 89

10 *Ibid.*

11 *Manchester Guardian*, 4 March 1941 p. 4

12 http://zythophile.co.uk, 'So what really happened on October 17 1814?'

13 *Guardian*, 16 March 2007

14 *Manchester Guardian*, 2 October 1940, p. 4

15 *The Observer*, 27 November 1927, p. 14

16 *The Times*, 21 November 1932, p. 19

17 Richard Rhodes, *The Making of the Atomic Bomb*, p. 13

18 *The Times*, 6 December 1939, p. 5

19 *The Independent*, Monday 6 June 2005

20 *The Times*, 28 March 1987, p. 15

21 Ed Glinert, *The London Compendium*, p. 195

22 *Picture Post*, 2 November 1940, pp. 18–19

23 *Manchester Guardian*, 4 March 1941, p. 4
24 *Picture Post*, 2 November 1940, pp. 18–19
25 Graham Greene, *Ways of Escape*, p. 107
26 Norman Sherry, *The Life of Graham Greene, volume 3*, p. 274
27 Graham Greene, *Ways of Escape*, p. 108
28 Judith Adamson, Mark Shechner, *Graham Greene: The Dangerous Edge: Where Art and Politics Meet*, p. 74 (the authors note that this scene is reminiscent of when Sarah finds Bendrix after the bombing in Greene's novel *The End of the Affair*)
29 Graham Greene, *Ways of Escape*, p. 111
30 Juliet Gardiner, *The Blitz*, p. 340
31 James Lee Milne, *Another Self*
32 *Diaries of E. J. Rudsdale*, http://wwar2homefront.blogspot.co.uk
33 Ray Pallett, *They Called Him Al: The Musical Life of Al Bowlly*
34 Beatrice Lillie, *Every Other Inch a Lady*, p. 255
35 Graham Greene, *Ways Of Escape*, p. 113

8 When Tallulah Bankhead Met Gerald du Maurier, and the Eton Schoolboys Scandal

 1 *The Manchester Guardian*, 14 April 1925, p. 6
 2 Tallulah Bankhead, *Tallulah!*, p. 146
 3 *Miss Thompson* was first published in *The Smart Set*, a magazine edited by H. L. Mencken and George Jean Nathan
 4 Tallulah Bankhead, *Tallulah!*, p. 119 – Tallulah describes the play as 'one of the all-time clinkers!'
 5 National Archives HO 382/9
 6 Paddington station is mentioned by Bankhead in her *Tallulah!* although its likely she meant Waterloo if she had travelled up from Southampton.
 7 Tallulah Bankhead, *Tallulah!*, p. 126
 8 Daphne du Maurier, *Gerald: A Portrait*, p. 149
 9 John Elsom, *Post-War British Theatre*, p. 26
10 John Sutherland, *Curiosities of Literature: A Book-Lover's Anthology of Literary Erudition*, p. 87
11 Tallulah Bankhead, *Tallulah!*, p. 116
12 Janet Aitken Kidd, *The Beaverbrook Girl*, p. 63
13 Tree was born in London, the eldest of three daughters of Herbert Beerbohm Tree and his wife, the actress Helen Maud Tree, *née* Holt. Her aunt was author Constance Beerbohm and an uncle was Max Beerbohm. Her sisters were Felicity Tree and Iris Tree but she also had seven illegitimate half-siblings, by way of her father's many infidelities, among them the director Carol Reed and Peter Reed, whose son became the actor Oliver Reed.
14 Tallulah Bankhead, *Tallulah!*, p. 164
15 Denis Brian, *Tallulah Darling*, p. 42
16 Marie Tempest, Gladys Cooper, Sybil Thorndyke and Evelyn Laye.

17 At one point, almost openly, Beaverbrook was in a relationship of sorts with Tallulah. Janet Aitken, his daughter, wrote about them: 'Father seemed to be getting too fond of Tallulah and I couldn't bear the thought of him hurting my beloved mother. Father was defiant, telling me to shut up and mind my own business.' Janet Aitken Kidd, *The Beaverbrook Girl*, p. 63.

18 She was named after her paternal grandmother, who was named after Tallulah Falls in Georgia.

19 Noël Coward, *Present Indicative: The First Autobiography of Noël Coward*, p. 196

20 Lee Israel, *Miss Talulah Bankhead*, p. 104

21 Philip Hoare, *Noël Coward: A Biography*, p. 145

22 Noël Coward, *Present Indicative: The First Autobiography of Noël Coward*, p. 145

23 Ibid.

24 Jonathan Law, *The Methuen Drama Dictionary of the Theatre*

25 Diana Souhami, *Radclyffe Hall*, p. 131

26 National Archives HO 382/9

27 *Independent*, 10 March 1993

28 Tallulah Bankhead, *Tallulah!*, p. 128

9 *The House of 'Cyn', Jimmy Graves and the Rise and Fall of the Luncheon Voucher*

1 *The Times*, 18 January 2013

2 *Daily Telegraph*, 16 November 2015

3 *The Scotsman*, 19 November 2015

4 *Guardian*, 18 November 2015

5 A fleet of passenger and cargo ships that ran between Southampton and Cape town from 1900 to 1977.

6 *Daily Telegraph*, 16 November 2015

7 *Guardian*, 21 November 1961, p. 24

8 *The Economist*, 2 March 1963

9 Jimmy Greaves, *Greavsie: The Autobiography*

10 Colin Shindler, *Four Lions: The Lives and Times of Four Captains of England*

11 *Hansard*, 17 May 1960 vol. 623

12 *The Times*, 15 August 1960, p. 9

13 *Daily Mail*, 17 November 2015

14 *Daily Telegraph*, 16 November 2015

15 *The Mirror*, 16 November 2015

16 *The Times*, 20 September 1976, p. 16

17 *The Sunday Times*, 22 November 2015

18 *Daily Mail*, 17 November 2015

19 *Ibid.*

20 A four-bedroom detached house on Ambleside Avenue is worth approximately £1.5 million in 2017.

10 Cocaine, the 'Yellow Peril' and the Death of Billie Carleton

1   *The Times*, 24 March 1879, p. 6
2   *Daily Express*, 22 November 1918 and *The Times*, 25 November 1918, p. 5
3   John Shepherd, *George Lansbury: At the Heart of Old Labour*, pp.131–2
4   Jonathan Schneer, *George Lansbury: Lives of the Left*, p. 168
5   *The Washington Post*, 5 January 1919, p. 8
6   Eve Golden, *Vernon and Irene Castle's Ragtime Revolution*
7   A keen sportswoman she played tennis at Wimbledon, learnt to fly and worked helping refugees during the First World War. *The Tatler* in 1917 applauded her activities in organising an aircraft exhibition which was first held at Grosvenor Galleries and subsequently travelled around Britain and Ireland to encourage men to join the RAF and to raise funds for charity.
8   Georgette (from crêpe Georgette) is a sheer, lightweight, dull-finished crêpe fabric named after the early twentieth-century French dressmaker Georgette de la Plante.
9   *The Syracuse Herald*, 15 June 1919
10 Marek Kohn, *Dope Girls*, p. 69. An average wage for a woman would have been less than £2 per week at that time.
11 *The Washington Times*, 15 June 1919
12 The castles were depicted in the Fred Astaire and Ginger Rogers movie *The Story of Vernon and Irene Castle* (1939).
13 *The Philadelphia Inquirer*, 22 June 1919, p. 5
14 *Washington Post*, 5 January 1919, p. 8
15 Eve Golden, *Vernon and Irene Castle's Ragtime Revolution*, p. 211
16 *The Times*, 4 December 1918, p. 3
17 Veronal was the brand name of Barbitone and was first marketed by Bayer in 1904. First synthesised in 1902 by the Germans Emil Fischer and Joseph von Mering, Barbitone was considered to be a great improvement over the existing hypnotics. Its taste was slightly bitter, but better than the strong, unpleasant taste of the commonly used bromides. It had few side effects, and its therapeutic dose was far below the toxic dose. However, prolonged usage resulted in tolerance to the drug, requiring higher doses to reach the desired effect. Pioneering aviator Arthur Whitten Brown (of 'Alcock and Brown' fame) died of an accidental overdose.
18 Eve Golden, *Vernon and Irene Castle's Ragtime Revolution*, p. 209
19 C. B. Cochran, *Secrets of a Showman*, p. 210
20 Beatrice Lillie, *Every Other Inch a Lady*
21 *Ibid.*, p. 77
22 Roy Porter, *London: A Social History*
23 Virginia Nicholson, *Singled Out: How Two Million British Women Survived Without Men*, p. 191
24 *Tatler*, 24 October 1917 p. 109

25 Marek Kohn, *Dope Girls*, p. 26 and Mrs C. S. Peel, *How We Lived Then, 1914–1918: A Sketch of Social and Domestic life in England During the War*, p. 66

26 C. S. Peel, *How we lived then, 1914–1918: A sketch of social and domestic life in England during the war*, p. 77

27 *Quex Evening News*, 3 January 1916, p. 5

28 Marek Kohn, *Dope Girls*, p. 71 and *The Times*, 4 December 1918.

29 Martin Pugh, *We Danced All Night: A Social History of Britain Between the Wars*, p. 217

30 Marek Kohn, *Dope Girls*, p. 32

31 James Morton, *Gangland Soho*

32 Marek Kohn, *Dope Girls*, p. 116

33 A particularly quiet month as far as British casualties were concerned. The average monthly British deaths during 1916 was over five times that amount.

34 *The Times*, 12 February 1916, p. 3

35 *The Times*, 16 February 1916, p. 9

36 *The Pharmaceutical Journal*, 31 December 2011

37 *The Washington Post*, 22 June 22 1919, p. 4

38 Marek Kohn, *Dope Girls*, p. 90

39 Raphael Samuel, *Patriotism: Minorities and outsiders*, p. xxi

40 *Daily Express*, 1 October 1920, p. 1

41 *The Times*, 25 November 1913, p. 6

42 *The Washington Times*, 22 June 1919

43 H. V. Morton, *H.V. Morton's London: being The Heart of London, The Spell of London and the Nights of London in one volume [1925 and 1926]*, p. 335

44 Thomas Burke, *Limehouse Nights: Tales of Chinatown*, pp. 155–58

45 Phillip J. Morledge, Sax Rohmer, *Fu-Manchu*, p. 171

46 Sax Rohmer, *Dope*, p. 157

47 According to *The Times* report on his retirement, Mead was still wearing Victorian side-whiskers when he retired, aged eighty-six, in 1933.

48 *Guardian*, 21 December 1918, p. 3

49 *Ibid.*

50 Marek Kohn, *Dope Girls*, p. 88

51 *The Times*, 24 January 1919, p. 3

52 *The Daily Telegraph*, 17 January 1919

53 *The Times*, 24 January 1919, p. 3

54 *Chicago Tribune*, 23 December 1908, p. 5

55 *The Times*, 24 January 1919, p. 3

56 Nicholas Connell, *Walter Dew: The Man Who Caught Crippen*

57 *The Times*, 24 January 1919, p. 3

58 Marek Kohn, *Dope Girls*, p. 97

59 Philip Hoare, *Noël Coward: A Biography*, p. 75

60 John Darlington Marsh died three months later in March 1919 and is buried in the same graveyard as Carleton.

61 *Daily Express*, 2 December 1918, p. 5

62 Lesley M. M. Blume, *Let's Bring Back: The Cocktail*

11 Judy Garland, Johnnie Ray and the Talk of the Town at the Hippodrome

1 Gerald Clarke, *Get Happy*, p. 417
2 Allan Warren, from a conversation with the author.
3 *Daily Mirror*, 20 January 1969, p. 1
4 Bob Stanley, *Yeah, Yeah, Yeah: The Story of Modern Pop*, p. 25
5 *Evening Standard*, 29 September 1955
6 *The Manchester Guardian*, 10 March 1959, p. 7
7 Tom Jones, *Just Help Yourself: Special Edition*, p. 140
8 George Savva, *For Whom the Stars Come Out at Night*, p. 52.
9 *Ibid.*
10 *Daily Mail*, 10 April 1951
11 *Sunday Despatch*, 15 April 1951
12 George Savva, *For Whom the Stars Come Out at Night*
13 Bernard Delfont in his autobiography recounts a story when the queen came to an event at the Talk of the Town: 'Throughout the evening I sat next to the Queen whose first visit it was to the Talk of the Town or, I guess, to any cabaret. Of all the illustrious guests, the most colourfully turned out was Barbara Cartland. As the novelist swept past our table, the picture of mature glamour, the Queen twinkled. "Who's that?" she asked. "Danny La Rue?"'
14 Bernard Delfont, *Bernard Delfont Presents*, p. 128
15 Scott Schechter, *Judy Garland: The day-by-day Chronicle of a Legend*, p. 365
16 *The Observer*, 19 Jan 1969, p. 26
17 Scott Schechter, *Judy Garland: The day-by-day Chronicle of a Legend*, p. 366
18 Rita Grade Freeman, *My Fabulous Brothers*, p. 93
19 Scott Schechter, *Judy Garland: The day-by-day Chronicle of a Legend*, p. 368
20 *Financial Times*, 20 August 1958, p. 4
21 Bernard Delfont, *Bernard Delfont Presents*, from notes on the inside cover
22 *Daily Mail*, 10 April 1951
23 Bernard Delfont, *Bernard Delfont Presents*, p. 129
24 Mickey Deans and Ann Pinchot, *Judy Garland: Weep No More My Lady*, p. 72
25 *Ibid.*
26 Gerald Clarke, *Get Happy*, p. 422
27 *TIME*, 4 July 1969
28 Allan Warren, from a conversation with the author
29 *Guardian*, 17 July 1974, p. 10

12 An Absolute Sirocco, Old Boy! Quo Vadis, Evelyn Laye, and the Story of Soho Girl Jessie Matthews

1 *Pictures*, 26 February 1921, p. 218
1 Barry Day (ed.), *The Letters of Noël Coward*, p. 156
3 *The Observer*, 14 December 1969, p. 40
4 Ben Macintyre, *A Spy Among Friends: Kim Philby and the Great Betrayal*, p. 46

5 Noël Coward, *Present Indicative*, p. 242

6 Jessie Matthews, *Over My Shoulder*, p. 89

7 *Guardian*, 21 August 1981, p. 2

8 *London Silent Cinemas* – londonssilentcinemas.com

9 Leslie Wood, *The Romance of the Movies*, p. 72

10 Minutes of the LCC Theatres and Music Halls Committee, meeting of 11 November 1908, LMA, LCC/MIN/10,729, Item 14, p. 523

11 James Harding, *Cochran: A Biography*, p. 125

12 James Ross Moore, *André Charlot, The Genius of Intimate Musical Revue*

13 The word 'spitfire' originally meant a feisty or quick-tempered young girl. The name of the famous fighter plane was first suggested by Sir Robert MacLean, director of Supermarine's parent company Vickers-Armstrongs, after his daughter who was known as the 'little spitfire' due to her fiery character. R. J. Mitchell, the designer, thought this a 'bloody stupid' name and preferred the name 'shrew'!

14 Jeffrey Richards, *The Age of the Dream Palace: Cinema and Society in 1930s Britain*, p. 210

15 Evelyn Laye, *Boo to my Friends*, p. 73

16 James Harding, *Cochran: A Biography*, p. 125

17 In March 1927, Rodgers and Hart had travelled to Paris from London to meet the with the arranger Robert Russell Bennett, also an American, to try to persuade him to orchestrate the songs for their upcoming London revue, *One Dam' Thing After Another*. On their way back to Paris from a sightseeing expedition to Versailles, a truck came within a hair of demolishing the cab the two songwriters, along with their two female companions, were riding in. As the truck rattled by, one of the young women cried out in apparent fright, 'Oh! My heart stood still!' Without missing a beat, Hart, apparently unaffected by what must have been a nerve-jangling moment, instantly urged the unfailingly conscientious Rodgers to make a note of her exclamation as a potential song title. Hart's partner faithfully jotted it down in his address book and upon coming across the note, only after they had returned to London, proceeded to construct a melody. When Rodgers played it for Hart, the lyricist loved the tune but claimed no recollection of the precipitating incident – via greatamericansongbook.net.

18 Jessie Matthews, *Over My Shoulder*

19 *greatamericansongbook.net*

20 *The Observer*, 22 May, p. 14

21 *historicengland.org.uk/listing*

22 *Gasbag* 231, p. 13

23 *Guardian*, 14 February 1928, p. 5

24 *New York Herald Tribune*, 31 December 1951

25 Jeffrey Richards, *The Age of the Dream Palace: Cinema and Society in 1930s Britain*, p. 211

26 Evelyn Laye, *Boo to my Friends*, p. 85

27   A quote by Nubar Gulbenkian from Peppino Leoni, *I Shall Die on the Carpet*, p. 239
28   Judith Walkowitz, *Lights Out: Life in Cosmopolitan London*, p. 111
29   *Ibid.*
30   Christopher Dilke, *Wine and Food*, 5, no. 17 (Personality in Food), p. 49
31   Evelyn Laye, *Boo to my Friends*, p. 92
32   Coward wrote the leading role of Sari with Gertrude Lawrence in mind, but he came to the conclusion the vocal demands of the part were beyond her capabilities.
33   Robert Ignatius Letellier, *Operetta: A Sourcebook, Volume II, Volume 2*, p. 981
34   Evelyn Laye, *Boo to my Friends*, p. 93
35   *Ibid.*
36   Philip Hoare, *Noël Coward: A Biography*, p. 209
37   *Daily Mail*, 27 June 2007
38   *Daily Mail*, 27 June 2007
39   *Daily Mail*, 14 August 2009
40   Michael Thornton, *Jessie Matthews: A Biography*, p. 143
41   Sheridan Morley, *Spread a Little Happiness*, p. 68
42   *Ibid.*, p. 69
43   Michael Thornton, *Jessie Matthews: A Biography*, p. 143
44   John Mundy, *The British Musical Film*, p. 65
45   *The Observer*, 30 October 1932, p. 14
46   *Daily Mail*, 26 October 1932
47   The stage musical was two words, 'Ever Green', while the film version was just one word.
48   Michael Thornton, *Jessie Matthews: A Biography*, p. 131
49   *The Observer*, 10 June 1934, p. 14
50   *Daily Mirror*, 6 June 1934, p. 4
51   Michael Thornton, *Jessie Matthews: A Biography*, p. 133
52   Victor Saville, *Saville's Musicals*, p. 48
53   Michael Thornton, *Jessie Matthews: A Biography*, p. 133
54   *Observer*, 10 November 1935, p. 14
55   Graham Greene, *The Pleasure Dome*, p. 101
56   *Daily Mirror*, 27 April 1940, p. 6
57   Ed Glinert, *West End Chronicles*, p. 174
58   Peppino Leoni, *I Shall Die on the Carpet*, p. 24
59   *Ibid.*, p. 19
60   Michael Thornton, *Jessie Matthews: A Biography*, p. 181.
61   *Ibid.*
62   *Ibid.*
63   *Ibid.*, p. 183.
64   *Daily Mail*, 27 June 2007

Index